Anonymus

Royal Commissioner on manual and practical Instruction in Primary Schools under Board of National Education in Ireland

First Report and Minutes of Evidence

Anonymus

Royal Commissioner on manual and practical Instruction in Primary Schools under Board of National Education in Ireland
First Report and Minutes of Evidence

ISBN/EAN: 9783741199806

Manufactured in Europe, USA, Canada, Australia, Japa

Cover: Foto ©Thomas Meinert / pixelio.de

Manufactured and distributed by brebook publishing software (www.brebook.com)

Anonymus

Royal Commissioner on manual and practical Instruction in Primary Schools under Board of National Education in Ireland

COMMISSION ON MANUAL AND PRACTICAL INSTRUCTION

IN

PRIMARY SCHOOLS UNDER THE BOARD OF NATIONAL EDUCATION

IN IRELAND.

FIRST REPORT

OF

THE COMMISSIONERS

AND

MINUTES OF THE EVIDENCE

TAKEN AT THE FIRST SEVEN PUBLIC SITTINGS.

Presented to Parliament by Command of Her Majesty.

DUBLIN:
PRINTED FOR HER MAJESTY'S STATIONERY OFFICE,
BY ALEXANDER THOM & CO. (LIMITED).

And to be purchased, either directly or through any Bookseller, from
Hodges, Figgis, and Co. (Limited), 104, Grafton-street, Dublin; or
Eyre and Spottiswoode, East Harding-street, Fleet-street, E.C.; or
John Menzies and Co., 12, Hanover-street, Edinburgh, and 90, West Nile-street, Glasgow.

1897.

TABLE OF CONTENTS.

Warrant appointing Commissioners to Inquire and Report with a view to determining how far, and in what form, Manual and Practical Instruction should be included in the Educational System of Primary Schools under the Board of National Education in Ireland.

Chief Secretary's Office,
Dublin Castle.

By the Lord Lieutenant-General and General Governor of Ireland.

CADOGAN.

Whereas it appears to Us to be expedient that a Commission should forthwith issue with a view to determining how far, and in what form, Manual and Practical Instruction should be included in the Educational System of the Primary Schools under the Board of National Education in Ireland:

Now We, George Henry, Earl Cadogan, Lord Lieutenant-General and General Governor of Ireland, do hereby nominate and appoint—

Somerset Richard, Earl Belmore, G.C.M.G.;
His Grace the Most Rev. William Conyngham, Baron Plunket, D.D., LL.D.;
His Grace the Most Rev. William J. Walsh, D.D.;
The Right Hon. Christopher Palles, LL.D., Lord Chief Baron;
The Right Hon. Christopher Talbot Redington, B.A.;
His Honor Judge Shaw, Q.C.;
The Right Rev. Monsignor Molloy, D.D., D.Sc.;
The Rev. Henry Evans, D.D.;
The Rev. Hamilton Wilson, D.D.;
Professor George F. FitzGerald, F.T.C.D.;
Stanley Harrington, Esquire, B.A.;
William Robert J. Molloy, Esquire;
Captain T. B. Shaw, late Royal Engineers, Inspector of Science and Art Schools under the Science and Art Department in England; and
J. Struthers, Esquire, Inspector of Schools under the Scotch Education Department;

to be Our Commissioners for the purpose aforesaid, that is to say, to inquire and report, with a view to determining how far, and in what form, Manual and Practical Instruction should be included in the Educational System of the Primary Schools under the Board of National Education in Ireland.

And for the better effecting the purposes of this Our Commission, We do by these presents authorise and empower you, the aforesaid Commissioners, or any three or more of you to be named by you, to call before you, or any three or more of you, such persons as you may think fit to examine, and by whom you may be the better informed in the matter hereby submitted for your consideration, and everything connected therewith, and generally to inquire of and concerning the premises by all other lawful ways and means whatsoever.

And also to call for and examine such books, documents, papers, writings, or records as you or any three or more of you as aforesaid, shall think useful for the purposes of the Inquiry.

And We also by these presents authorise and empower you, or any three or more of you as aforesaid, to visit and personally inspect such places as you or any three or more of you may deem expedient for the purposes aforesaid, and also to employ such persons as you may think fit to assist you in undertaking any Inquiry for the purposes aforesaid as you may deem expedient to make, and Our pleasure is that you or any three or more of you as aforesaid, do from time to time and with all convenient speed report to Us what you shall find concerning the premises.

And We further by these presents ordain that this Our Commission shall continue in full force and virtue, and that you Our Commissioners do from time to time proceed in the execution thereof, although the same be not continued from time to time by adjournment.

And for your further assistance in the execution of these presents, We do hereby appoint James Dermot Daly, Esquire, B.A., to be the Secretary to this Our Commission, whose services and assistance We require you to use from time to time as occasion may require.

Given at Her Majesty's Castle of Dublin, this 25th day of January, 1897.

By His Excellency's Command,

D. HARREL.

COMMISSION ON MANUAL AND PRACTICAL INSTRUCTION

IN

PRIMARY SCHOOLS UNDER THE BOARD OF NATIONAL EDUCATION IN IRELAND.

FIRST REPORT.

TO HIS EXCELLENCY GEORGE HENRY, EARL CADOGAN, K.G.,

&c. &c. &c.

LORD LIEUTENANT-GENERAL AND GENERAL GOVERNOR OF IRELAND.

MAY IT PLEASE YOUR EXCELLENCY,

We, the undersigned Commissioners, appointed to inquire and report with a view to determining how far, and in what form, manual and practical instruction should be included in the Educational System of the Primary Schools under the Board of National Education in Ireland, availing ourselves of Your Excellency's permission to report our proceedings from time to time, desire to submit to Your Excellency the minutes of the evidence that we have taken up to this date on the subject of our Inquiry.

As the matter is one in which a wide interest is taken in this country, and as we think it will materially assist us to keep the Public informed of the progress of our Inquiry, we request Your Excellency to authorize the immediate publication of the evidence appended.

We have the honour to be,

Your Excellency's faithful servants,

BELMORE.
PLUNKET DUBLIN.
✠ WILLIAM J. WALSH,
Archbishop of Dublin.
C. PALLES.
C. T. REDINGTON.
JAMES J. SHAW.
GERALD MOLLOY.
HENRY EVANS.
H. B. WILSON.
GEO. FRAS. FITZGERALD.
STANLEY HARRINGTON.
W. R. J. MOLLOY.
T. B. SHAW.
J. STRUTHERS.

JAMES DERMOT DALY,
Secretary.

Dated this 25th day of February, 1897.

INDEX TO WITNESSES EXAMINED UP TO FEBRUARY 26, 1897.

COMMISSION ON MANUAL AND PRACTICAL INSTRUCTION.

MINUTES OF EVIDENCE.

FIRST PUBLIC SITTING.—THURSDAY, FEBRUARY 4, 1897, AT 11 O'CLOCK, A.M.,

In the Royal University, Dublin.

Present:—The Right Hon. the EARL of BELMORE, G.C.M.G., in the Chair; His Grace the Most Rev. the LORD PLUNKET, D.D., LL.D.; His Grace the Most Rev. WILLIAM J. WALSH, D.D.; The Right Hon. C. T. REDINGTON, M.A.; The Right Rev. Monsignor MOLLOY, D.D., D.Sc.; Rev. HENRY EVANS, D.D.; Rev. HAMILTON WILSON, D.D.; STANLEY HARRINGTON, Esq., B.A.; W. R. J. MOLLOY, Esq.; and Captain T. B. SHAW,

with J. D. DALY, Esq., B.A., Secretary.

Mr. ALEXANDER HAMILTON, M.A., Chief of Inspection under the Board of National Education, examined. Feb. 4, 1897. Mr. Alexander Hamilton, M.A.

1. CHAIRMAN.—Before I begin to examine Mr. Hamilton, I may state in a few words that the reason for putting the questions which I am going to put to him, and which may seem to some people unnecessary, is that persons who are likely to read our reports—and indeed I may say, I, myself—have not the experience of the working of the National Board, which many of the members of the Commission have, and which, possibly, many of the gentlemen who are in the room, may have; and therefore to get the thing properly on the notes and properly before the public, it has been considered better that I should ask a certain number of questions, which will be introductory to the subject of our inquiry. And when I have gone through them other Commissioners will put further questions to the witness. I will, therefore, Mr. Hamilton, begin by asking you some questions, which possibly many of those in the room may know the answers of, but which, it is desirable for the sake of those who do not, to ask. Will you inform us what is the office you hold?—I am senior Chief of Inspection.

2. How long have you been an Inspector?—I was appointed in April, 18[illegible].

3. Mr. MOLLOY.—Then was as District Inspector?—As District Inspector.

4. Mr. REDINGTON.—Your position as Chief of Inspection gives you the control together with your colleague, Mr. Downing, of the Inspectorial staff?—Yes.

5. And you yourself were an Inspector until you became Chief of Inspection?—Yes, I was.

6. Mr. MOLLOY.—And you have served also as Head Inspector, that is one of the intermediate grades?—Yes.

7. CHAIRMAN.—I will ask you first, Mr. Hamilton, into what classes are the National schools divided?—They are divided into two classes, vested and non-vested.

8. Under what control are they?—They are under the control of patrons and managers.

9. With regard to the vested schools, are they again subdivided?—Yes, those that are vested in the Commissioners, and those that are vested in trustees.

10. How are these schools spoken of, as distinguished from Model schools?—They are spoken of as Ordinary schools; the word Ordinary is sometimes used to exclude Model schools only, and sometimes it is used to exclude also Convent schools, Monastery schools, Workhouse schools, and Evening schools.

11. Now will you tell us how many schools were on the roll in the year 1895 and how they were divided?—There were [illegible], I believe. There were [illegible] schools in operation on 31st December, 1895.

12. How many of those schools were vested and how many were non-vested schools?—[illegible] vested schools and [illegible] non-vested schools.

13. Of the vested schools can you give us the number that were vested in trustees?—[illegible].

14. And vested in the Commissioners?—[illegible].

15. Do these numbers include the Model schools?—They do.

16. How many Model schools are there?—There are [illegible].

17. With regard to building grants do the Commissioners award aid towards the building, fittings and furniture and so on?—Yes they do, for vested schools only.

18. And with regard to the salaries?—They award aid in respect of salaries to both classes of schools, vested and non-vested.

19. And also as regards teachers' residences?—They also award aid to both classes of schools.

20. Is that towards building or towards making them?—Towards building houses, they can only recommend in the case of non-vested schools a loan; and then the Commissioners contribute one-half of the annual sum towards the repayment of that loan. In regard to vested schools the Commissioners can make a grant up to £100.

21. Then that leads to this question, in what way is this aid given to both classes of schools, vested and non-vested?—For aid for residences?

22. Either for residences or for the payment of teachers?—For the payment of teachers, to both classes of schools, the Commissioners award a personal salary to the teacher.

23. And then with regard to residences?—In the case of non-vested schools they can recommend a loan for the building of the residence.

24. Who is the loan provided by?—The loan is provided by the Board of Works.

25. And for vested schools?—They can make a grant for the building of a residence in connexion with a vested school.

26. They make the grant themselves?—They make the grant themselves.

27. Mr. REDINGTON.—The grant cannot exceed £100?—It cannot exceed £100.

28. Or half the expense?—It may be less than £100, if half the expense is less than £100.

29. The Commissioners contribute one-half the annual instalment to pay off the loan for a teacher's residence?—Yes.

30. Or else they give a grant not exceeding £100 for a teacher's residence?—In connexion with the vested schools.

B

31. A loan can be given for a Teacher's Residence?—It can.

32. A loan can be given for a residence in connection with either a non-vested or vested school?—Yes.

33. Now as regards building school houses, the grant for building amounts to how much?—Two-thirds of the estimated cost.

34. And that grant is only given in the case of vested schools?—Only for vested schools is a grant given for building.

35. In the case of non-vested schools a loan only is given?—A loan may be given for building.

36. And no aid is given towards the repayment of that loan?—No, not for school-houses. The residence for which repayment is made may belong either to vested or non-vested schools.

37. The loan for a residence is repayable in thirty-five years at 5 per cent.?—Yes.

38. CHAIRMAN.—Will you tell us with regard to non-vested schools what aid is given, for what purpose is aid given?—For the payment of salaries and for the supplying of books and requisites.

39. And supplying also, I have here results fees, gratuities, and the benefits of inspection and training; are these also included?—Yes, they are.

40. What conditions are required before aid is given?—For non-vested schools or vested schools?

41. For non-vested schools?—The school must be in operation; it must deserve assistance; it must have reason to expect an average attendance of at least twenty; it must have sufficient local aid, as the Commissioners may require; it must have house and offices suitable; and it must not be owned by the teacher or any relative or anyone in his interest.

42. Then as regards the Model Schools, how many classes are there?—There are three classes, the Central and Metropolitan Model Schools, the District Model Schools, and Minor Model Schools.

43. How many of each are there?—In the Central and Metropolitan Model Schools there are [illegible] departments; there are nineteen District Model Schools, including forty-seven different departments; and seven Minor Model Schools, with twenty departments.

44. With regard to ordinary National Schools under what management are they?—They are placed under local management—local managers.

45. And how are the teachers appointed?—The teachers are appointed by the managers, subject to the approval and sanction of the Board.

46. How are the managers appointed in the case of non-vested schools?—Generally speaking the manager is the person who makes the application to have the school taken into connexion.

47. What is the distinction between the manager and the patron?—The manager has certain local duties in connexion with visiting the school and signing the agreement with the teacher and signing the quarterly returns. He may be the patron of the school.

48. Or he may be appointed by the patron?—Or he may be appointed by the patron.

Rev. Dr. EVANS.—But, of course, it ought to be brought out that while he may be appointed by the patron his appointment has to be recognised by the Commissioners of National Education.

49. Mr. REDINGTON.—The manager should be a suitable person living in the locality?—Yes.

50. CHAIRMAN.—And does the Board of National Education require that their assent to the appointment of the manager should be given?—Yes.

51. Mr. REDINGTON.—In schools vested in the Commissioners who is the patron?—The Commissioners.

52. And in schools vested in trustees?—The trustees are the patrons.

53. And if there is a school committee?—That committee is taken as the patron.

54. The Commissioners reserve to themselves the right of removing the patron or manager?—They do.

55. After full inquiry?—Yes.

56. Is that procedure often carried out?—Very rarely indeed.

57. Monsignor MOLLOY.—In schools that have a patron the patron appoints the manager, subject to the approval of the Commissioners?—Yes.

58. But there are some schools that have no patron. Who appoints the manager in that case?—The manager in such cases is considered to combine in himself the offices of patron and manager.

59. Who appoints the patron and manager?—Usually the patron and manager, if the offices are combined, is the person who makes the application to have the school taken into connexion with the Board.

60. He is accepted as the patron and manager by the Board?—Unless stated to the contrary in the application, as sometimes is the case.

61. Mr. REDINGTON.—That can only be in the case of non-vested schools?—In the case of non-vested schools.

62. In the case of vested schools, either the Commissioners or the trustees are the patrons?—Yes.

63. Most Rev. Dr. WALSH.—Technically every school has a patron as well as a manager, but the two offices may be held by the one person?—Yes; I take it that is the view.

64. Mr. MOLLOY.—What trouble does the manager go to before applying to the Board. Just explain the preliminary steps that have to be taken by him to get up the school?—He writes to the Board stating he wishes the school to be taken into connexion, and applies for the necessary forms. These are sent to him. He fills up these forms, answering the queries, and returns them to the Board.

65. But prior to that would he not have the trouble of getting pupils and getting a house, or arranging about a house?—Oh, yes, the school must be in operation.

66. CHAIRMAN.—The school must be in operation before it is taken into connexion?—A non-vested school must be in operation before a manager applies.

67. Mr. REDINGTON.—Are the vested and non-vested schools worked in exactly the same way?—Yes, so far as teaching is concerned.

68. Most Rev. Dr. WALSH.—There are different rules as regards the use that may be made of the schoolhouse according as the school is vested or non-vested, they differ a little. There is a greater latitude in the use of the non-vested school than in the case of the vested school?—There is.

69. The use of a vested school is more subject to the control of the Commissioners?—It is.

70. Rev. Dr. EVANS.—You said to us that there were three classes of Model Schools, (1) Central and Metropolitan School, (2) Provincial Model Schools, and (3) Minor Model Schools.—District Model Schools is the second class.

71. Are they all subject to the same code?—Yes.

72. Are they all inspected in the same way, or does the inspection of these schools differ in any respect?—There is a slight difference in the inspection so far as the Central Model Schools are concerned; that is, the duty is discharged by a Head Inspector.

73. Does the inspection of these Model schools differ in any way from the inspection of the Ordinary Schools?—Not so far as their results examination and things of that kind are concerned.

Mr. REDINGTON.—The manager of the Model School under the Commissioners is the District Inspector?—Yes.

74. And he is also the Inspector of the Model School?—He is.

75. Therefore so far as the two offices are combined in one person there is a difference between the Model Schools and Ordinary Schools?—There is.

76. Rev. Dr. EVANS.—Is there any parallel to that in the National system, outside the Model Schools, viz.: of the manager and inspector being the same person?—I don't know any case precisely at present.

78. Mr. Molloy.—Has it not happened that a manager has expressed a wish to the Commissioners that the Inspector should act as local manager and have not the Commissioners complied with that request?—In a few cases they have.

79. Chairman.—Does that apply only to vested schools or to non-vested schools?—It applies to non-vested schools.

80. Most Rev. Dr. Walsh.—Was that made as a permanent arrangement or merely as a temporary one?—Only a temporary one.

81. Most Rev. Lord Plunket.—In the Central Metropolitan Model Schools the Professors have, also certain control and supervision, have they not?—At present the Professors are recognised as the managers of the Central Model Schools, but not as the Inspectors.

82. The District Inspector in that case is not the manager?—No.

83. It is the Professors?—The Professors are the managers, and until the beginning of 1888 the Professors were also the Inspectors of the Central Model Schools.

84. Chairman.—Now, Mr. Hamilton, I want to ask you some questions with regard to school farms and school gardens. I believe that certain Ordinary National Schools have such farms and gardens attached to them; is not that so?—Yes.

85. Can you tell me how many there are?—On the 31st December last there were forty-seven Ordinary Schools having school farms attached, and eighty-two schools that had school gardens attached.

86. Can you give me any particulars as to the size of these farms and gardens?—The largest is as much as forty-eight acres.

87. Where is that?—In the Co. Monaghan. Cur... is the name of the school having the largest farm.

88. And the smallest?—The smallest is only 1a. 3r. 10p.

89. Monsignor Molloy.—What would be the general run. Can you say what is the usual amount of land in these gardens or farms?—I am speaking only of the farms now.

90. You have given us the largest, 48a., and the smallest, 1a., but what would you say is about the ordinary size of these farms?—It would be very hard to say as they differ so much.

91. It would be very easy to strike an average, but it is not an average I want; what I want is the usual size, if there is anything that can be called usual in character. Would it be 5a. or 8a., or thereabouts?—There are ten of them that have less than 5a.; all the others are above that, and some of them considerably above that, but ten of the farms have less than 5a. each.

92. How many would there be between 5a. and 10a. can you say?—I could not say without reference to the lists; ten more probably.

93. Will you make a note of it and send us in a memorandum showing how many there are under 5a., how many between 5a. and 10a., how many between 10 and 20, and how many over 20?—Yes.

94. Chairman.—I won't ask you any questions in detail about these farms and gardens. I will come to another subject. How many Convent Schools are paid by capitation, and how many by class salaries?—There are 183 Convent Schools paid by capitation and 10 in which the teachers are paid by class salaries. The Nuns are classed teachers. There are three Monastery Schools paid by capitation and 47 paid by class salaries.

95. How many special industrial departments for girls are there in 53 Convent Schools?—There are 53 special industrial departments, one industrial department in each of 53 Convent Schools.

96. How would you describe the industrial department? What does the industry consist of?—Embroidery and other advanced kind of needlework. There must be a class of extern or within pupils who have passed sixth class under the instruction of this special industrial teacher.

97. How many Workhouse Schools were there in 1896 in connexion with the National Board?—There were 153 Workhouse Schools.

98. Was that one for each workhouse. I don't know how many workhouses there are. I suppose that is about the number?—I am not sure.

99. Or was it one boys' and one girls'?—I take it that it is the separate departments that are returned in that number.

Mr. Molloy.—There are about 160 workhouses in Ireland, and I should say there is one school in each, with two departments—boys' and girls', as a rule.

Chairman.—Are there some workhouses with no schools?—Yes.

Mr. Molloy.—Some two or three workhouses have schools which are not in connexion with the National Board.

100. Chairman.—How are the salaries determined of the Workhouse Schools?—The salaries are determined by the Poor Law Authorities. Except the salaries of the teachers of these Workhouse Schools, and they are paid from the Consolidated Fund. The Commissioners of National Education have nothing to do with the payment of those teachers.

101. Then what connexion have the National Board Commissioners with them, and in what way do they maintain their connexion?—The schools receive books and requisites and the benefit of inspection.

102. And do they give result fees?—They determine the amount of the result fees which the Poor Law Guardians may, if they choose, pay the teachers.

Most Rev. Dr. Walsh.—Out of the rates.

103. Mr. Redington.—As regards books, they are not given free, but are sold at cost price to the Workhouse authorities?—Yes, just in the same way as in the other schools.

104. Mr. Molloy.—And a free grant in the first instance?—Yes, all schools taken into connexion receive a free grant.

105. Chairman.—Would you give us the number of school hours for secular instruction, and on how many days in the week?—There must be not less than 4 hours on 5 days of the week for secular instruction, but those 4 hours may include an interval for play of not more than half an hour.

106. And in practice are the hours limited to 4 hours or are they longer in the Schools through the country generally?—The hours are a little longer in the majority of cases; I believe in some schools they are limited to exactly what is laid down.

107. Mr. Redington.—Some subjects must be taught in school hours, and others outside school hours?—Yes, most of the extra subjects must be taught outside the ordinary school hours.

108. And then there are some subjects which may be taught either in or out of school hours?—Yes, there are.

109. Could you tell us the subjects of the school curriculum that must be taught in the ordinary school hours?—Reading, writing, arithmetic, grammar, geography, needlework, if it be a girl's school, or there be a workmistress, agriculture in the case of rural schools under a male teacher; those are the subjects that must be taught.

110. Did you mention spelling?—Yes, I should have mentioned spelling.

Chairman.—Agriculture must be taught within school hours?—Yes.

111. Mr. Redington.—You mean the text book?—Yes, the theory of agriculture.

112. What subjects may be taught either in school hours or out of school hours?—There are certain optional subjects; drawing may be taught inside or outside school hours, algebra, geometry, and mensuration may be taught inside or outside school hours.

113. Mr. Molloy.—You omitted to mention book-keeping, does not that come in, in town schools?

Feb. 4, 1897.
Mr. Alexander Hamilton, M.A.

Jan. 3, 1897. — Mr. Alexander Hendren, M.A.

—Yes, it takes the place of agriculture. It is an optional subject in all schools.

114. Mr. Redington.—It would be desirable to have the three lists, viz.: the compulsory subjects in the curriculum, the subjects that may be taught either in or out of school hours, and the subjects that can be taught only out of school hours. Are not there three different categories?—They are.

115. Chairman.—Can you put a list of those subjects in at your leisure?—Yes.

116. Mr. Redington.—Under what category would drawing come?—Drawing is an extra subject, but it may be taught inside school hours, or it may be taught outside school hours.

117. Handiwork?—Handiwork may be taught inside school hours or outside school hours.

118. Cookery?—Under the present regulations cookery may be taught inside school hours.

119. And laundry work?—And laundry work also.

120. Chairman.—How is cookery taught? Is it the theory only, or practically?—Both theory and practice.

121. In school hours?—Yes.

122. Captain Shaw.—Has any individual scholar to learn all those compulsory subjects; would any boy learn the whole seven subjects you have mentioned?—Yes, in certain classes every pupil would learn these subjects; there are some classes that do not take all those subjects.

123. There are some that do?—And some that do.

124. Chairman.—Will you tell us how teachers are appointed?—The teachers are appointed by the local managers of the schools, subject to the approval of the Board.

125. And what are their ages, the minimum and the maximum?—The minimum age is 18 and the maximum age 35.

126. Does that apply to both male and female teachers?—Yes.

127. Most Rev. Lord Plunket.—That is at the time of their appointment?—At the time of their appointment.

128. Chairman.—But is there any exception to that rule of age?—There is. The exception is if a teacher from another educational organisation comes into the service of the Board the age for appointment might be extended up to 40 instead of 35, provided the teacher had been employed from 1st of January, 1895, in this other organisation.

129. Rev. Dr. Evans.—On that point is there any exception in the case of [illegible] schools?—Not that I know of.

130. May not a teacher be appointed to an [illegible] school outside these limits of age?—Not so far as I know.

131. Chairman.—Into what classes are the teachers divided?—Into three classes—third class, second class, and first class, and each of these is divided into a second and first division.

132. How would you describe the teachers?—They are divided into principal teachers, assistants, junior literary assistants, work mistresses, and teachers of special industrial departments.

133. What persons are eligible for appointment as teachers?—Persons eligible for appointment as teachers are those who have been trained, or monitors or pupil teachers who have obtained classification at the end of their course, or teachers already holding classes.

134. How are teachers promoted?—Promotion from the second division of third class to the first division of third class is made on the recommendation of the District Inspector on account of the efficient conduct of the teacher during a year's service; and similarly from second division of second class to first division of second class teachers are promoted on the recommendation of the District Inspector.

135. Mr. Redington.—Under the old programme?—That was under the old programme.

136. Chairman.—I want to ask you a question now arising out of that—When a teacher has been appointed to a non-vested school or in a rural district, and that teacher is promoted, does that teacher, as a rule, remain in the same class, or is the teacher promoted to some other class of a more important character?—Oh, no; his promotion does not affect his position in the school, it becomes a personal matter. He receives a higher salary if it be such promotion as carries a higher salary. There is no difference between the salary of second division of third class and first division of third class, but there is a difference between third class salary and second class salary.

137. Mr. Redington.—But in a very small school he cannot get more than third class salary?—No.

138. In schools under 30 third class salary is the maximum, and between 30 and 35 second class salary is all he can get, whatever his classification may be, and first class salary can only be given where the average is over 35?—Yes.

139. Chairman.—In point of fact, if a person wishes for promotion who is in charge of a small school he can only obtain that promotion by seeking another situation; is that so?—Within certain limits he may obtain the promotion, but if the attendance is very small he may not obtain the salary that attaches ordinarily to that promotion.

140. He may obtain the rank without the pay?—In certain cases he does.

141. A Teacher promoted in classification may look for a more advantageous and profitable school elsewhere?—Yes.

142. Mr. Redington.—How many Training Colleges are there for teachers?—There are five.

143. Can you name them?—The Marlborough-street Training College, under the Commissioners, with two departments, for Male Teachers and Female Teachers; Drumcondra, for Roman Catholic Male Teachers; Baggot-street, for Roman Catholic Female Teachers; Kildare-place, for those of the Irish Church, both Males and Females; and Waterford or De la Salle Training College, for Roman Catholic Male Teachers.

144. What is the length of the course of the Training Colleges?—It begins in September and continues until about the end of the following June.

145. For how many years is the course?—There may be a two years' course or only a one year's course.

146. Who enter for a one year's course?—Teachers already classed, and in charge of schools.

147. And who enter for a two years' course?—Candidates who offer themselves for that course; they may be teachers under certain circumstances, teachers in charge of schools, but they resign their schools.

148. Or those who have been monitors?—Or monitors at the end of their course.

149. Or pupils who have not been monitors?—Or candidates who have not been monitors, who simply offer themselves for examination.

150. You said Marlborough-street College is under the management of the Commissioners?—Yes.

151. The others are under local management?—Yes.

151a. Is it compulsory for teachers to be trained?—No, it is not.

152. Monsignor Molloy.—It would be impossible I suppose to make it compulsory, because the number of trained teachers at present available is not sufficient for all the schools in Ireland?—No.

153. Mr. Redington.—The curriculum in the Training Colleges is determined by the programme for the promotion of teachers?—It is.

154. Are any subjects taught in the Training Colleges that are not included in the curriculum for the promotion of teachers?—Yes, there are some subjects taught that are not included in the curriculum for promotion.

155. What are those subjects?—Music and drawing are taught; they do not enter into the curriculum for promotion; handicraft does not enter into it.

156. In future, music will be an optional subject for all teachers seeking promotion?—It will, be under the new programme.

157. And in future, drawing will be a compulsory subject for all teachers seeking promotion?—It will.

158. And needlework will be a compulsory subject for all female teachers seeking classification as well as promotion?—It will. In a certain sense it has been compulsory, that is to say, the teachers were obliged to submit to examination, but the marks were not reckoned in the trial for class classification; they were obliged to take needlework and attend and be examined.

159. What kind of drawing is required from the candidates who are going in for promotion under the new programme?—Freehand drawing; then there is also model drawing and geometrical drawing.

160. Most Rev. Dr. Walsh.—The first [illegible] not compulsory?—Freehand I think is compulsory.

161. Mr. Redington.—Will you put in the programme?—Yes.

162. Most Rev. Dr. Walsh.—One point I wish to have cleared up, Mr. Hamilton; training is not compulsory for teachers?—No, it is not.

163. Is training compulsory for promotion to first class?—It is now.

164. But that was not always so?—No, it was not always so.

165. When was it made compulsory, about 1887 I think?—1887 it was.

166. And even at present teachers who were in the service before 1887 can obtain promotion to first class without being trained?—If they were of a certain age.

167. And in the service of the Board before that date?—Yes and [illegible].

168. But for other teachers training is a necessary condition now of promotion to first class?—It is.

169. Mr. Redington.—Is there a special teacher of drawing in the Marlborough-street Training College?—There is.

170. And of music?—Yes.

171. Both vocal and instrumental?—Both vocal and instrumental.

172. Mr. Molloy.—And in the other colleges, the denominational colleges, are there any special teachers of drawing?—I believe there are, but I know very little of other colleges, they are under the management of my colleague.

173. Mr. Redington.—By instrumental music what do you mean?—The piano and the harmonium are the instruments.

174. Chairman.—Supposing a teacher who was very good at certain subjects, above the average, was yet unable to learn anything of music or drawing to come up to the standard required, would that be a bar to his promotion to first class?—Under the new programme failure in any subject that is compulsory will certainly be a bar to promotion; these subjects have not affected the promotion of teachers up to the present, for they did not enter into the course for their promotion.

175. Most Rev. Dr. Walsh.—The minimum standard for passing in a particular subject is 30 per cent.?—It is.

176. And in order to pass the general classification they must get 50 per cent of the marks assigned?—Yes.

177. That is taking the subjects all round?—Yes.

178. Fifty per cent. of the aggregate of obtainable marks and 30 per cent. in each particular subject?—Yes, that is the standard.

179. Chairman.—What is the distinction between teachers and assistant teachers?—In regard to payment, teachers are paid according to their rank and classes if the attendance is sufficient.—

180. But will you first tell me what is understood by an assistant teacher, does it imply that there is a head teacher as well?—It does.

Feb. 4, 1897.

Mr. Alexander Hamilton, M.A.

181. And therefore it necessarily follows that where there is an assistant teacher, in that school there is more than one teacher?—Yes.

182. They are not a different class from ordinary teachers?—Oh, no.

183. I mean an assistant could become a principal next day if he got another school?—Yes. There is no difference except difference of position and employment.

184. As long as they are assistants they only get third class salary?—There is a fixed salary for assistants no matter what their class.

185. Does promotion go on the same lines as that of the principal teachers with regard to assistant teachers?—Almost on the same lines.

186. Most Rev. Dr. Walsh.—Is not the qualification for assistant teacher precisely the same as the qualification for principal teacher?—So far as their examination is concerned it is.

187. Rev. Dr. [illegible].—May I ask you do the assistants in Model schools get full class salaries?—Yes, assistants in Model schools and in Training schools get full class salaries.

188. So in Model schools they are not limited to third class salaries as they are in Ordinary schools?—No.

189. Mr. Redington.—There are also other exceptional advantages given to Model school teachers in the shape of supplementary salaries?—Yes, in certain cases.

190. Will you explain the principle on which results fees are paid?—For each particular class there is a programme laid down, which is placed before the teacher. At the end of the results year a list is prepared of all pupils in the school who during the results period have made at least 100 attendances; they are arranged according to the classes, beginning with the infants and going up to the highest class in the school. The Inspector examines these different classes according to the programme provided, and assigns a mark in each particular subject, writing it opposite the name of the pupil.

191. Assigns a mark?—Assigns a mark, either No. 1 pass or No. 2, or 0 for failure.

192. No. 1 being the highest?—The higher degree of excellence. Then he sends up this marking paper to the Education Office, the marks are tabulated in the Education Office and the values given to them are summed and computed, and they determine in the Education Office in what proportion these payments are to be made to the different teachers, principal and assistant, or to more assistants than one if there be more.

193. What is the usual division of results fees between principal and assistant?—The principal teacher gets twice as much as the assistant.

194. And each assistant gets the same amount?—Each assistant gets the same.

195. Do the fees for each subject differ considerably?—Oh, yes, they do.

196. Will you mention the highest fee given?—The highest fee given for any ordinary subject is 3s. for a pass.

197. What is that for?—Agriculture gets that fee; drawing also may get that fee.

198. Could you mention the fees for drawing?—The fees in drawing are, third class, 2s. 6d.; fourth class, 3s. 6d.; fifth class, first stage, 3s., second stage, 4s.; and sixth class, 4s.

199. And the fees in needlework?—They begin in second class; the fee for second class needlework is 6d.; for third class, 1s.; for fourth class, 2s.; for fifth class, both stages, 2s. 6d.; and for sixth class, 3s.

200. For handicraft?—For handicraft there is a [illegible] fee.

201. What is the lowest class that can take it?—The fifth.

202. Can a fee be paid a second year for handicraft?—Yes, the fee is paid twice for handicraft.

Oct. 4, 1897.
Mr. Alexander [illegible], M.A.

203. Would you give us the fees in each class for agriculture?—Agriculture cannot be taken up before the fourth class; the fee there is 4s., in first stage of fifth, 5s., in second stage of fifth, 5s., and in sixth class, 5s.

204. Are the fees in cookery 4s. for the fourth, and 5s. for the fifth?—I believe the fee is 5s. for fifth or sixth class.

205. CHAIRMAN.—With regard to the fees for agriculture, and also for cookery, is the examination only in the theory of agriculture and the theory of cookery, or where there is the opportunity of a test of practical examination, as in the case where there are those farms and gardens, is there any practical work included as well as what can be learned from books?—As far as the ordinary results reports are concerned the examination in agriculture is purely on the theory; it is held by the District Inspector of each district. But in the case of school farms and school gardens there is a special examination dealing also with the practical part.

206. And are there any results fees attaching to that?—Yes; results that are a much higher scale attaching to practical proficiency.

207. And with regard to cookery how is that done? Is there any practical way of teaching cookery?—Oh, yes; there is a practical teaching of it, and practical examination.

208. And the results fees are increased where there is an opportunity of practical examination?—In cookery examination and teaching are always practical.

209. Monsignor MOLLOY.—What examination is held in handicraft at present? What is the nature of the handicraft?—The only handicraft that I know anything of is woodwork, planing and sawing, and something of that kind.

210. Then the examination is a practical examination?—A practical examination.

211. Mr. REDINGTON.—Besides fees for practical work in agriculture, does not the teacher get a special fee for the way in which the garden or farm is kept?—Yes; where there is a school farm or school garden there is a special fee for that.

212. Are these not higher than given for some literary subjects, such as Latin and Greek?—Yes; ten shillings is the fee.

213. Mr. MOLLOY.—In connection with the principal examination in cookery are there not also demonstration lessons given, and an examination on the demonstration lessons by the Inspector?—The demonstration lessons are given by these itinerant instructors, and the Inspector's examination comes later.

214. Most Rev. Dr. WALSH.—You were asked by Lord Belmore about the practical teaching of agriculture. I wish to ask your attention to this passage in one of the Inspector's reports:—"Very little intelligent instruction is given in agriculture; the prescribed chapters of the text book are occasionally learned, or rather committed to memory; but it is very seldom indeed that I find the subject efficiently taught." Does that correspond to the results of your examination?—Not quite; I should not go so far as that.

215. Here is another extract:—"Judging from the results of the examination in agriculture, the study in the schools here is neither intelligent nor calculated to serve the pupils in after life." Does that fall in with your experience?—I think that is too strongly put; certainly my experience would not lead me to say that.

216. "The teachers rarely illustrate their instruction by reference to the actual work in the fields around." Does that correspond with your experience?—I think it is true to a considerable extent.

217. Monsignor MOLLOY.—Can you say roughly in how many schools cookery is carried out?—No; I have no statistics on that point.

218. Captain SHAW.—Does the teacher's payment for teaching these extra subjects depend entirely on results fees?—Yes.

219. Mr. REDINGTON.—What proportion do results fees bear to the total income of the teacher?—I think not more than one-quarter, if so much.

220. Rev. Dr. EVANS.—I think you said in the division of the results fees the principal teacher got twice as much as the assistant?—Yes; I think so.

221. In a school then in which there are five assistants how would results fees be divided?—The principal teacher would get twice as much as any one of the assistants.

222. Does that mean that the principal teacher gets half?—Oh, no.

223. Capt. SHAW.—How are the utensils and the kitchens provided for the cookery? Where do the funds come from for providing whatever is necessary?—From local resources.

224. Most Rev. Dr. WALSH.—But where do they come from in the Model schools?—I think in one or two cases——

225. In Marlborough-street where do they come from?—They must have been provided from the College funds.

226. You don't think they are provided from local resources in the school at Marlborough-street?—No; not in that case.

227. Do you think they are provided from local resources in any of the Model schools? But perhaps you don't go outside the Marlborough-street establishment; we can ask one of the other Inspectors.

228. Mr. REDINGTON.—With reference to the income of the teachers would you kindly say from what sources it is derived? First, the salary?—Yes; salaries.

229. Secondly?—Results fees; then the residual grant.

230. Explain, please, what the residual grant is?—It is a division among the teachers of a certain sum of money from Parliament awarded by the Act of 1892.

231. When school fees were abolished?—When school fees were abolished.

232. Then is there not an addition of 30 per cent. to the salaries given under that same Act?—There is.

233. Then there is a capitation payment under the Customs and Excise Act?—There is, also.

234. Most Rev. Lord PLUNKET.—You spoke of No. 1 pass and No. 2 pass. Does No. 1 imply greater proficiency? Do the results fees differ proportionately to the passes?—No; there is no difference; the fee is the same.

235. Monsignor MOLLOY.—The fee is independent of the proficiency if the pupil passes?—Yes.

236. Most Rev. Dr. WALSH.—There is a notable difference between the value of a No. 1 pass and a No. 2 pass from an educational point of view?—There is a difference.

237. What is the qualification for a No. 2 pass? What percentage for answering?—About 40 per cent.

238. And what is the qualification for a No. 1 pass?—About 60 per cent. or upwards.

239. But it may go from 60 per cent. to 100 per cent.?—Yes.

240. So you may have a difference of between 40 per cent. and, it may be, 60 per cent. or 80 per cent., representing the difference between No. 1 and No. 2 pass?—There may be. The No. 1 pass, however, may represent only 61 per cent., while the No. 2 pass may represent 59 per cent.

241. And there is no difference in the results fees?—There is no difference in the results fees.

242. When we find it stated in the published reports of the Board that a certain number of pupils have passed, does that give any idea as to whether the pupils passed as No. 1 or No. 2 passes?—No; there is no means of distinguishing.

243. A pupil may pass in the sense of our published reports without getting a No. 1 pass in any subject?—Possibly.

244. Monsignor MOLLOY.—When these returns come up to the office what use is made of this distinction between No. 1 and No. 2 passes? What does it avail for?—It avails to some extent in determining the character of the school, determining whether the school is efficiently taught or not.

8th Jan. 1896.

Mr. Alexander [illegible], M.A.

245. If they get No. 2 passes, the pupils pass, and that shows efficient teaching, but a school gets a better reputation if it has a large number of No. 1 passes?—Yes, it does.

246. Most Rev. Dr. Walsh.—Allow me to ask you, as regards the money paid in fees, is distinction made in any class of schools? What about the Convent schools? In their case does the payment depend on the proportion of No. 1 passes that the Convent school has on the results examinations?—I think not.

247. It merely depends on the results of the examination, irrespective of whether the passes are No. 1 passes or No. 2 passes?—I think so. It depends on the percentage of passes.

248. So that in no case does the payment to the school depend upon whether the passes are No. 1 or No. 2 passes?—It makes no difference in the payment.

249. Mr. Redington.—If the actual passes obtained bear the relation to the total possible passes of 80 per cent. in a Convent school, it is considered to be an efficient school and gets a higher merit capitation grant?—Yes.

250. A grant of 11s. per head?—Yes.

251. And if less than 80 per cent. 10s.?—Yes.

252. Most Rev. Dr. Walsh.—If what is less than 80 per cent.?—If the percentage of actual passes on possible passes is less than 80 per cent.

253. Mr. Redington.—What subjects are taken into consideration in calculating those averages?—The ordinary subjects of the course.

254. The extra subjects are left out?—The extra subjects are left out.

255. Chairman.—Will you explain what is the distinction between ordinary and optional and extra subjects?—Ordinary subjects are those which a teacher is required to teach in his school, to instruct all the pupils of his school.

256. And what are optional subjects?—Those which he may, or may not teach. He is not required, but he may, if he chooses, take them.

257. Give an example?—Vocal music is an optional subject, and agricultural instruction in certain cases.

258. In certain cases only?—In certain cases it is a compulsory subject which the teacher must take.

259. I suppose that depends upon whether the schools are town or country schools?—Yes.

260. But do I understand that in all the country schools the theory of agriculture is supposed to be taught?—Yes, if the school is under a male teacher.

261. Mr. Redington.—Cannot optional subjects be taught in or out of school hours?—Yes.

262. Chairman.—What are extra subjects—Latin and Greek?—Oh, yes; there is a long list of extras, but it includes Algebra and Geometry, which may be taught in or out of school hours.

263. Mr. Hamilton.—What regulates the teaching of these extra subjects? Does it entirely rest with the decision of the teacher or Manager, or does it rest with the parents of the children?—Practically it is to a large extent in the hands of the teacher. If he is unwilling to teach them it is difficult to coerce him. If, on the other hand, he desires to teach them, the Manager may object and say he is taking up too many. The Manager has the right to interfere, but practically it rests with the teacher.

264. Chairman.—In the case of agriculture I understood you to say that in some cases it is compulsory?—Yes.

265. Does that imply that in the class of schools where it would be a compulsory subject the teacher should have a practical knowledge, or merely what he can learn from books?—It implies only that he has the knowledge which he obtained in his examination for his office of teacher.

266. He need not know how to practically carry on operations in the garden or farm?—No, that part is not tested.

267. Mr. Redington.—Is not the number of extra subjects taught limited by the Commissioners?—They interfere when they think the number is excessive.

268. What is considered to be the number that ought not to be exceeded?—Two or three, unless where there is a large staff of teachers.

269. Can a teacher teach an extra subject if he has not got a certificate of competency?—Generally speaking such a certificate is necessary for the teaching of an extra subject.

270. If there is no certificate are steps taken to see that he is competent?—Yes.

271. Rev. Dr. Evans.—In the list of teachers you mentioned you included junior literary assistants, is there any considerable number of them?—No, the number is small.

272. About how many?—I don't know; they are dying out. No new appointments are being made and the class is rapidly disappearing.

273. Mr. Redington.—How many classes or standards are there in National schools?—Well, there is the infants' class, then the first class, the second class, the third class, the fourth class, the fifth class in two stages, and the sixth class, also consisting two examinations—for which the pupil may be presented for promotion in the ordinary subjects.

274. There is a separate programme for each of these classes?—There is.

275. Chairman.—Is it possible for a small school to have a sixth class and no fifth, a fourth and no third if there are not enough pupils?—It may happen in certain cases.

276. Would a pupil in a school of this class who became too old or too advanced for third be promoted to fifth if there was no fourth, or would his promotion involve the making of a fourth class?—Probably if the school was very small that boy himself would constitute the class.

277. Captain Shaw.—A student must spend a year in each class?—Not necessarily; a teacher may and does, in some cases, promote him two steps in one year; it is not frequently done but sometimes happens.

278. Chairman.—It is possible in promoting a pupil to skip a class?—A teacher may under certain circumstances.

279. Will you kindly put in evidence the programme for teachers and for pupils?—Yes.

280. Monsignor Molloy.—Am I right in supposing that as a general rule each pupil goes steadily from class to class upwards and spends one year in each class?—That is so as a general rule.

281. And wherever there is a fifth class as a general rule there are four classes actually below it—would that be true as a general rule, and that wherever there is a fourth class there are three below it, and so on?—Yes, as a general rule.

282. There are a great many schools I suppose in which there may not be a fifth or a sixth?—There are some schools.

283. Mr. Hamilton.—I don't know if you stated the limit of age with regard to the sixth class?

284. Most Rev. Dr. Walsh.—Is there any limit?—For admission or promotion?

285. Mr. Hamilton.—For remaining in it?—Practically we call on the managers or conductors of the school to withdraw pupils at 18 years of age.

286. Mr. Redington.—How much time is usually given to extra subjects, after the ordinary school hours are over?—That varies very much, some take one hour, and some an hour and a half, sometimes more.

287. Most Rev. Dr. Walsh.—For extra subjects?—Yes.

288. Mr. Redington.—Would one and a half hours be the longest time pupils ought to be kept after school hours?—I think it would.

289. I don't know if you told us that the four hours of school time are broken by an interval for play?—Yes, an interval of not more than half an hour.

290. Are they not generally so?—Yes, usually, almost invariably.

Feb. 4, 1897.
Dr. Alexander Hamilton, M.A.

291. Chairman.—What is the ordinary hour in a rural school for commencing the instruction?—Ten o'clock is the common hour.

292. Monsignor Molloy.—Then the hours are from 10 to 2?—10 to 2.30, or 3.

293. But the four hours that are necessary are from 10 to 2. Extra time would be taken in some cases?—Yes.

294. Most Rev. Dr. Walsh.—The half-hour for recreation or for religious instruction may be taken in the middle of the day?—Yes.

295. So the necessary school hours for secular instruction may begin at 10, and continue until half-past two from the interposition of that additional half-hour?—Owing to the half-hour for religious instruction it would be necessary to continue to half-past two.

296. Religious instruction can only be given at one time during the school hours?—At one intermediate time.

297. Monsignor Molloy.—But that time is not fixed for any particular hour?—No.

298. Does it happen that some schools have evening classes for extra subjects?—We have no evening classes for extra subjects.

299. Most Rev. Dr. Walsh.—There are evening schools?—There are evening schools, but they are quite different.

300. Mr. Redington.—With reference to that question, I think there has been a modification in the last few weeks of the rule allowing evening classes to be held in cookery after the lapse of an hour or two from the termination of the ordinary school business?—I was not thinking of that change.

301. When are the rolls marked?—The marking should be completed by eleven o'clock.

302. If a pupil comes in at a quarter to eleven o'clock that pupil will have satisfied the obligation of four hours school attendance by being there until two?—It is taken so; if he gets credit for attendance when the rolls are marked at eleven o'clock, there is nothing further.

303. With regard to the Compulsory Attendance Act, are you aware in how many places in Ireland it is in operation?—Not exactly. I think about 40.

304. You will get us, perhaps, that return?—Yes.

305. Mr. Molloy.—What is your opinion of postponing the marking of the roll until eleven o'clock, is it not a disadvantage to the pupils?—In some cases I think it is.

306. Would you be of opinion that marking it at ten o'clock would be more advisable?—I would be afraid to propose that.

307. Mr. Harrington.—With regard to the ages, what is the general age up to which boys remain in schools—town schools and country schools—can you say as a general rule?—Not with any degree of confidence; in some of the country schools, particularly in the south and west, we have boys and girls remaining considerably over 15; at all events a great many.

Rev. Dr. Evans.—In mentioning the grades or classes in the schools you did not say anything about Kindergarten?

Chairman.—I understand the next witness will give us information on that point.

308. Most Rev. Dr. Walsh.—There are one or two points that I want cleared up—first about compulsory attendance—the limit of compulsory attendance is the fourth class?—Yes.

309. In places where the law is at present in operation there is no compulsion affecting the attendance of the fifth and sixth classes?—No, it does not affect them.

310. You mentioned, I think, that there are about 40 places where the Compulsory Act is in operation at present?—Yes, I think so.

311. But the Act applies to a larger number of places?—Yes, it applies to 116 places.

312. And it rests with the local authority to put it into operation?—Yes.

313. The Municipal Councils or Town Commissioners or whatever the local authority may be?—Yes.

314. And in a large number of towns through Ireland the local body in the exercise of its discretion has not put the Act in force?—That is so.

315. In the majority of places to which the Act applies has that occurred?—I cannot speak with any confidence as to numbers, but there are a considerable proportion of those where it is not in force.

316. Next about the management of the schools, the ordinary National schools as distinct from the Model schools are under local management?—Yes.

317. Are the Model schools in any case under local management?—They are under local management by the District Inspector stationed in the place.

318. Are they under local as distinct from official management?—No, there is no local management apart from that.

319. All the Model schools are under the management of some official of the National Board?—They are.

320. Who is the Manager of the Model schools throughout the country outside Dublin?—The District Inspector in each case.

321. Who are the Managers of the Model schools in Marlborough-street?—The Managers there are the Professors.

322. Rev. Dr. Evans.—You mean, of course, the Professors as the agents of the Board?—Oh, yes.

323. Is not the Board itself the Manager of the Central Model Schools?—Well, yes, in a certain sense it is.

324. Most Rev. Dr. Walsh.—But it has deputed or delegated the duty of management to the Professors?—So I understand.

325. You mean by the Professors the four Professors of the Training College in Marlborough-street?—Yes.

326. Monsignor Molloy.—Do they act as a body or individually, when they exercise their special functions?—They act as a body.

327. They hold a meeting—what number forms a quorum in order that their action would be legitimate?—I don't think that has been considered.

328. Most Rev. Lord Plunket.—I was led to understand that the Professors never held any stated meetings, is that in accordance with your knowledge of the case?—I think in fact I understand that the Professors appointed one of the four in turn to discharge certain duties—signing certain returns that are required from time to time and that they all take it in turn.

329. Monsignor Molloy.—Then in fact an individual Professor exercises the functions and they take it in turn?—Yes.

330. Rev. Dr. Evans.—With regard to the management of Model schools by District Inspectors, do they ever exercise the functions of appointing or removing teachers?—No, they do not either appoint or remove.

331. Most Rev. Dr. Walsh.—In those schools the appointment or removal of teachers rests with the Board?—Yes, in all cases.

332. Rev. Dr. Evans.—Do the Professors in Marlborough-street schools exercise the function of appointing or removing teachers?—They exercise the function of recommending the appointment or removal of teachers.

333. But the appointment and removal in all Model schools rests with the Board itself?—Yes, it does.

334. Most Rev. Dr. Walsh.—With regard to these capitation payments, we have it from you that there are two systems of paying teachers, either by class salary or capitation?—Yes.

335. The Convent schools are probably the principal representatives of the system of payment by capitation?—Yes.

336. Can you state which of those two systems results in the payment of a larger sum to a school, the capitation system or the salary system?—I have never compared them.

337. Take the case of a school with 100 pupils, what would the payment be—a Convent school—supposing the school to be an excellent one, they

would receive a capitation grant of twelve shillings per head?—Yes; there is an addition to that of three shillings and sixpence a head.

338. That would amount to £20 with this addition; perhaps you are not in a position to tell us which of those two modes results in the payment of the largest amount to the school?—I have not worked out the figures in such a way as to be clear about it.

339. It is stated in one of the returns that the average payment per pupil is £1 14s. paid in these Convent schools, we may take that as an official statement?—Yes.

340. And that in schools paid by classification—Convent schools—the payment is £1 1s. 8d. per head, we may take that also as official?—Yes.

341. And that in ordinary schools as distinct from Convent schools, that the payment is £1 3s. 10d., we may take that also as accurate?—Yes.

342. And that the average payment in Model schools is £2 for 3d. per head?—I have no doubt that is correct.

343. Captain Shaw.—Are there any special courses teachers can attend except when in training at the Training College?—There is a course at Glasnevin in agricultural instruction.

344. Any others?—I don't remember.

Mr. Molloy.—They can attend Science and Art Classes at the Technical Schools in Kevin Street.

345. Mr. Redmond.—The classes at Glasnevin last six weeks?—About that.

346. And during that time what becomes of the school?—Special permission may be given to close the school by notifying the vacation or a substitute may be put in charge.

347. Rev. Dr. Walsh.—One main thing here is to inquire how far manual practical instruction can be introduced in the system of primary education in schools; can you form any estimate of the number of teachers qualified to give this instruction?—I have not the [illegible] that [illegible] certificates [illegible] in a [illegible].

348. Do you think that the pupils would have time to get through the programme of literary education and also take their manual and practical instruction, would we have to [illegible] the programme of literary [illegible] in order to—in my opinion in small schools where there is only one teacher (I suppose I am asked for my opinion about it) the programme is one as it stands is rather heavy, and if [illegible] or anything like that be added something must be dropped when there is only one teacher to teach everything.

349. Monsignor Molloy.—Too **heavy for the** teacher or the pupils?—For both.

350. Chairman.—You mean that four hours instruction is too heavy for the teacher and pupil?—No, but that the programme is [illegible] in schools where there is only one teacher for the teaching of all subjects that are compulsory.

351. Rev. Dr. Walsh.—The programme is beyond the power of the teacher and pupil to get up provided you have only manual instruction?—Yes.

352. Monsignor Molloy.—Do you think it would be a much greater strain on the pupil to learn to use a piece of wood regularly in school than it would be to [illegible] at home; don't you think that a good deal of handicraft could be taught to pupils so that it would be a recreation rather than a strain on the mind?—Yes, I think it possible, but the hours for teaching, if the present programme is to be kept up, with this addition, must be extended, that is, the hours of compulsory teaching.

353. They would [illegible] hours?—I think so.

354. Most Rev. Lord Plunkett.—Or some of the other subjects would have to be omitted?—Yes, I think so.

355. Then the question would arise between the value of one subject and the other?—Quite so.

356. Monsignor Molloy.—You spoke of teachers having certificates for manual and technical instruction, how are they obtained?—There is an examination held yearly.

357. Will you explain why they get the certificates?—There is a regular programme, and the examination is conducted by an official of the Board of Works.

358. In agriculture, for instance, do they get their certificates on a purely theoretical examination?—Yes; there is no special certificate for agriculture, it is [illegible] of the subjects of classification, in which a teacher is examined; if he obtains his classification he is [illegible] qualified to teach in all those subjects.

359. What are the subjects in which there is a special certificate given?—Drawing and vocal music. Special certificates are given for French and Latin, and [illegible] other extras.

360. Is there one for **handicraft?—Yes, a special** certificate.

361. How is the examination conducted for giving that special certificate?—There is a written paper and a practical examination, by an expert.

362. Is that expert an official of the Board or an outsider?—He is an outside expert.

363. Captain Shaw.—Is he an expert as a teacher or an artificer?—He is an official of the Board of Works.

364. Does he know anything about teaching?—I don't think he has any acquaintance with teaching.

365. Most Rev. Dr. Walsh.—Is he a trained teacher?—He is not a teacher at all.

366. Is he a [illegible] in the office of the Board of Works?

367. Is he an officer who works with tools?—I don't know if he is a practical worker himself.

368. Monsignor Molloy.—Does the Board give certificates for teachers of cookery?—I think not.

369. I think they have got three teachers of cookery from [illegible]?—Yes, they have.

370. Do you know how many teachers they have for all branches?—There are at present four [illegible] teachers employed.

371. Is that the whole amount of teaching in cookery up to the present, the teaching given by these four teachers?—No, it has been taught [illegible] in a number of schools before the employment of these teachers.

372. And the pupils also gave these lessons certificates?—I think not; it was taught in a number of the Convent schools in which the teachers were considered competent, but no special certificate was required.

373. Mr. Redmond.—Can you give us the name of the expert who examines for certificates in handicraft?—Mr. Robinson.

374. Is he not an architect inspector of buildings under the Board of Works?—I think so.

375. Mr. Molloy.—The teacher has another paper—Yes, but Mr. Robinson only examines the practical part of the examination.

376. Most Rev. Dr. Walsh.—Who is the teacher?—I don't know his name.

377. Is he a person of any educational experience except teaching handicraft to the children in Marlborough-street?—It is not he who does that; handicraft is taught to the children by the teachers of the school.

378. One of the literary staff of the school?—Two of the ordinary literary staff teach it to the children.

379. I see one of the questions put in the examination for this certificate in handicraft is "State how you would sharpen a saw;" a written explanation has to be given of this operation, is that so?—I suppose it is, I don't know the question.

380. Has the person going in for this certificate to sharpen the saw, or merely to give a written statement of how the thing should be done?—I should say both.

381. Most Rev. Lord Plunkett.—You have said that the result of the introduction of manual instruction into schools would be to displace or deteriorate the instruction given in other subjects. Have you con-

Dec. 4, 1897. Mr. [illegible], M.A.

Oct. 1, 1897.

Mr. [illegible] Hamilton, M.A.

sidered yourself as to whether, taking into consideration the disadvantages, it still would be desirable that such instruction should be introduced into the schools?—I think the introduction of manual instruction into schools might seriously determine the present disadvantage, unless the hours were considerably extended. If that were done it might be possible to introduce it without injury.

382. CHAIRMAN.—Would you expect the manual instruction should be given only occasionally once or twice a week or more often?—I think it should be given more frequently if it were to be of much value, and then it should take the form of an addition to the minimum four or four and a half hours a day.

383. Monsignor MOLLOY.—Do you think it would be seriously injurious to the schools to omit some of the subjects at present taught and compulsory?—No, I don't think it would be a serious injury.

384. What subjects do you think could most conveniently be omitted if any were to be omitted?—I am inclined to think that in our present programme probably the teaching of grammar in lower levels, it is less effectually taught and less useful in those cases.

385. Perhaps the analysis of sentences could be omitted?—I think it might.

386. Mr. [illegible].—Grammar for the third class pupils?—I think so.

Mr. EDMOND DOWNING, Chief of Inspection under the Board of National Education, examined.

Mr. Edmond Downing.

387. CHAIRMAN.—You are, I believe, Chief of Inspection under the Commissioners of the National Board?—Yes, my lord.

388. How long have you held that office?—Very nearly two years.

389. What were you before?—I was Head Inspector of schools for about three years and District Inspector for eighteen years.

390. Will you tell us from your experience the varieties of manual and practical instruction at present imparted, more or less, in the Irish National schools?—I will begin with kindergarten, which is the basis of manual instruction; then we teach drawing.

391. I have got another subject before we get to kindergarten. The question is, what are the varieties?—The varieties of manual instruction taught more or less in our schools are kindergarten, drawing, handicraft, practical agriculture, practical gardening, needlework of different kinds, the use of the sewing machine, cutting out of garments, knitting, lace-making, embroidery of various kinds, cookery, laundrying, dairying, management of poultry, weaving, a little; treatment of flax, a little; [illegible], a little; type-writing and shorthand, very little. Instrumental music I would include as manual training; others may hold a different opinion.

392. What are the scientific subjects relating to those you have mentioned, and which are taught in some National schools?—I would name book-keeping, for book-keeping is necessary for agricultural and dairy purposes; I would also include mensuration, chemistry, botany, physiology, mechanics, hydrostatics, light and sound, heat and the steam-engine, electricity and magnetism.

393. With regard to kindergarten, when was it introduced?—In 1885.

394. How is it encouraged?—Results fees are paid for it in infant schools—a special fee of 2s. being allowed in addition to other results fees.

395. What do you understand by kindergarten?—It is a peculiar method of amusing and interesting children at a very early age, and turning their own amusements to account in an educational way. It appears to be mere play, but this play is wisely constructed to lead the children to think and form ideas that they might not otherwise have. They are taught by means of it colour and form and number; and then there is physical training; the children go through calisthenic exercises, and they are taught to sing. It is a very varied kind of instruction. One principal part of it is an object lesson. A conversational object lesson is a most important feature of it.

396. What aids are given for the development of it?—In the Training Colleges the teachers are being trained in the practice of kindergarten, and there are two organisers who introduce it into schools when we are asked for their assistance—two organising mistresses.

397. Monsignor MOLLOY.—Who asks you?—Any Manager asking will get the assistance.

398. CHAIRMAN.—In what number of schools is it taught?—In 1896 there were [illegible] schools. It had increased from 376 in 1891. There is a slight progress, very slight, but still continuous since then, and in 1896 we had [illegible] schools or departments in which kindergarten was taught.

399. What number of children are there under instruction?—In 1896 the number was 57,100. It had increased within these five years from [illegible] to 57,1[illegible]—a very considerable increase.

400. Can you tell us anything about the payment for such instruction?—The payments amounted in 1895 to £1,613 in results fees for that object. The payments had increased from £[illegible].

401. Can you tell us the proportion of schools into which that kind of instruction has yet to be introduced?—There are more than 7,000 schools in which there are infant children that are not taught kindergarten.

402. What proportion would that be to the whole?—In about seven-eighths of all the schools in which there are infants kindergarten is not taught.

403. That is to say that there are only two-ninths in which it is introduced?—Yes.

404. Most Rev. Dr. WALSH.—You said that the number of schools in which it was taught was 523, and there are 7,000 in which it is not taught—are you speaking of seven-eighths?—We must omit some [illegible] schools in the calculation. With these 523 schools where the kindergarten is taught, there will be seen [illegible] girls' schools and [illegible] boys' schools. We have a good many schools in which there are no infants.

405. Monsignor MOLLOY.—What was the figure, 7,000? I understand you to say that the system was already taught in 523 schools, and that it has yet to be introduced into 7,000 others?—These numbers are approximately correct.

406. Most Rev. Dr. WALSH.—You said it was 222 boys' schools and [illegible] and girls' schools—is that so? I thought that 523 was the total number?—523 is the total number.

407. Including both boys and girls?—Yes; they are almost always mixed.

408. Monsignor MOLLOY.—They are infants?—Yes.

409. Then what was the figure 7,000 that you mentioned?—About 7,000 schools in which there are infants and in which there is no kindergarten instruction given.

410. Most Rev. Dr. WALSH.—So the proportion is not 2 to 7, but 523 to 7,000?—Yes; that is the proportion of schools in which it is taught as compared with those in which it is not taught.

411. Monsignor MOLLOY.—With regard to pupils, the figures you have given us, 523 schools and 57,100 pupils learning the system, would give an average of 115 pupils learning the system in each school where it is taught?—Yes.

412. Does that mean that there are 115 actually learning it, or does it mean that there are 115 pupils in the school where it is taught?—There

trained?—The number of women admitted in 1884-5 was 327, 310 remained to the close of the session. Out of 181 examined finally, 63 obtained certificates in kindergarten. The numbers are given at page 35 of the last report.

440. I think you will find it is 174 women who passed out your students and 111 [illegible] students?—That is passing the examination. I was referring to the kindergarten when I said 63 obtained certificates.

441. Yes, out of 174 who passed the examination at the close of their course?—Or 181 all examined.

442. Most Rev. Dr. Walsh.—The appliances that are required for kindergarten teaching and everything else, are a considerable cost to [illegible]?—Yes, a considerable cost is well-provided.

443. One of the difficulties of introducing or extending the system in Ireland is the cost?—Yes, the original cost.

444. Who has to bear the cost of introducing those appliances?—The manager in the ordinary schools. It is more possible than on the teacher.

445. Do you know whether these kindergarten departments are to be found in the Convent schools as a rule?—Oh, yes.

446. Who bears the expense there?—The nuns.

447. Who bears the expense in the Model schools?—The Commissioners.

448. In the Model schools local managers have not to [illegible] for that purpose [illegible].

449. Are the Model schools the only schools in Ireland where the appliances for kindergarten are provided at the public expense?—They are the only ones.

450. Monsignor Molloy.—What is the cost of the equipment for a kindergarten system, would it depend on the number of the pupils to some extent?—Oh, yes, entirely.

451. Supposing you had 100 pupils under the kindergarten system, what would be the cost of the complete equipment?—Very considerable, and of course a room must be provided if you start from the very beginning, it is very expensive; a room of a [illegible] must be provided, and it must be supplied with rather costly furniture. The desks are made in a special way and figured, divided into squares and circles for the laying of the different little blocks of wood, then there must be a provision of charts and a large gallery, a very expensive thing to get up in a school.

452. What would that cost, over and above the school room itself?—I have not an idea, in schools of such great variation.

453. A complete equipment including furniture for 100 pupils?—I should say if you include the furniture it would cost £100.

454. Most Rev. Dr. Walsh.—Can we get from the [illegible] how much has been already expended out of the public funds for the establishment of kindergarten in each of the Model schools?—I think that could be got, I will try to get it.

455. Mr. Molloy.—Do you think the providing of a separate room for the kindergarten essential? Is it not a great hindrance to the starting of kindergarten classes to require a separate room?—I think the kindergarten in its integrity a separate room is required, but I think there should be a modified scheme. In fact the kindergarten we practise is not the kindergarten of Froebel, it is largely modified, and with a further modification there might be a scheme adopted in the ordinary schools by which it could be taught widely, the same views.

456. Mr. Hamilton.—Is there a general desire amongst the managers of [illegible] schools to have this system of kindergarten established?—I think so, I think it would be very popular, if the necessary funds were available.

457. Rev. Dr. Evans.—Is there any means of knowing whether the pupils who begin with kindergarten progress better in their course of education than those who did not so begin?—I should think so, I don't think there is any proof of that. I have no idea

what proof could be given that they had progressed better at the later stages.

458. Would the results of examinations show in infant classes whether the teaching of kindergarten had served those pupils or not?—If you mean in increasing their proficiency in literary instruction, I should say not, no great result in [illegible] of that, but it is in itself of very great value, of much more value for infants than the literary instruction. I think the literary instruction of children under seven is of comparatively little importance.

459. Have we any practical evidence at all that it has served the children or the schools in which it was taught?—Oh, I should say so. There is clear evidence of that, that it has served the pupils.

Rev. Dr. Evans.—I should like you to indicate what that evidence is, how it could be got hold of so that we could bring it forward here to bear upon our present inquiry.

460. Monsignor Molloy.—Have the Inspectors reported on the general development of the intelligence of the infants under this system?—I think there could be copious quotations bearing on that point.

461. Rev. Dr. Evans.—You don't give any opinion now in answer to my question. My own opinion is that it is exceedingly beneficial, but I want to know what means we have of obtaining information that might aid our present inquiry more than opinions; we can give you, I fear, nothing but opinions.

462. Would not the results papers disclose something in the way of information on this matter?—I think not.

463. Captain Shaw.—Could you not get an average age of children, say in the first class, that had been through kindergarten, and others in a school that had not been through it, and see what the average age of the classes were, and the relative numbers of passes, and so compare the results?—Yes, we could do something like that, but then that is not a fair comparison, for you are comparing one school with another.

464. Monsignor Molloy.—The result would be very much influenced by local circumstances?—Yes.

465. Captain Shaw.—Could you not pick out an average school where they don't teach kindergarten and the rest of the education is as good?—My view is that the teaching of kindergarten does not affect the passes at all afterwards, nothing will come of an inquiry of that kind.

466. Monsignor Molloy.—I think you said that you considered the effect of the kindergarten system was to train their intelligence while passing through that system?—Yes.

467. Would they not have the advantage of a trained intelligence over the others?—I am very sorry to say that our teaching papers don't give much evidence of intelligence at all, it is a great deal of rote work.

468. Most Rev. Dr. Walsh.—Take it in this way, do you consider that the evidence we get through those percentages of passes and the results system really gives any useful information as regards the efficiency of the schools?—I believe that as a test of intelligence it is not worth the paper it is written on, my lord.

469. Most Rev. Lord Plunket.—As regards your own experience as an Inspector, and having seen a great many schools, some in which the system has been carried out, and some in which it has not, as regards your own experience, have you observed anything more in the way of intelligence or of love of study among those who have passed under this system than among the others?—The desire of the children to attend the kindergarten school is obvious to all of us. They get to love the school. Children are forced to go to other schools, but they go to the kindergarten schools without any compulsion. In fact in Derry, while I was there, on several occasions children were sent to the school when suffering from infectious and infectious diseases, and when I remonstrated with the

teachers have got their certificates a very long time ago, and not having practised they are practically incapable of resuming the teaching of drawing. Perhaps 30 years ago they got their certificates and they have not taught or practised drawing since.

511. Rev. Dr. Evans.—Coming back to the Central Model schools, has there been a special teacher of drawing there from their foundation?—There has.

512. Was the appointment of a drawing master in these schools made with a view to the benefit of the teachers in the training college?—I should say so.

513. So that through the advantages obtained by the teachers in training there would be a benefit done all over Ireland in the schools in which those teachers afterwards were?—I take it so; at that time there was no other training college.

514. And that appointment of a drawing master in the Central Model school was not made with the intention of creating there to have an advantage over other schools in Ireland?—At the time that was done it was not so intended.

515. Most Rev. Dr. Walsh.—You know there are other Training Colleges in Dublin besides Marlborough-street?—Yes.

516. And there is a practising school attached to each of these Colleges?—Yes.

517. One in Kildare-place, one in Baggot-street, and one in Drumcondra. Is there a special teacher of drawing attached to these, paid by the State in the same way as the teacher of drawing is paid in Marlborough-street?—No.

518. Although the connection between the practising school and the Training College is the same as the connection between the Model schools and Marlborough-street?—That is so.

519. Then the teacher of drawing in Marlborough-street is paid, and he is not paid in the other cases?—Yes.

520. Chairman.—Is there any director of instruction in drawing?—No, my lord, and I think that is one of the drawbacks.

521. Most Rev. Lord Plunket.—I suppose one of the difficulties is that even a certificated teacher who has the whole charge of a school finds it very difficult to introduce the teaching of drawing among the other subjects that he or she have to impart?—Our children will not attend, up to this, at all events, we have no chance of getting them for school for longer hours than at present. It would be very injudicious of the teacher of a small school to take up any optional branch within the four obligatory school hours.

522. Mr. Harrington.—Do you consider that drawing ought to be taught in practically all schools?—I think so; a simple course of drawing, with this qualification—I would not like to see it taught in a school where there was any marked want of taste evinced in the teaching of it.

523. Most Rev. Dr. Walsh.—You would not consider that the possession of the certificate by a teacher was a necessary condition for allowing him to teach drawing?—No.

524. If he was able to teach drawing, and produced results that satisfied the Inspector, would you consider that to be a sufficient provision for allowing drawing to be taught in the school?—I would.

525. You would regard competency attested by the results of his teaching to Inspector as good a qualification as competency attested by a certificate?—I think so.

526. Most Rev. Lord Plunket.—Then you think a modified system in regard to drawing might be applied to these small schools just as you think a modified system in regard to kindergarten should be applied?—We are not overcrowding in drawing, and what we are getting done at present, I think, would be quite possible in all schools, and I think then that there should be more advanced drawing as an extra branch along with that.

527. Chairman.—Do you think that kindergarten and drawing are equally suitable for boys and girls?—I do, my lord.

528. And with regard to manual instruction what do you say?—In manual instruction they diverge at once; the occupations suitable for boys and girls branch off at once. When you have done with kindergarten and drawing other occupations are different for boys and girls in almost all cases.

529. The girls, of course, use their hands in the way of work?—They do at needlework. Every girl must spend an hour a day at needlework.

530. What do the boys do?—There is nothing to correspond for boys. The only practical instruction given to boys is practical farming, practical gardening, and handicrafts, and these are limited to very few schools. Handicraft is taught but in fifteen schools. The number of pupils examined in handicraft in 1895 was but 253.

531. Would you point to the page of the report at which that is given?—Page 32.

532. Monsignor Molloy.—In how many schools is cookery taught?—Cookery was taught in 60 schools in 1895.

533. Chairman.—With regard to shorthand and type-writing?—Taught only in two schools, and in no school at all in 1895. It dropped out after 1894.

534. Mr. Harrington.—Until lately was there a single course combining shorthand and type writing?—Yes.

535. And it was found inconvenient to have it combined, and lately they have been made separate courses?—Yes.

536. Do you anticipate that there will be more teaching of shorthand now?—There will be more teaching of both I expect.

537. Most Rev. Dr. Walsh.—While these two subjects were combined could shorthand be taught in any school unless the Manager provided a type-writing machine?—No.

538. How could a Manager provide a type-writing machine for his school?—Out of his own pocket.

539. And in no other way?—No other way.

540. He would get no grant for it from the Board?—No.

541. When type-writing is taught in the Model school who provides the machine?—We have not gone that length in providing a machine.

542. It is taught in Marlborough-street?—I am not quite sure.

543. It has been reported to the Commissioners at all events that it is taught there. Supposing it is taught, who do you think provided the machine?—I suppose the Commissioners supplied it.

544. It was very hard to have shorthand-writing taught in the schools so long as it was necessary to begin by buying a type-writing machine; that is no longer necessary?—No, it can be taught separately.

545. Rev. Dr. Evans.—You are aware that the Commissioners' stores supply instruments?—Yes.

546. Do they supply type-writers?—They do not.

547. Most Rev. Dr. Walsh.—You have given us figures to show the extent to which drawing is taught in the schools. I should wish to know whether, in your opinion, the teaching of drawing that goes on in our schools is worth very much. Is it really teaching?—It is not good teaching, but it is of some value.

548. I find in one of the Inspector's reports a paragraph on which I should wish to get your opinion—"The results obtained in drawing are as yet poor." You agree with that?—I think so.

549. Do you agree with this—"No great amount of supervision appears to be given to this subject; copy-books, pencils, and the harmful accessory India-rubber is supplied, and, provided the pupils remain quiet, they are left to their own devices"?—That would apply to that man's own district.

550. It is the Coleraine district. Do you think that is a fair description of how it is taught there?—It is not taught much there.

551. "About a third of the time is devoted to

drawing, the remainder in rubbing out what has been done." Is that what goes on under the name of teaching drawing in our National schools?—There is a good deal of it, but the defect is a little overstated.

[illegible]. Chairman.—Could you put in Tables showing the number of schools in which each kind of manual instruction was given in 1891-95, the number of pupils examined yearly in these subjects, and the amounts paid in result fees in these subjects?—Yes; this is it:—

—	Number of schools in which taught.					
	1891.	1892.	1893.	1894.	1895.	1896.
Kindergarten,	279	294	300	312	322	
Drawing,	1,047	1,149	1,295	1,318	1,401	
Handicraft,	14	14	11	10	15	
Sewing Machine, &c.,	452	447	461	426	460	
Cookery,	48	52	53	56	60	
Poultry,	8	9	9	8	12	
Dairying,	6	5	8	6	8	
Weaving,	2	1	2	3	5	
Net-mending,	-	-	1	1	3	
Type-writing,	-	-	3	3	-	
Shorthand,	-	-	2	3	-	
Instrumental Music,	156	158	145	158	163	

—	Number of Pupils examined.					
	1891.	1892.	1893.	1894.	1895.	1896.
Kindergarten,	30,437	31,037	33,743	35,117	37,160	.
Drawing,	18,301	30,416	54,731	62,216	67,167	.
Handicraft,	259	224	197	238	250	.
Sewing Machine, &c.,	4,138	4,050	5,077	4,752	5,514	.
Cookery,	963	986	1,025	1,320	1,432	.
Poultry,	150	114	113	154	190	.
Dairying,	73	61	64	97	79	.
Weaving,	46	43	57	107	75	.
Net-mending,	.	.	8	8	33	.
Type-writing,	.	.	16	20	.	.
Shorthand,	.	.	14	10	.	-
Instrumental Music,	1,034	1,011	973	907	1,103	.

—	Money paid in Fees, even pounds only given.					
	1891.	1892.	1893.	1894.	1895.	1896.
Kindergarten,	£2,918	£2,592	£2,241	£2,470	£2,519	
Drawing,	4,775	6,438	7,807	8,538	8,519	
Handicraft,	46	51	41	40	46	
Sewing Machine,	530	563	585	540	545	
Cookery,	207	232	260	312	313	
Poultry,	35	31	38	35	43	
Dairying,	19	19	15	21	17	
Weaving,	11	20	18	24	18	
Net-mending,	-	-	2	3	8	
Type-writing,	-	-	3	1	-	
Shorthand,	-	-				
Instrumental Music,	216	253	239	213	259	

The Commission adjourned to next day.

SECOND PUBLIC SITTING.—FRIDAY, FEBRUARY 5TH, 1897, AT 3 O'CLOCK, P.M.,

in the Royal University, Dublin.

Present:—The Right Hon. the EARL OF BELMORE, G.C.M.G., in the Chair; His Grace the Most Rev. the LORD PLUNKET, D.D., LL.D.; His Grace the Most Rev. WILLIAM J. WALSH, D.D.; The Right Hon. C. PALLES, LL.D., Lord Chief Baron of the Exchequer; The Right Hon. C. T. REDINGTON, M.A.; The Right Rev. Monsignor MOLLOY, D.D., D.SC.; Rev. HENRY EVANS, D.D.; Rev. HAMILTON WILSON, D.D.; Professor G. F. FITZGERALD, F.T.C.D.; STANLEY HARRINGTON, Esq., M.A.; W. R. J. MOLLOY, Esq.; and Capt. T. B. SHAW;

with J. D. DALY, Esq., M.A., Secretary.

CHAIRMAN.—Before calling the first witness the Commissioners desire to make it publicly known that they will visit some of the provincial centres for the purpose of taking evidence. They propose to visit Belfast, Cork, and Galway, and possibly a few other places, if found desirable later on. They invite the evidence of those who have practical experience to make, and who live in the neighbourhood of the centres named. Communications should be addressed to the Secretary.

Mr. ARTHUR PURSER, Head Inspector of National Schools, examined.

553. CHAIRMAN.—You are a Head Inspector of National Schools?—One of the Head Inspectors.

554. How long have you held that position?—Nearly six years.

555. What position did you hold previously under the Board?—That of District Inspector for about twenty years.

556. We will first deal with the subject of drawing: how far is drawing taught in National Schools generally?—Only freehand drawing is taught as a rule.

557. What provision was there for teaching it in the Training Colleges?—The Board's Rules require arrangements to be made for teaching drawing, the course in actual work includes little more than freehand drawing; in one or two Colleges a few of the students take a little more, some model drawing and a little geometrical drawing.

558. Would you explain what you mean by geometrical drawing?—Drawing with a ruler.

559. Like drawing [illegible]; I don't mean that they teach, but that would be like geometrical drawing?—Yes, Euclid's figures.

560. With regard to ordinary schools what is taught there?—Freehand drawing only.

561. And is that taught to any extent?—About one-twelfth of the schools, I think, learn drawing, not much more than one-twelfth at all events.

562. The larger schools?—The larger schools much more than the smaller ones.

563. Is drawing taught in infant schools?—Kindergarten drawing is taught in infant schools up to second or third class where they happen to have children so highly placed.

564. Is it continued from kindergarten to senior class without any break?—As a rule children will leave the infants' school after passing in first class, and when they get to the senior school they don't take up drawing until they get to the third class, so that there is a break of two or three years.

565. And then do you find they have forgotten what they already learned?—To a certain extent, yes.

566. How is drawing taught?—In most of the schools the teacher uses copy-books containing a pattern on one side and the pupil draws it on the other side; the teacher simply puts the copy-book before the children and lets them draw away. Some teachers who teach it correctly will go among the children when they are drawing and point out defects showing them how to hold their pencils and what errors to avoid, but as a rule that is all that is done. Some teachers, more latterly than formerly, make them draw from a distance, so that they cannot measure with bits of paper.

567. Are they allowed with the pattern in the copy-book, to measure?—They do always measure.

568. Do they draw at all from anything but flat patterns—models, for instance?—No, scarcely ever.

569. Not even in the higher classes?—Well, there might be some odd schools where they do, but practically not; in most of them certainly not.

570. Are model drawing, object drawing, and geometrical drawing taught?—Not in our schools.

571. What encouragement is given by the Commissioners in the way of fees?—They gave a fee for every pupil, from the third class up, who passes in drawing; it was mentioned yesterday. I think it is 1s. 6d. in third class, and it goes on up to 3s. in sixth class.

572. What you call Results fees?—Yes.

573. On what conditions are the teachers paid?—They are paid on condition of having a certificate of competency in black drawing.

574. And what are the conditions on which the certificates are granted?—They undergo an examination in freehand, geometrical and model drawing, and if they get 50 per cent. of the total marks allowed for any one of the three subjects they get a certificate in that division of the subject.

575. And is it necessary to obtain a certificate that they should pass in all three subjects?—No; if they pass in one they can teach that one.

576. Could this percentage be lowered?—I think the percentage of 50 could be lowered.

577. What would you suggest to lower it to?—You allow a teacher to teach agriculture if he answers 30 per cent., and you allow him to teach algebra if he answers 30 per cent., and a great many other things if he answers 30 per cent. I think for a certain amount of drawing you might accept a lower certificate and not give the full fee perhaps that you allow for a full certificate.

578. Do you think the lowering of the scale would lead to the more general teaching of the subject?—I am certain it would.

579. Is it at a certain point optional now?—Quite optional, except in so far as the Manager may desire him to teach it.

580. Is drawing more generally taught abroad?—Yes, a great deal more.

581. For example?—It is compulsory both in France and Germany.

582. Is manual training always combined with drawing?—There is no manual training abroad where drawing doesn't enter into it. If they have any manual training to do they have to draw sketches of it.

583. Have you yourself a knowledge of manual training?—To some extent. I was at the Leipzig Training School, the training school for manual handicraft.

584. MR. REDINGTON.—Who is the Principal there?—Dr. Götze.

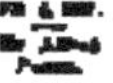

this I would not lower, because I don't think we want them in our schools: Latin and Greek scarcely come into primary education.

630. You said that drawing was taught in one-tenth of the schools in Ireland; if it is not taught in one-tenth, would you suggest that was a pity?—I should have said one-sixth.

631. Monsignor Molloy.—Is drawing usually taught by a teacher who teaches other subjects as well?—Yes.

632. Is that universal or is it only general?—It is universal in ordinary schools; it is not generally the case in the larger Convent schools, and it is not the case to a certain extent in the Central Model schools.

633. Part of the difficulty in making drawing universal would be the difficulty of getting a teacher who could teach drawing and all the other subjects as well?—Yes.

634. Have you considered whether it would be possible to establish a special teacher for drawing alone in a centre, and let him teach the schools in the locality at special times, giving him a certain number of schools?—would that be possible?—Quite possible.

635. Would it be desirable?—If the teachers of the school could teach it, I think it would be better done.

636. As I understand at present the number of certificated teachers is hardly more than one-half of the number of schools, therefore it is not possible that all the teachers could teach in their own schools?—A good many could get certificates if the standard was lower.

637. Is it desirable to lower the standard?—You would still only be paying for the work done.

638. We were told yesterday that the number of certificated teachers, including those who got certificates many years ago and who now, because they are out of practice, would be incompetent, there [illegible]. I take it that the number of teachers competent to teach drawing is quite insufficient?—That is so.

639. Would it be possible under your system to establish centres, and appoint masters to teach drawing and drawing only?—I don't think you could establish them in a country place without great expense.

640. In the large towns?—In the large towns, as a rule, you would not require it because there will nearly always be a teacher there who will have a certificate, or the manager could very readily at the first change in his staff introduce someone who would have a certificate.

641. What size of town do you include in that statement?—I mean a town of 10,000 inhabitants and upwards.

642. There are only a very small number of such towns in Ireland?—That is so.

643. If you went down to 3,000 say?—It would become very expensive.

644. In a town of 3,000 people might you not have some schools in the town itself and some within a distance of three miles to which he could go?—That would add very much to the expense—going to one of these schools, and teaching would occupy him the better part of the day.

645. Where there is a teacher of drawing how many hours in the week are given to drawing?—One hour to one and a half hours as a rule. There is that

had got his certificate many years ago, would it not be a help to him as stimulating to give him notice?—It would be a great help, but I doubt if it would pay the cost.

646. Monsignor Molloy.—But surely the object of teaching is not to make money?—Certainly not.

647. Then what about your objection?—I mean that the advantage of drawing would not be equal to the expense.

648. Mr. Redmond.—You say you would lower the standard?—For the present.

649. And yet you would require an examination to be passed?—Yes.

650. Do you anticipate that if you do that, many teachers who have not certificates now will get them?—A considerable number would. You must remember every day you meet a considerable number of teachers who fail below sixty per cent. and yet some above thirty per cent.

651. Can you suggest any other way of increasing drawing except by lowering the standard for certificates?—I know of no other way unless you make it a compulsory subject, but until you have more teachers competent you can hardly oblige them to do that.

652. Professor Fitzgerald.—I see that Professor Sullivan, of Cork, states that "drawing in primary schools should, in all cases, be restricted, so far as the payment of results fees is concerned to outline-drawing from the flat and common objects from the round." We say in our summary of proficiency now in Ireland "that the programme commences with free-hand drawing of the simplest character and advances to practical geometry, shading from the flat, shading from the round, perspective, and painting in water-colours." There is a very great difference, is there not, between Dr. Sullivan's opinion and our programme, which begins with free-hand drawing and ends with painting in water-colours—which do you think ought to govern us?—I think your programme is a good deal that has not been adopted; we have not got to that; we have not got even to drawing from the round.

Chairman.—We were told by a witness the other day that there is nothing but drawing from the flat.

Monsignor Molloy.—They get their choice and take the easiest.

653. Professor Fitzgerald.—Don't you think we ought to insist on drawing from the round?—I think so.

654. How far does our present arrangement—the plan with—proceed?—Free-hand of the simplest character.

655. Does it advance to practical geometry?—Not in the case of pupils.

656. Nor shading from the flat or shading from the round?—Shading from the flat perhaps a little more advanced than that.

657. I see in this book of Mr. Barter's, on "Woodwork" in London Schools, there is a matter thought of great importance, namely—drawing from models by measurement, mechanical drawing. Is there anything of that kind in our schools?—No, nothing.

658. Would it be difficult to make arrangements by which the teachers could be taught drawing from the flat, mechanical drawing, and drawing from the round, by bringing them to centres and teaching them?

teachers and teaching them that drawing was made compulsory, or by compelling them to go to the Science and Art classes?—Probably they may have had that.

667. Would not that be better than lowering the standard, bringing the teachers up to the standard?—I said I would only lower the standard temporarily.

668. Is our standard higher than in England?—I don't know what the standard in England is.

669. You said there was only one hour and a half given each week to drawing in our schools?—To the utmost.

670. How much is given to each child per week in writing?—In the lower class certainly more than three hours.

671. Would it not be well to diminish the time for writing and increase the time for drawing?—The writing is bad enough without it.

672. Would it not improve their writing to make them learn drawing?—A teacher often finds a difficulty in getting time for drawing, and I may often suggested to him to take it from the writing hours.

673. Mr. Haughton.—With regard to manual work, in order to introduce it into schools it would be necessary I suppose to omit certain of the subjects now being taught or to extend the time of teaching?—I think it would to a certain extent.

674. Which would you do, extend the time or reduce the subjects?—I would do both.

675. What subject would you omit?—Grammar, to begin with.

676. Chairman.—Would you omit it altogether or only partially?—I would omit it altogether as a special subject; grammar should go along with reading and explanations.

677. Most Rev. Dr. Walsh.—Grammar is not obligatory in England?—I think not.

678. Mr. Harrington.—You mentioned French; to what extent are modern languages taught?—To a very trifling extent; they are taught in a few Convent schools.

679. Chairman.—And a few Model schools?—Very little in Model schools.

680. Mr. Harrington.—What languages are taught besides French?—Practically no other. I have some German classes being taught once or twice, but only two or three pupils at a time.

681. What about Latin and Greek?—There is a little Latin taught.

682. In Convent schools only?—Latin and Greek are never taught in Convent schools.

683. In what class of schools is Latin taught?—It used to be largely taught in certain schools in the south of Ireland; I only came across it in one or two schools where the teacher had a knowledge of it himself—going through College he would take up Latin as one subject.

684. Professor Fitzgerald.—Do you think it is any use to a child to learn geography, to learn where the Hoang-ho or the Irrawaddy is?—If you taught them a knowledge of the places around them instead of the ordinary geography it would be extremely interesting.

685. I have made an effort every year, since I was a member of the Board, to get a knowledge of their own parish to be the first thing they should learn, rather than a knowledge of the world—would you approve of that?—I would.

686. The ordinary geography that they read out of their reading books about the Congo and India would be sufficient for them to learn?—Quite sufficient.

687. Most Rev. Dr. Walsh.—You are aware Geography is not obligatory in England?—Yes.

688. Captain Shaw.—How do you propose the teacher should qualify for the modified certificate?—Much the same way as at present—he gains a medal to draw.

689. He has to teach himself?—He gets practice.

690. If there was a centre that the teacher could attend, every Saturday afternoon under a regular master, would that be practical?—Yes; I think so.

691. Chairman.—That would be done in Model [illegible] Schools?—Yes.

692. Captain Shaw.—If the master would hold the class somewhere to a group of schools?—Yes.

693. Chairman.—Do you think there are in Ireland such convenient centres?—You could make a convenient centre for a dozen teachers, particularly on a Saturday.

694. Take a county like Donegal, would it not be difficult? There would be very few places where the difficulty would be great, but those would be quite exceptional.

695. Rev. Dr. Wilson.—Do you think it would be important that they should learn less in the literary and more of the industrial or arts side?—It depends on what you mean by the industrial.

696. Manual instruction?—I think manual instruction would be very useful, and a good training.

697. And you think it would be important that there should be somewhere, a centre where the teacher would learn, say on the Saturday, what he is to give in instruction to their pupils—do you think that a good arrangement for the Government to adopt?—Are you talking of drawing or manual instruction?

698. Of everything relating to woodwork?—I think the Saturday work would be of little use; the interval is too long; it would be better to have a three or six weeks course.

699. Mr. Molloy.—I should like to ask Mr. Nesbitt is he aware that the Commissioners have at this time special teachers of drawing, who are employed in teaching their—(illegible)—not only taught in the Model schools but gave instruction to the ordinary schools surrounding?—I was not aware of that; I was aware they taught in the Model schools.

700. Most Rev. Dr. Walsh.—What is the qualification in regard to any ordinary subject in the National schools?—Twenty per cent.

701. And the qualification in drawing is sixty per cent.?—Yes, sixty per cent.

702. Is there any reason for maintaining such an extraordinary discrimination as that, as against the teaching of drawing?—I don't think there is.

703. No such reason occurs to you?—It was made high, it seems to me, because it was an optional subject, and didn't come into the classification certificate, and therefore it was an inducement to one like to qualify better in that than in a series of subjects, where he had to pass in all without failure.

704. Apart from that, you see no reason to justify the maintaining of a sixty per cent. qualification in drawing, when twenty per cent. answers in bookkeeping or geometry?—There is some reason for having a higher standard, because he must have a practical knowledge to teach it.

705. Must he not have a practical knowledge of book-keeping or writing to teach it?—Not to the extent that it is taught in our schools; a man may be a very bad writer and yet by making his pupils take very great care, he may be able to make them write fairly well, but he may not understand the technique of drawing at all.

706. Do you think it would be advisable to have the same percentage for the teachers in drawing that we have in the other subjects, or do you think it advisable that a higher qualification should be insisted on?—I think it ought to be something higher.

707. How much higher?—I would not at present go beyond forty per cent.

708. That is twice as high?—Yes.

709. Mr. Harrington.—It is not merely in drawing that the percentage is sixty?—No.

710. What is it in modern and ancient languages, isn't it sixty per cent.?—Yes.

711. So that this high percentage is not required in drawing alone?—Yes.

712. Most Rev. Dr. Walsh.—But as the proposal is to make the teaching of ancient or modern languages obligatory, it is proposed to make drawing obligatory?

Feb. 8, 1898.

Mr. Alfred Nesbitt.

Oct. 8, 1896.
Mr. Alfred Purser.

—Yes; you have a somewhat similar case with regard to geometry and algebra. A male teacher need only get twenty per cent. in those subjects, but if a female teacher wanted to teach them she must get sixty per cent.

713. CHAIRMAN.—With regard to the kindergarten system, in what proportion of schools is it taught?—One-twelfth.

714. Is the inspection full and satisfactory?—I would say it was too mechanical.

715. How would you suggest it could be improved?—Well, I think the teachers want to be taught it better, in the Training Colleges where they learn it; chiefly to be taught that it is not merely letting children to build a castle with bricks, it must have more meaning, they should be taught the meaning of it and to teach it intelligently.

716. Is drawing taught as part of the subject now?—It is, to a small extent, practically however only with the second class; the first class have a little slate-drawing.

717. Could kindergarten teaching be more generally introduced?—I think they could; they have been introduced in French schools.

718. And what advantage would that secure?—It would make them handier, and would be a good preparation for manual training.

719. They teach these things more in France and Germany than we do?—Kindergarten is not part of the German course: there is a good deal of it taught at the infant stages, but the State doesn't compel it to be taught or encourage it very much. In France it is part of the school course from the top to the bottom.

720. Do they teach things in France and Germany which we do not teach here?—Well, yes; they teach more about things than we do; they teach history a good deal, and natural history in these continental schools, and anything that will train the character of the children.

721. But coming back to Ireland will you tell us if [illegible] cooking, dairying, laundry and cooking, are taught to any extent?—The first three are very little, but cooking is taught more extensively. In some of the schools a great deal of it is taught in Dublin.

722. How is that managed for—have they a kitchen?—It is generally taught in schools that have more than one room; one of the classrooms is devoted to it on so many afternoons in the week. In a few cases of course they have a special kitchen for the purpose.

723. To what extent is it taught—do they for instance take a fowl with its feathers on?—I have never seen them carrying it quite so far as that; they take a fish just as it comes from the fishmonger, and they prepare it for the pot, and the same way with the meat. I have never seen them take a fowl, but they do actual cooking.

724. I have got in my paper "Industrial scheme for VIth class;" explain this?—Well a few years ago our instruction was almost entirely literary except needlework for girls from the second class to sixth, the Commissioners proposed that the sixth class girls instead of having so much literary work should spend two hours a day at industrial work of some kind, different classes of needlework chiefly.

725. Does this include shirt making?—Yes. Dress making, and lace making.

726. In about how many schools of the total number in Ireland was this done?—I think last year 1,500.

727. Was this scheme a success?—No, I don't think it was popular in the country, a great many schools got leave to give it up and return to the literary programme; there was a difficulty in procuring the material, it generally fell on the teacher, and it was too great a tax on her, she could not afford to provide the materials for so much sewing.

728. MR. REDINGTON.—Have you heard complaints of too much time being given to industrial subjects?—At first, yes; a great many schools thought they should give three hours.

729. What is the amount of time they are bound to give if they take it up?—Two hours.

730. Are they two consecutive hours?—Not necessarily; very often not.

731. Would you begrudge out of a school day of four hours to five, would—two hours a long time to industrial work?

732. Schools that don't take up the Commissioners' scheme devote one hour a day to needlework?—Yes.

733. What do you think the longest time that should fairly be given?—An hour a day is quite enough for needlework.

734. With reference to your statement in answer to His Grace that 20 per cent. entitles a teacher to teach a subject, is it not the case that in addition to getting 20 per cent. in each subject he takes up he must get 50 per cent. of the whole number of marks?—Certainly.

735. CHAIRMAN.—Do you consider agricultural instruction practical?—No, it is only taught from the text-books; the children don't understand anything about what they are reading.

736. We had it stated here that in a few schools there were gardens?—In those cases the instruction is practical.

737. Is it well taught in those cases?—I have seen very few; in some cases the instruction was fair enough.

738. MR. REDINGTON.—It is the duty of the Inspectors to examine the school gardens and of the Agricultural Superintendent to examine the school farms?—Yes.

739. Are many of the Inspectors experts in gardening or practical agriculture?—A few are.

740. Do you think it would be better to have an agricultural expert to inspect the gardens as well as farms?—Yes.

741. CHAIRMAN.—To what extent is manual instruction carried out in Training Colleges and schools?—In the Training Colleges I have to deal with it is only practised in Kildare-place, the Church of Ireland Training College. All the male students there have to go through a course laid down for them, chiefly carpentry work. As far as schools are concerned I only know one or two—one is Kildare-street, in a small school in Swords boys' school, and I saw a very good class at [illegible] quite lately. That is not in my circuit.

742. What is the nature of the inspection, and what teachers are employed?—In the Kildare-place school it is an instructor, the same man who teaches the Queen's Scholars. In the Swords school it is the teacher of the school that teaches.

743. Most Rev. Dr. WALSH.—I see in your reports you recommend that some modification of kindergarten ought to be introduced into the practising schools attached to the Training Colleges for males?—Yes.

744. Do you think it would be useful?—I think it would.

745. In the interest of the Training College or of the practising school?—It was in the interest of the college. I was thinking that the students coming out from there might be able to teach the infants intelligently in their schools.

746. What source do you think the funds should come from for getting up this kindergarten apparatus—from the school funds or the college funds?—From the college funds; it would be a trifling thing.

747. What would it come to, I have no interest in this question, I am the manager of one of the Training Colleges?—For the very small amount they would have to learn, it would not cost £5 to provide the materials.

748. What was expended in the Model Schools in Marlborough-street?—I don't know.

749. Out of what funds did that come?—Out of the Commissioners' funds I should think.

750. You mean out of the public taxes?—Oh, certainly.

Feb. [illegible], 1897. Mr. Alfred [illegible].

Monsignor Molloy.—We had it stated yesterday that for a school of 100 the equipment over and above the usual outfit would cost £100.

751. Most Rev. Dr. Walsh.—You were asked about the subjects that might be omitted to make room for manual instruction—with regard to grammar and geography; are you of the same opinion as many of the Inspectors that it would be a great advantage if neither of these subjects was obligatory?—I was not aware they went as far as this, I thought the Inspectors considered grammar might be postponed.

752. How could we ascertain the views of the Inspectors generally on that point?—You would have to ask their opinion or get a special report from them.

753. I have here a number of special reports in which they speak very strongly in favour of making grammar optional; some taking not quite so many, but still a good many, of the Inspectors are in favour of making geography an optional subject; does that fall in with your own view?—Geography in the sense that we have it at present I certainly think might.

754. You think it would be no loss to education, if these two subjects were made optional, and manual instruction compulsory?—I don't think it would be any loss.

755. What about history?—It is taught in our schools, but to a very trifling extent.

756. Is it taught to boys or girls or to both?—I suppose it is; I have only had one or two examined in history all the time I am in the service.

757. Is it really taught, or is it only on paper?—I found it was supposed to be taught in one school, but they knew nothing about it.

758. Only one school in all [illegible] that I examined.

759. As an Inspector you can give no reason for confining it to girls' schools and not teaching it to the boys?—Oh, none.

760. With reference to what has been called the alternative scheme, how many hours are occupied in needlework where it has been adopted?—Two hours a day.

761. Mr. [illegible].—Can you describe the handicraft practised in the schools you have examined?—They do a little sawing, and planing, and joining boards.

762. Altogether wood work?—Yes.

763. No cardboard work?—None.

764. Is it taught in connection with drawing?—No; they don't make a sketch of the thing beforehand.

765. Would that be of more educational value than the present system?—I think they should make a sketch of everything they are going to do.

766. Is that the case in Germany?—I think it is, of course in the Training College they had plans of the things they were going to make.

767. Monsignor Molloy.—Is there any form of manual or practical work at present compulsory in the training colleges?—Drawing is compulsory and needlework.

768. Handicraft is not compulsory?—No.

769. In the kindergarten system?—No.

770. Practical work in the physical laboratory is not compulsory?—No.

771. Do you think it desirable that that kind of practical training ought to be made compulsory in the training colleges?—Yes, certainly.

772. And do you see any difficulty about making these three, handicraft, kindergarten, and work in the physical laboratory of an elementary kind, compulsory?—I see no difficulty.

773. And you think it desirable?—Yes, I do.

774. Professor FitzGerald.—You said it would be desirable to make the kindergarten more intelligent, how would you propose that we should arrange to make the kindergarten more intelligent, is it by making it compulsory in the training colleges?—Partly that, but partly I think your programme should be drawn up on more different lines, your programme seems to be very mechanical.

775. You think it is partly the fault of the programme that the teachers are not trained in the theory of it sufficiently?—I think the teachers are not trained in the theory, they get very little credit for knowing anything about it.

776. Under our new arrangement won't they get more credit?—I think they will.

777. Could cooking, generally, be taught in all classes throughout the country?—I think it could, it would be very hard where there is only the one room however, unless you allowed them to dismiss the rest of the pupils for a part of the day, so that they could go to such centres in the evening.

778. Do you think it might be introduced into boys' schools as well as girls' schools?—I [illegible] our teachers are capable of teaching it.

779. In the Technical Schools in England they were trying to get the boys to cook and they could not get them?—I superintended the cookery examination at [illegible], and I had the superintendence of [illegible] men, Major [illegible] and his son. I think we gave Major [illegible] a certificate.

780. In the Army now the cooks and the sergeants [illegible] it is very desirable that the soldiers should know how to cook. In the Regimental Technical School it was thought desirable. Do you think it would be the plan to try and arrange that in country towns, there should be classes of boys for cooking?—That might be useful, but I think it would be more useful to teach them how to [illegible].

781. It was stated that two hours was rather too long to keep girls at sewing under our present industrial programme, do you think that the industrial programme might be modified by introducing something besides sewing, which would occupy them for two hours at industrial work?—I think it might be better to introduce some work of a different kind—some manual work.

782. But you think it would be possible to introduce some manual work for girls?—I think it would be quite possible.

783. And then two hours would not be too much?—I think not.

784. Chairman.—You would shorten the sewing hours, say, take only one hour for sewing and the other hour for manual work?—Yes.

785. Professor FitzGerald.—I see there is one school in which botany is being taught in Ireland, has there been any attempt made [illegible] to agriculture by teaching some botany along with it?—No; none at all. A few teachers may teach agriculture practically, even where they have not a garden. I have one teacher [illegible] and he has a nice collection of grasses for specimens, and he has a collection of seeds and such things, and he teaches it practically. If you asked his boys to go out into the field and bring you [illegible] grass, or timothy grass, or any other grass, they will go out and bring you in the right grass.

786. That shows that this kind of instruction is possible in schools?—Yes.

787. Most Rev. Dr. Walsh.—Is he paid anything more for teaching it in that way than if he taught it out of a book without a specimen?—He is a good teacher; gets nearly 100 per cent. of passes, and nearly all his [illegible]; he is a first-class teacher.

788. Professor FitzGerald.—It is encouraging to us to know the thing is possible?—He is very practical.

789. I see it is proposed, and it has been done in England, to arrange for school museums, [illegible] this [illegible] is very much like that?—Yes.

790. Does he encourage the children to collect for his school museum?—I think they collected most of these things.

791. Does he change them every year—what does he do with the old ones?—He encourages them to bring in specimens themselves; they must have done that as they could not bring it for the Inspector.

792. This is practically meant to encourage

Feb. 1, 1897.

Mr. Alfred Purser.

children to collect things for themselves?—Yes; things they read about in the books.

793. Do you think it would be desirable to encourage that everywhere else in Ireland?—It would be a great advantage if all teachers would do it—the teaching would be far more useful.

794. You think boys might learn botany and that it would not be derogatory to their dignity, as the Intermediate Commissioners seem to think it would?—I think not, I think the best botany books are written by men.

795. Is it not desirable that boys in an agricultural country should know botany?—I think it is very desirable they should know all the plants they find mentioned in their books.

796. And how they grow?—And how they grow.

797. I see that extra grants in handicraft can be earned by pupils in the 5th and 6th classes, could those subjects that are at present in our handicraft course be introduced in earlier classes—3rd and 4th classes?—I think they could be introduced into the 4th certainly. The average age of children in the 3rd class is rather young. It would be better to fix an age limit than a class limit.

798. Could Sloyd be taken earlier than our classes in handicraft?—I don't understand what Sloyd is exactly, it is a name given to a great many things.

799. I mean the Swedish Sloyd. We have nothing at present between kindergarten and the fifth class of a practical character for boys, we don't even allow them to learn sewing?—No.

800. It is stated here that the subject has not been taken up "as generally as might be wished, principally owing to a want of knowledge on the part of the teachers, the difficulty of procuring the necessary materials and appliances, and the shortness of the school day." Which of those three reasons do you think is specially the reason why the teaching of handicraft is not taken up?—I think the first two, the inability of the teacher to teach it and the expense of procuring materials.

801. Under our rules cannot a special instructor in handicraft be obtained in a school, like the way a workmistress is obtained to teach sewing, and who would earn results fees?—Yes, but the results fees would be too small, you pay a workmistress a fixed salary.

802. Then there is no way in which handicraft for boys can be subsidised in the same way that the workmistress is subsidised for girls?—Not at present.

803. I have heard it stated that one of the reasons why the results fees are not sufficient to provide a teacher in handicraft for fifth and sixth classes is because they cannot earn results fees on boys that they teach in the fourth class, and unless a boy has begun in the fourth class there is no chance of their getting results fees in the fifth?—He means it would take two years to qualify them for first year's fees, two years teaching. I don't think that is the case where they are properly taught at all, I don't think there would be any difficulty in earning fees the first year.

804. Is our present course in handicraft of educational value or is it only a sort of bread and butter subject, putting on locks and planing and sawing?—I don't think it is on a regular system.

805. Most Rev. Dr. Walsh.—That was one of the objections to the alternative system in the sixth class, that it was rather practical or utilitarian than educational?—Well, I never heard that complaint made, I heard it was not utilitarian, that the children really did not do any work worth anything.

806. Captain Shaw.—One question as regards the cookery, would you say the cookery which is taught is such as would be required in the homes the students come from?—Oh, yes, it is quite practical.

807. Do they use the material that would be available in their own homes, you talked about fish and fowl?—Oh, yes, they do.

808. Is there any domestic economy taught to the girls or management of homes such as they occupy themselves?—Yes, it is taught in a book to a certain extent, that was part of the industrial scheme for sixth class.

809. Are the results fees obtainable under this scheme as large as they were for an ordinary sixth class education?—Precisely the same, but they are divided in a different manner for the industrial and literary work.

810. Then with regard to the manual work is there any test for the accuracy of the work which the boys do as it is now taught?—The Inspector sees the finished work that is produced to him.

811. Do they work to measurement to begin with in the work which they do?—Not any which I have seen. I told you there is very little of it; five or six boys in two schools is all I have seen, except in Bray, which is outside my district.

812. Do you consider that clay modelling, card-cutting, paper folding and wire working would be suitable instruction up to the fourth standard?—Oh, yes, and even beyond it.

813. Rev. Dr. Evans.—I think you told us that there were 1,600 schools in which the industrial programme was taught?—I take that from the Commissioners' Report.

814. This includes the Model Schools, does it?—Some of the Model Schools.

815. Not all?—Not all.

816. What other class of schools is included?—It includes Convent Schools.

817. All the Convent Schools?—Oh, no; some Convent Schools and some of the ordinary schools.

818. Can you say in what counties of Ireland these schools are situate?—I can tell you of my own circuit. Those in my circuit are mainly situated in the county Longford, in the south-western part of the King's county, and in county Westmeath.

819. Can you say to what extent the schools may be found in Dublin?—They are very rare in Dublin.

820. Do you know anything about Belfast?—I do.

821. Are any Belfast schools included in the 1,600?—I think very little.

822. Is there one school in all Belfast that teaches this industrial programme?—I could not tell you.

823. I want to know the localities in which the industrial programme is in operation that we may see where it is appreciated, and why? Do you know anything of Cork or Waterford?—A little of Waterford.

824. Is the industrial programme in operation there?—It may be in operation in one or two schools, but I think that would be all.

825. But your impression is that it is more in the rural schools than in the city schools or large town schools?—It is more in the rural schools. I think most of the important schools got exemption very early.

826. In the schools that you examined where it was in operation, are you able to say that marked good has resulted from it?—No.

827. Now, will you convey to the Commission your impressions about it?—It seemed to me that the girls had not enough to do as a rule. There was an insufficient supply of material, and consequently they were idling a great part of the day, and, I think, spent a good deal of that idle time in gossiping to one another.

828. Monsignor Molloy.—What time does the industrial programme come into operation at a school? At what stage of the pupil's progress?—At the final stage, when they reach the 6th class.

829. Up to that time they have been following a programme which is almost entirely literary?—They gave one full hour every day to needlework.

830. But there is no special industrial programme until they come to the sixth class?—No.

831. Then do you think that the fact of the industrial programme being reserved until their ideas have been formed and habits acquired in the lower classes—do you think that operates unfavourably towards their taking up the industrial programme when

they have advanced to the highest class in the school?—I think it does to a certain extent.

832. Mr. Molloy.—Is there any reason for confining the kindergarten to the youngest class? Do you see any difficulty in extending it to first, second and third classes?—Not the least; I would have kindergarten operations going through the whole school if possible.

833. With regard to drawing. Under the National Board rules drawing begins with the third class. Do you see any difficulty in commencing it earlier?—No.

834. There is a very large proportion of our pupils in second class?—I see no reason why they should not. Where you have kindergarten classes you may have pupils from learning drawing, but only where there is kindergarten taught.

835. But I mean drawing with a view to earn results fees?—I see no objection to pay them fees from second class upwards.

836. Would not that bring a very large number of additional pupils for drawing?—A very large number, and would be an encouragement to teachers to take it up.

837. Lord Chief Baron.—I observe by our last report the number of schools returned as teaching cookery is sixty?—Yes.

838. And the number of schools in operation was 8,507?—Yes.

839. That is considerably under 1 per cent.?—Yes.

840. In your opinion is cookery effectively taught in those sixty schools; of how many of those sixty schools have you any experience?—I could hardly answer that, but I think I have seen it in a dozen schools at least.

841. In the general mode in which cookery is taught what provision is made for providing materials?—The teacher of the school provides the material in most cases.

842. Does he pay for them himself?—In some cases what the teacher does is, he makes the children bring the things there to cook; if the child is going to make a cake the child brings the materials.

843. But are you aware that the difficulty in providing the materials is one of the reasons why there are so few schools in which cooking is taught?—I can quite imagine it to be, particularly in country schools, where there would be a difficulty in the children bringing the materials from their homes where they have a long way to come.

844. But having regard to the figures I have given you I suppose I may say that practical cooking is not taught under our system at all?—Except in some of the large Convent Schools, I think you may say so.

845. Most Rev. Lord Plunket.—You said that in the places where the industrial scheme was working it was not doing much good, I assume that that was not because of its being an industrial scheme introduced into the curriculum, but because of the way it was worked?—Yes, it was the difficulty of providing materials I think.

846. But if an industrial scheme were worked in a different way you think it would be an advantage?—I do; I think it would be an advantage not to make the industrial scheme exclusively needlework, where the pupils are kept two hours at one subject; it is too long.

847. One of the reasons why you thought it was not working well was the want of materials, can you make any suggestion as to an alteration in the method of work that would be likely to make it profitable?—That is the present industrial scheme, having the needlework for two hours?

848. I mean the industrial scheme generally; can you make any suggestion as to some alteration whereby instead of doing very little good, as you say, it might become profitable?

Professor FitzGerald.—An industrial scheme.

Witness.—I think you would have to take up some other subject instead of needlework, altogether different from needlework.

849. Rev. Dr. Evans.—Before we pass away from that altogether I should like to ask whether the Commissioners alone do not furnish all sorts of sewing material requisite for that industrial scheme.

Chairman.—Sewing?

Rev. Dr. Evans.—Oh yes, but on terms similar to those on which they supply books?—They do supply the materials, but a great many teachers say they can get them better and cheaper elsewhere and in greater variety. It is obvious since to suppose you can get a greater variety elsewhere, in a big shop like Pim's for instance you would have a greater variety than you could have in your little store.

850. But in view of the fact that the stores send samples to the teachers, furnish requisitional forms, and deliver the parcels everywhere, are not the stores more accessible to people in the country?—I don't know.

851. At any rate we do furnish all that is requisite for that industrial programme?—As far as I know, yes.

852. We do provide materials, and the teachers can purchase them on as cheap terms as books?—Yes, but it is very expensive, and they get no return for it. A teacher spends perhaps £10 on materials to be worked up, and cannot sell the clothes and there it is lost to her.

853. Were the Commissioners to ask you for suggestions as to how that programme could be improved, what answer would you give?—I am afraid I would ask for time to consider.

854. Most Rev. Dr. Walsh.—There is one point on which I am afraid there may be some misconception, a number of questions have been put to you about the industrial scheme; that expression has a technical meaning in our system of rules?—Yes, certainly.

855. It does not mean the general provision that is made for industrial work in our system of national education in Ireland?—Oh, no.

856. It means a special provision that is made for the girls of the sixth class?—Yes, only for girls of the sixth class.

857. And it is in that particular sense that you have used the word when you spoke of the industrial scheme as not working well, you did not intend to say that the general provision that we have made for industrial work in the schools, as far as it goes, had not done a certain amount of good?—No.

858. You would wish to see that extended?—I would wish to see it extended.

859. But the particular thing that you say has not done good is this special industrial scheme, taking the word in its technical sense?—Yes, this industrial scheme of needlework.

860. For girls of the sixth class?—Yes.

861. Girls of the sixth class might learn needlework under two different arrangements, one is the ordinary arrangement of having one hour in the day, the other is this special industrial scheme of having needlework for two hours in the day?—Yes.

862. Therefore this special industrial scheme is also called the alternative scheme?—Yes.

863. And it is only of that alternative scheme that you have been speaking unfavourably?—Yes.

864. Mr. Redington.—The Lord Chief Baron quoted some figures about cookery, am I not right in saying they refer to the year 1895?—I have not the statistics before me.

Lord Chief Baron.—Yes, they do.

865. Mr. Redington.—Since then are you aware that special teachers of cookery have been appointed who have increased the amount of instruction in the country generally?—Oh, yes, I understand four have been sent round to different centres.

866. Their salaries are paid by the Government?—I believe so.

867. And the expenses of travelling and the cost of a certain supply of utensils are paid for; do you think that a good system?—I have not come across any of the four you appointed lately.

Feb. 4, 1897.

Mr. Alfred Purser.

[868]. You know that they are certificated teachers?—Oh, yes.

[869]. They have got the diploma of the National Union, as it is called?—So I heard.

870. Professor FITZGERALD.—Do they teach children or grown up people?—They have not been in any classes at all.

871. CHAIRMAN.—I want to ask you one question with regard to agriculture. You told us that you knew of one teacher in one district or another who did teach the boys to distinguish between the different grasses and the [illegible] of [illegible]. Has that teacher got a garden plot or a farm where he could teach practical work, for example, getting the ground ready for turnips, sowing [illegible], and afterwards thinning turnips?—Not attached to his school, he may have a small plot around his dwelling-house, he has a little residence.

872. But you don't know as a matter of fact?—I know he has a small plot around his residence, but it is not large enough for anything beyond gardening on a small scale, but his neighbour's [illegible] [illegible] all around him, and the boys can be [illegible] [illegible] there.

[873]. Professor FITZGERALD.—I want to ask a little about the reason why this industrial programme was not accepted in more schools; is it not the case that it was arranged at first that the industrial programme or the old programme might be accepted, it was not to be possible to have some girls taking one and some girls taking the other?—Yes.

874. Was it not the case that the sixth class girls, at the time the industrial programme was projected for them to take, were learning the old programme, which was not suitable necessarily as an industrial programme, but was more suitable for girls going to be accountants or telegraph clerks, and so on?—Yes.

[875]. Was it not the case that the teachers were afraid of losing all their sixth class and not getting any others instead; was not that one reason that would have prevented a teacher from changing from the existing state of affairs to one about which they did not know what would happen?—As a matter of fact a large number of sixth class children did leave the schools as soon as you introduced that scheme, you did not give the teacher the option of taking it or not at first, you said they should take it, they lost a considerable number of girls. Some schools were exempt, and in cities girls went from schools that were not exempt to schools that were exempt.

876. Was not that programme rather in the nature of a home industry than suitable for girls that wanted to make their livelihood by industry such as the girls that go into the factories in Belfast?—Yes.

877. So that it was not an industrial programme suited to girls that wanted to make their livelihood by industry in a place like Belfast?—No, it was not.

Mr. SAMUEL E. STRONGE, A.B., Head Inspector of National Schools, examined.

878. CHAIRMAN.—You are I believe one of the Head Inspectors under the National Board of Education?—Yes.

879. How long have you filled that position?—Three-and-a-half years.

880. What were you before?—District Inspector.

881. For how long?—For eighteen years.

882. Will you give the Commission your opinion with regard to some heads which you have put before me here, and firstly, as regards the principles of agriculture?—I would first dwell on "principles" because it is principles, it is not a technical subject, we don't teach it practically, and therefore I call it principles of agriculture, because it is really not a technical subject.

883. With regard to school gardens?—With regard to school gardens I have seen a good many of them, they consist from half a rood up to one rood, and they are cultivated by the teacher, and he has to exhibit them at the results examination every year. The boys are supposed to spend in these about half an hour every day, that is, at recreation time, time not taken from the school hours, they assist the teacher in cultivating the ground, that is practical gardening. The other agriculture is I think principles of agriculture, it is book-work.

884. Have you formed any opinion as to whether as a rule the instruction given by the teachers is of a practical nature, that they really teach the boys?—Not in agriculture, but in the school gardens it is of a practical nature, but in agriculture it is merely words, they don't see the things corresponding to the words.

885. But do they teach the boys merely to keep the garden in order and tidy, or do they teach them in such a way that they could take situations as gardeners afterwards?—No, not as far as that, but the boys assist them, using the ordinary horticultural implements in order to assist the teacher during that half hour.

886. In fact they merely teach them what would be enough to make them labourers, not enough to make them gardeners?—No, not enough to make them gardeners, if they had a garden of their own afterwards they could follow what the teacher taught them.

887. They could put in potatoes?—Yes, or peas or beans.

888. But they could not take the care of a flower garden?—No.

889. With regard to handicraft what do you say?—Handicraft I think I have seen in only two schools, one in county Wexford and another here in Dublin, of course it is merely carpentry, building boxes and nothing [illegible].

890. Anything in the shape of mending [illegible]?—There is nothing in the shape of [illegible] work, and nothing educational in what they do, they learn to put on [illegible] and to put in a broken pane, to take out the old putty and put in the new putty.

891. To cut the glass?—No, that is not part of it, they are supposed to measure the pane in inches, they [illegible] that, but of course this is all merely carpentry, it is not anything like educational Sloyd.

892. Then what do you say with regard to drawing?—Then the drawing we have at present is really [illegible] [illegible], it does not appear to me to be any good, it is simply drawing from [illegible]. I shall be happy to hand you round some of the drawings of a school, not part of it but the whole of it, two schools are probably these drawings handed in).

893. Rev. Dr. EVANS.—Do you say that these are fair samples?—These are average samples of drawings, and they are all there, every one drawn in the school.

894. Well, I must say particularly bad or particularly good specimens?—I know.

895. CHAIRMAN.—Then with regard to kindergarten?—I beg your pardon for one moment: with regard to drawing if I might be allowed to finish with regard to it. This drawing is all from the flat, an example is set alongside you or an example often hung on the gallery, which you copy, instead of beginning as they might begin at the very beginning with a cube and drawing the cube on the board and let the children imitate it. Begin with objects from the very first and then your drawing will lead somewhither, this drawing leads nowhither.

896. There is no perspective taught?—No, there is nothing practical in that drawing.

897. Then with regard to kindergarten?—With regard to kindergarten we stop it just about when it begins to be useful, that is practically at the end of the second class, because there are very few of the third class in an infant school. Now the third year is the most important kindergarten of all, it is modelling in clay.

We stop it altogether, they pass in to a higher class, and there is no more, so that we have lost pretty much all the work we did in kindergarten when they pass into a higher class and it is not continued.

898. You think the kindergarten is a useful branch of the school work?—So far as it relieves the children from the pressure of the continued literary strain, but as an education that lasts, leaving a permanent effect behind it, when you drop it after leaving the infant school it does not leave a permanent effect behind it.

899. Most Rev. Dr. Walsh.—Suppose the kindergarten was followed up by a system of educational Sloyd in a higher class, then would you consider kindergarten an important part of our school training?—Yes, as an introduction to what you mentioned.

900. Do you think work of this kind could be introduced into our schools without a thorough overhauling of our present system of payment by results? [illegible]

901. Why do you say you are afraid not?—If you wish me to put it stronger I am sure it could not.

902. But you would not consider it a [illegible] or an objection to the introduction of this practical work into the schools, that it would necessitate a thorough overhauling of the results system?—I would not, your Grace.

903. On the contrary would you not think it an advantage?—I think it a very decided advantage.

904. Mr. Redington.—What is the reason why the teaching of drawing is so bad?—The usual thing in a school is to hand out the drawing books, just the same as you would do copybooks, and the pencils and rubbers and [illegible], and the children begin to work at it while the teacher is engaged somewhere else. There is no teaching, it is merely [illegible] of a pattern. There is a case for your [illegible].

905. But the results are such that a large number of pupils pass?—That is under the conditions under which we teach; that is the programme.

906. Monsignor Molloy.—They pass because they are fairly good under the circumstances?—They are fairly good under the programme laid down, and we have no choice.

907. Mr. Redington.—Is the fault in the programme itself?—Yes. I consider the fault to begin with is in the programme.

908. Are the teachers inefficient?—They are not inefficient; they could teach it well enough, provided the system under which they work would enable them to begin at the right end. I saw it twice taught properly. One in the Ursuline Convent in Waterford, where the nun went up to the board, it was a large flower, and holding the pattern in her hand, she took the chalk and drew the design on the board, and showed the class where it began; that was a well-taught lesson. That was the only instance in which I saw it taught that way.

Most Rev. Lord Emly.—I suppose you are aware that, in the Kildare-place Training College they teach drawing in the Queen's Scholarship the way you suggest; they have got models that they place on the desk, and they have also models to exemplify the rules of perspective, not merely on the flat, but in such a way as to bring it very vividly before the minds of the teachers; that principle is strictly followed out there, that it should not be merely drawing on the flat but from solid models such as you suggest.

909. Mr. Redington.—It has been suggested by Monsignor Molloy that teachers of drawing might be established in certain centres to teach drawing in the schools around, what is your opinion about that?—I don't see why that could not be done. There is another thing that might be done, you might have special courses for teachers.

910. Kindly keep to one thing at a time, do you see any difficulty in carrying out that suggestion?—That would depend upon how many schools he could have around him, he could go to, the amount of time he would give to each.

911. Chairman.—Could a teacher do you think practically attend to more than one school in the day?—Oh, yes.

912. He is country districts, and allowing for the time he would take to get from where he would live to the school?—Suppose he gave three hours a week.

913. No, no, I am speaking of a teacher living in the locality, as was suggested by Mr. Fraser just now, and visiting half a dozen schools besides work in the town in which he lives?—I was about to point out how many he could visit. He would only have to give three hours to each school, that would be [illegible].

914. That would only allow him [illegible] schools?—He would probably get on to eight or nine schools in the week under those circumstances, giving an hour to each.

915. I don't quite follow you?—There are four or five school hours in the day.

916. Take the case of a teacher in a country town. How many hours would you suppose he would give in the school or schools in the town?—Ten might allow him four hours a day, [illegible] a week.

917. How many hours would you give to each school?—Three hours a week.

918. I am supposing he had a group of schools and could only visit each school once a week?—That would be insufficient.

919. Could a man practically visit more than one school a day?—Oh, yes, there are four or five school hours in the day.

920. I understand they begin about ten and are over about two or three. If a man lived in the town, and the schools were four or five miles distant, he could practically only go to two each day?—He would lose half his time going to and fro. There is a case at present, Mr. Ashbrook, who is doing experimental work in Limerick, round about Newcastle, and it was found that the number of schools to which he could give an hour a week would be eight schools.

921. Professor Fitzgerald.—We would want 1,000 teachers?—Yes.

922. Mr. Redington.—What do you think of the other plan, viz., to have lectures on drawing on Saturdays to which teachers in the neighbourhood would go?—How many Saturdays would you have in the year. You would require to give them forty lessons to make them proficient, and that would be the whole year if you took the holidays out.

923. Why would they not have more than an hour?—Yes, certainly.

924. Suppose they had one hour for twenty Saturdays?—That would be quite insufficient.

925. Do you think the teachers would avail themselves of the opportunity of getting certificates in drawing?—I think they would.

926. What do you think of another plan, viz., to have an Inspector of drawing to go round and advise the teachers as to how they should teach the pupils?—And examine the drawings as well. I think that would be a very good plan. He would be better or more qualified to judge than an ordinary Inspector.

927. I suppose it is only a minority of Inspectors who are experts in drawing?—I should say so.

928. It is not one of the subjects taken up in examinations for Inspectorships?—It is not.

929. Monsignor Molloy.—You have examined the pupils in the schools where there are school gardens?—Yes.

930. That was a practical examination?—That was a practical examination.

931. Will you explain to the Commissioners how you conducted it. In the case of potatoes, the potatoes ought to be half grown, that is, they ought to be in progress of growing, ought have reached the stage of flowering or not, the boys ought to know the date of planting, when it was put down and the amount of manure required for the plantings. And the same when you went to peas, the class of peas, were there Hardy Emperor, or any other kind. Then the sticking of peas, what time they should be staked, and so on.

932. Did you generally find that they were able to answer?—Oh, yes, fairly enough, showing that they had properly gone through the process they were then describing.

933. Do you think that that system of practical teaching was so far as it went a success?—Yes, I think that has been productive of good.

934. Professor FITZGERALD.—Is there any experimental gardening carried on in the schools?—What am I to understand by that?

935. Putting down plants without any manure and seeing whether they won't come up?—No, I don't know that.

936. Do you not think that it would be instructive to the children to see experiments in gardening carried out?—It would, but I would rather see experiments that would be productive of good results rather than those that would fail.

937. It was only as an example of experimental gardening I was giving you that, but is it not desirable that the children in our schools, the future generation of farmers, should be taught how to learn from experiments of their own in gardening and in agriculture?—Yes, I say nothing against it.

938. Is there any way in which you can teach people to make experiments except by making them?—There is no way in which you can learn how to use a rule unless you get it.

939. Is there any making of things to drawings from scale?—No.

940. Would it not be desirable from an educational and also useful for the candidates themselves to know how that was done?—Yes; if a teacher were to draw a cube from an actual cube on a blackboard.

941. Is there not a great difficulty in arranging that the point of view of the teacher shall be the same as the point of view of the children?—The cube could be put at an angle with one edge to the children at the same angle as another was to the teacher.

942. There is a certain amount of difficulty in having it in the same position with reference to all?—I quite admit that.

943. Could teachers learn to draw on boards in that way without having special teaching in it?—No, a teacher would require certainly in that case to have had instruction how to do it, it is not one of those things he would pick up of himself.

944. There would it not be more important to teach the teachers than merely to send round Inspectors to see how they taught?—Yes, I thought the proposition we were talking of was how to teach the teachers.

945. It was proposed I thought to send an Inspector round, I did not understand that your proposal of sending round Inspectors was a method of teaching the teachers?

Mr. REDINGTON.—Advising the teachers and examining the pupils for results, was the idea I threw out.

946. Professor FITZGERALD.—But it would not be a substitute for teaching the teachers. Then you don't think that the teacher who does not himself know how to could teach drawing?—I think not.

947. You think teachers might be brought to centres?—Yes, or might be brought to Dublin here for a short course of drawing every day for an hour a day under a skilled teacher.

948. CHAIRMAN.—Do you think it would be on the whole more practical to teach the teachers to draw in ... certificates in drawing, would it not be a help to them rather to have their pupils' work inspected by an expert?—Certainly.

951. And would not the advice that would be obtained on these visits be a help to the teacher?—Yes.

952. Monsignor MOLLOY.—Don't you think it would be a greater advantage to have the pupils taught by a teacher who had a taste for drawing and was specially selected to teach them that and nothing else?—You would not teach your teacher in that case but only teach the pupils and you would have to keep your teacher on the spot.

953. Yes, but before he was sent to the spot he would have been selected as a thoroughly efficient teacher of drawing, whereas in the other system the pupils are taught by a teacher who teaches everything else as well as drawing, and may not have any special faculty for drawing?—An expert teacher would be better of course than a blunderer, but how many of those would you require in Ireland—you would require a large number.

954. The question is of supplying a want that at present exists; at present not half the teachers are able to teach drawing. If that want is to be supplied the question is whether it could not be better supplied by providing special teachers who would teach drawing in a number of schools at the same time rather than by imposing the duty on ordinary teachers imperfectly qualified?—That would start the drawing at once.

955. It would afford a means of starting the drawing classes in the neighbourhood of all the towns of considerable size in Ireland?—Could the other be done pari passu, have the teachers up here and have them taught?

956. Certainly, but what do you think of the system I propose, in itself, as a beginning in connection with the large towns?—I should be very glad to see it indeed.

957. Mr. HARRINGTON.—With regard to the agricultural portion of this question, have you experience of school farms as well as gardens?—No.

958. With regard to gardens are they considered in the districts where they are good models of teaching by the farming people around?—They are so far as I know.

959. With regard to the introduction of manual work into the school what are the difficulties in the way, where there is only one teacher with a number of classes under him?—First of all you are assuming that the teacher is skilled in handicraft.

960. Yes, assuming that?—Then you would have to reduce the amount of work that the teacher has to do at present in order to enable him to introduce handicraft.

961. That applies to the great majority of schools?—That would apply to two-thirds of all the schools in Ireland.

962. What subjects do you think could be omitted to make room for manual work?—There are two ways in which that could be done, a reduction in the programme of all the subjects or the elimination of some of the subjects or an elimination of part of the subjects. I am not quite sure you could eliminate grammar, because how are you to teach them to write a letter, and the writing of a letter nowadays is considered of some importance. And then as regards geography it would

them are attended?—No, the school farms have a regular course of cropping.

965. I am speaking of the theoretical teaching?—The school farms differ from the school gardens from the fact that in the school farms you have got a system of cropping and rotation of crops, as it is called, it might be the 3, 4, 5 or 6 course; while in the school garden it is only garden plants you have.

966. I don't think you quite understand the drift of my question; is the book which is used in the school while the subject is taught in school there the same in both cases?—Yes.

967. Are the same portions of the book used in both cases?—Yes.

968. Do you consider an examination a good test of the teacher's ability to impart instruction?—No.

969. Could you suggest any other way of considering a teacher?—Seeing the teacher at work, seeing him teach his class, seeing how he keeps up the attention of the class and what the result of it is, see the methods rather than the result.

970. Rev. Dr. Wilson.—In replying to His Grace, Dr. Walsh, about drawing, you said that the result-fees examination should be condemned, would you apply that to the result fees generally of the National system?—Yes, all round.

971. You don't consider that the system of result fees contributes to promote general education?—It contributes to promote possibly the very opposite.

972. That is to say, it selects the bright boys and bright girls and leaves the others very much neglected?—Not exactly that, on the contrary more time is devoted to the dull children under a results system than to the bright, and they are all taken at the same pace. It is because it does not develop the intelligence at all, the intelligence of the children is neglected, that is the objection to it, it is purely mechanical in its way of working.

973. As regards grammar, I am glad to agree with you that you would not recommend the teaching of it, what have you to say further on that subject of grammar?—That we begin the wrong way about teaching it. Many people [illegible] and they [illegible] with [illegible] and know nothing about trigonometry; in the same way you might learn to write a very good letter and know nothing about how to analyse a sentence or know the rudiments of grammar.

974. You would think it essential really in an educated boy that he should know grammar?—That he should know it to that extent that he could write a letter which is not grammar as we understand it.

975. To write a letter and speak correctly?—And speak correctly like you or me.

976. Rev. Dr. Evans.—You know Belfast?—Yes, fairly.

977. And you also know something of the south of Ireland?—Yes.

978. Did you hear the statement made here that Kindergarten was taught very extensively in Belfast?—Yes, I heard that yesterday, I think.

979. Do you agree with that statement?—Well, it is not taught extensively in Belfast, those infant schools that I had under my own charge had no Kindergarten; I have a very small district.

980. When you say your own charge you mean your own district as an inspector?—Yes.

981. Might it not be so that in a place like Belfast if some of the large schools introduced kindergarten other schools would be obliged to introduce it also in order to retain their pupils?—Yes, there is no such competition in Belfast than that is so.

982. So that the introduction of kindergarten into a large number of schools in Belfast would not necessarily mean that in the prevailing spheres there it is highly valuable?—Yes, that would be so. With this exception that Belfast is so well divided into the denominations that the denominational schools don't compete against each other, but there is a competition within each denomination.

983. Do you know that the Industrial schemes for girls of the Board [illegible] in Belfast?—Yes. [illegible]
Mr. Robert [illegible]

984. Is there a single school in all Belfast in which it is working?—Not that I know of.

985. Can you tell the Commission why it was objected to in Belfast?—I think that in the beginning when the Industrial programme was introduced, the managers of Belfast sent up a memorial to the Commissioners of Education to say they would not have it at any price, and then they all claimed exemption. Any new schools that arose since in Belfast applied on the ground that the others had claimed exemption and they had to get exemption too.

986. Have you heard any reasons mentioned by managers of schools adverse to the Industrial programme?—The only thing I heard with regard to this is that they say that if they want to make their daughters dressmakers or needlewomen they know the place to send them to; it was not to the National Schools they would send them to learn.

987. Did you hear here it said that the early years of school life were the only years these children would have for acquiring literary knowledge, and if the time were occupied in this way otherwise they would fail to get sufficient literary instruction?—I heard that said.

988. You know of a school in Waterford that objected to the programme?—Yes.

989. That was of a different type to the schools in Belfast, why would they not like it there?—They send their children to school, they said, for the purpose of learning to read and write, and geography, and grammar, and not for the purpose of making dresses and so forth.

990. But they would get that knowledge better taught elsewhere?—Yes.

991. Most Rev. Lord Plunkett.—May I interrupt you for one moment; when you are speaking of the Industrial programme, are you speaking of what is technically called the Industrial Scheme or the industrial training generally?—Yes, the alternative scheme.

992. Rev. Dr. Evans.—You have some experience of the school gardens?—Yes.

993. Do they teach the distinction between annuals, biennials, and perennials in these school gardens?—Yes.

994. Do they teach how to grow plants from cuttings?—No, I have not seen that.

995. A question was asked about experimental gardening, did you ever know an instance in which a teacher tried to show whether it would be advantageous to plant potatoes in autumn as distinguished from spring?—No, I never knew a case of that.

996. Have you ever seen an instance of a plot or part of a garden treated so as to show what class of manure had suited onions, cauliflowers, or other kinds grown in the garden?—No.

997. And the children are not taught the difference in point of utility between one kind of artificial manure and another?—No.

998. Or the value of artificial manure as distinguished from stable manure or farmyard manure?—The only thing they use in cottage gardens is farmyard manure; I never saw anything else.

999. Do you think that there is really useful instruction given in these school gardens?—I think there is; if it were only for the neatness with which the plot is kept and the method in which it is laid out, it would be educative to the children.

1000. Do you think that children in the country would learn garden work as well from their fathers at home?—That would depend on the part of Ireland. In the north-east of Ireland there would probably be as nicely trimmed gardens as the school garden, but in the south or west of Ireland they have not any gardens to speak of.

1001. Monsignor Molloy.—You are aware that ordinary teachers occasionally come up to Dublin for a course of six weeks at the Albert Farm, Glasnevin;

e of practical education
nothing, only about five

1019. Not technical?—Not technical.

1020. Do you think it has anything in common with a system of educational Sloyd?—No: I should

[illegible] 1896.
Mr. Samuel E. [illegible]

teacher who had a certificate for cookery?—This teacher was very practical; the first thing she asked the girls to do was to wash the utensils.

1037. Do you think that the plan of having highly qualified teachers is better than that of having the subject taught by ordinary teachers who may not be so highly skilled?—That is my opinion.

1038. How many schools did this instructress in cookery visit in the week?—She did but two, but there were sixty girls in one school and sixteen in another, that was as much as she could take giving four hours to the work.

1039. I understand by the regulations she can only teach sixteen girls?—A practical lesson is only sixteen, but at a demonstration she may have sixty.

1040. Chairman.—What is the distinction?—In a demonstration the girls sit in the gallery, and the teacher does the cookery herself, the girls taking notes. In the case of a practical lesson the girls do the work themselves.

1041. Mr. Redington.—Does the practical lesson follow the demonstration?—The demonstration lesson is a lesson of two hours, and then there would be two hours of a practical lesson for sixteen girls.

1042. Monsignor Molloy.—How many classes of sixteen girls is each teacher authorised to take?—As many as will fill five days, two lessons each in which each pupil gets, in a week; that will bring you up I think to eighty all told in the week that she could instruct. There is a fixed number of classes authorised by the National Board for each teacher to take.

1043. Mr. Redington.—How many demonstration lessons, and how many practical lessons is she bound to give a day?—Two lessons a day for two hours each.

1044. Monsignor Molloy.—How many classes does she give in the day?—Two.

1045. On how many days in the week?—Five.

1046. That is ten in the week?—Yes.

1047. Mr. Morley.—And any number may attend the demonstration lessons?—Yes, that brings it out; she would have eighty different girls under her during the week, I understand.

1048. Of course for the demonstration lesson any number of girls may be present?—Yes.

1049. Monsignor Molloy.—I think the teacher in Carrickfergus, besides teaching in the National Schools, gave demonstrations to the townspeople?—She did in the evening.

1050. How was that arranged?—I had nothing to do with that, and I don't know how she arranged it, her time outside our hours is her own, I take it.

1051. Professor Fitzgerald.—Are these classes at Carrickfergus popular?—They were very popular.

1052. Did you hear the same sort of objection raised to them as to the industrial programme in Belfast?—No, no objection was raised to them. On the contrary the girls were very keen, and the chef of the Olderfleet Hotel at Larne sent his boy down every day with the girls to learn cookery.

1053. They did not object that they were being made into cooks and housemaids?—They did not.

1054. You mentioned that there was an objection to the present method of paying results fees, do you mean that you object to all results payments or to the present method of giving results fees on individual examinations of the pupils?—The objection is to the system of teaching that is fostered by the system of payment we have.

1055. That is payment on individual children?—Exactly.

1056. Then you would not have the same objection to payments on examinations of classes?—I would rather pay as in England, on the average attendance, so much if the subjects are satisfactorily taught, and then an increased grant if more than satisfactorily taught, if excellently taught.

1057. That is an examination of the classes?—That depends upon an examination of the classes of course.

1058. Then the success of the results fees in England depends upon an examination of the classes?—Not that alone, but also on the manner of conducting a school. The instructions advise the Inspector to which, for the chief fees, what is done in the school. The work, the discipline, the moral tone and the style of the children all enter into the payment in England.

1059. Then it depends on the personal opinion the Inspector forms of the way the work is done and partly on the examination?—That is so.

1060. And that plan you consider a great improvement on the present arrangement?—Yes.

1061. But do you not think that it would be desirable that some of the teacher's salary should depend on results?—Not at all, if there is sufficient supervision a teacher will do his work as well as if he were tempted by a money payment at the end of the year.

1062. Do you think the teachers are sufficiently good to give up our whole results system?—There were excellent schools in Ireland before results fees came in at all.

1063. Was there not a great temptation to keep children too long in the junior classes?—That could still be checked even if you had not the results system, there was a temptation and it was done, but the Inspector when he came round always checked that. Now every child whether dull or bright is forced on by the system we have, you make them walk together.

1064. But that might be modified too?—Then you would have to allow the teacher freedom of classification, at present he has not.

1065. A modified freedom of classification is what you would advise?—Yes.

1066. Do you think that any geography that is necessary in order to make a person an intelligent inhabitant of the world, do you think that that might be taught by means of a reading book without requiring him to know where Cape Comorin is or the Straits of Babel-Mandeb?—Yes, if you begin with your surroundings as they do in Germany.

1067. You mean they ought to be taught to read a map of their own locality?—Yes.

1068. Once they had done that would it not be sufficient to teach them geography from reading books?—Yes.

1069. As to teaching grammar do not a large number of school teachers speak bad grammar in their own conversation?—Yes, some do.

1070. Although they know grammar very well?—Theoretically they know grammar well enough. The conversational grammar that we speak every day does not come from books, it is from the people we associate with, and sometimes habit is too strong.

1071. The grammar that is at present taught in schools does not make the children speak correctly?—It does not.

1072. Then one of the objects of teaching grammar in the schools is not obtained?—It is not obtained.

1073. Is not the objection that was raised by the Belfast people to the industrial programme practically an objection to it, because it was competing with technical education, instead of being an educational subject it was a technical subject?—I never heard it objected to as competing with the industries of the town.

1074. I don't mean because it was in competition with them, but if a person has two ways of learning a thing, I call these two ways competing with one another. There were two ways of learning dressmaking, one by going to a dressmaker and the other by going to the schools. Was it not because the schools were trying to supply something of a purely technical kind that it was objected to and not because our course was not of educational value?—I am not able to say that, because the objection to the industrial scheme was taken up in Belfast before I went there, and the whole schools of the town were exempted at once, so the whole was over before I went to Belfast.

1075. Was not the objection that if they wanted them to learn dressmaking they would send them to a dressmaker, was not that saying that our course was arranged to make dressmakers instead of to make educated young women?—Practically it was.

1076. Ought not our course be arranged to make educated young women?—Yes, but you have qualified what "educated" is, educated might take in both manual and intellectual training.

1077. Therefore, the objection that we were teaching them to be dressmakers is not an objection against a course of manual training which was chosen for its educational value?—No, it is not.

1078. Mr. [illegible].—With regard to laundry work, to what extent is it taught in the schools?—I never saw laundry work taught in the schools.

1079. It is not taught in any schools?—It may be, but I never saw it.

1080. Captain [illegible].—With reference to the difficulty of disposing of the made-up material, has it ever been attempted to make the student's own clothes in these schools?—The only thing of that class I ever saw done was bringing some of their own stockings or dresses to mend.

1081. But they never made new articles for themselves?—Well, I remember one day at the examination of the Dungarvan Presentation school, before I left the school they had cut out and put together an entire dress for a girl, and she walked home in it that evening.

1082. Would not that overcome the difficulty of disposing of the materials?—Yes.

1083. Rev. Dr. [illegible].—From your experience would you not think it very important if by a prudent arrangement technical instruction could be added to our National School system?—Yes, I should. Yes, I should be glad, as I said before, if the drawing we have in the kindergarten could be continued up to the higher classes so as to train the hand and the eye both, but they are both rather badly trained among boys at present, rather better among the girls.

1084. Rev. Dr. Evans.—Do you know the programme of work that is prescribed for female Queen's Scholars in the Training Colleges?—Yes.

1085. I do not mean the literary work, but the manual work, to qualify them to teach the Girls' Industrial Programme?—That is you mean cookery for one, and needlework and cutting out.

1086. Are they not required to learn to cut out dresses?—Yes, they are.

1087. And make them up?—Yes.

1088. And to wear them?—I don't know about the wearing of them. I rather think a girl is afraid to wear a dress she makes herself.

1089. I think, in the course of your duties at the Training Colleges, you will see Queen's Scholars wearing dresses made by themselves?—I should be very glad to see it indeed.

1090. Lord Chief Baron.—I believe the schools in which cookery lessons are given are comparatively few, the National Schools?—You mean those that we have not special teachers in?

1091. In which cookery lessons are given in any form?—These are few.

1092. They were 60 in 1888?—Well, I have seen three of them.

1093. I believe the number has been something increased since 1888, but in a very small proportion of the schools is cookery taught?—Yes.

1094. Are you aware that one of the great difficulties in teaching cookery in the National Schools generally is the difficulty of paying for the materials for the cookery?—I should say that that would be one of the chief difficulties. In a case I know of the children provided the materials and brought them in on Saturday, and they were cooked, and they took them home and re-heated them for the Sunday's dinner. That was the most practical thing that could be done.

1095. Then when you go a little lower down in the class of life there is even a difficulty in getting the children to bring materials for a future dinner?—There is to be sure, they would not have the means.

1096. Have you considered what remedy could be applied to that?—I have not.

1097. Most Rev. Dr. Walsh.—In reference to the question I put to you about the results system you don't mean that no portion of the teacher's income should be dependent upon how he does his work in the school, you don't mean that all his income should be independent of how he does his work?—Well, there was a time when it was, and when we had very good schools too. The results system when it came in stimulated very much the weak teachers, but that stimulus is gone and now they have fallen back and you could not maintain it because the system we work would not maintain it to advantage. We would not get advantage from it, and the system that they have in England is almost without results, that is, there is only a matter of 1/8 dependent upon results in England, in the principal grant.

1098. Do I understand you to mean that what we should pay for is the method in which the teacher does his work in the school, and not the actual results produced by that method?—Largely so.

1099. If he does his work well, you would pay him even though he may fail in producing good results with stupid pupils?—Quite so.

1100. If he does his work well you would pay him, as if his work was successful, you would not punish him for the stupidity of the pupils he has to teach?—Certainly not.

The Commission adjourned.

THIRD PUBLIC SITTING.—SATURDAY, FEBRUARY 6, 1897, AT 11.30 o'CLOCK, A.M. Feb. 6, 1897.

In the Royal University, Dublin.

PRESENT:—The Right Hon. the EARL OF BELMORE, G.C.M.G., in the Chair; His Grace the Most Rev. the LORD PLUNKET, D.D., LL.D.; His Grace the Most Rev. WILLIAM J. WALSH, D.D.; The Right Hon. C. PALLES, LL.D.; Lord Chief Baron of the Exchequer; The Right Hon. C. T. REDINGTON, M.A.; The Right Rev. Monsignor MOLLOY, D.D., D.Sc.; Rev. HENRY EVANS, D.D.; Rev. HAMILTON WILSON, D.D.; Professor G. F. FITZGERALD, F.T.C.D.; STANLEY HARRINGTON, Esq., M.A.; W. R. J. MOLLOY, Esq.; and Capt. T. B. SHAW;

with J. D. DALY, Esq., M.A., Secretary.

Professor THOMAS CARROLL, M.R.I.A., Agricultural Superintendent, Albert Farm, Glasnevin, examined. Professor Thomas Carroll, M.R.I.A.

1101. CHAIRMAN.—I believe you are the Superintendent of the Agricultural Department of National Education in Ireland, and Inspector of the Agricultural Schools?—Yes.

1102. What is the nature of the evidence that you are prepared to lay before us to-day?—I should like to describe what is done in the department with which I am connected, my lord.

1103. Will you hand in a prospectus of the Albert Agricultural Institution?—Yes, my lord (prospectus handed in).

1104. Will you kindly explain the objects of the institution?—At the present time there are at the Albert Agricultural Institution (a) classes for young men who study agriculture; also (b) special classes for teachers who are engaged or about to be engaged in the teaching of agriculture in schools; (c) classes for young women in the theory and practice of dairy work; (d) classes for instruction in training in the Marlborough-street and Kildare-place training establishments. Perhaps I might give the attendance of these different classes. For the male agricultural pupils the attendance from 1891 to 1896 have been twenty-four[?], forty-three, ... forty-seven, an average of about forty-five each year. The female dairy pupils. There has been an enormous increase in the number attending in this section, it has gone from forty in 1888 to ninety-four in 1896. Queen's Scholars attend. We have the whole of the Queen's Scholars from the two training colleges, and the average attendance of those will be 150 from the Marlborough-street Training College, and thirty from the Kildare-place Training College. The Marlborough-street students attend two days per week during their course at the Training College. The Kildare-place students attend one day in each week.

The attendance of National School teachers, who are already engaged in teaching schools, has been rather varying, mainly because when these classes were first established, the Commissioners paid the travelling expenses of the teachers to and from the institution. This class commenced in 1891[?], when there were seventy[?] teachers. This number was not kept up; and in 1893[?], when the payment of the travelling expenses was discontinued, there were about thirty teachers. In subsequent years, up to 1896, when again the Commissioners thought well of paying the travelling expenses, the numbers averaged about eight per session. In 1896, in consequence of the payment of expenses, the number went up to thirty-nine[?].

In 1893[?] the Commissioners thought well to establish a class for young men, either those who were already engaged in creamery management or who were about to be engaged in creamery management; these men come for a session of five weeks, the object being to give them knowledge in science as bearing upon the treatment of milk in creameries; in 1893[?] there were four in attendance. In 1896 there were fifteen. I shall hand in some statistics, showing the attendance for each year, 1880 to 1896, and shall hand them in to your secretary. At the Munster Dairy School there has been an enormous development. In 1886 the attendance was thirty-nine; next year forty-six, fifty-four, and so on until 1895 and 1896, when the attendances were 102 and 116. The attendance of the male agricultural pupils at the Munster Dairy School has not been so successful, mainly because more attention was given to instruction in dairying for young women, principally because the school is situated in a dairying district, and the Commissioners thought it advisable to give more attention to the special circumstances of the district.

1105. Where is it situated?—Within three miles of the city of Cork. The attendance of the male agricultural pupils averaged for the last three years, twenty-four, fourteen, and eighteen. There is also a class for creamery managers, established in 1893, and the attendance has been ten, ten, thirteen, and twelve. Perhaps the Commission would like to ask questions upon these schools before I go to the agricultural schools, my lord.

1106. MR. REDINGTON.—What are the details of the arrangements for teachers?—Teachers come up for a six weeks' session, the arrangements being [illegible] that they may come up during the periods given for holidays at their schools, and the Commissioners have allowed an extension of a fortnight to make up a six weeks' time.

1107. What are they taught at Glasnevin?—They are taught the practical work on a farm where opportunity serves, and where the class are equal to it, they do some labour with the object of getting them to acquire a proper use of their hands in agricultural and garden work.

1108. Are they taught any science?—Yes, at the ordinary lectures now going on, by Sir Charles Cameron, Dr. McWeeney, Mr. Moore, and Mr. Shaw.

1109. What do these gentlemen lecture in?—Sir Charles Cameron lectures on agricultural chemistry and geology, Dr. McWeeney on natural history and bacteriology, Mr. Moore lectures on botany and vegetable physiology, and Mr. Shaw on elementary veterinary science.

1110. They lecture for the students who are in residence for eight months?—Yes.

1111. And the teachers who come up for a six weeks' course attend such of the lectures as are given during the six weeks?—Quite so.

1112. Therefore, they do not get a course of lectures for themselves?—No, but only a course of lectures to them would be more useful.

1113. Do they derive much benefit from attending in that way?—Not very much. I have asked the lecturers to give more attention to these teachers with a view of improving their knowledge, but very much cannot be done, as at present. In fact, there ought to be a special course in these subjects for these teachers.

1114. Unless that is done, the scientific agricultural instruction they get is defective?—It is not as good as it might be, of course they get what may be called a scientific course, but it is not equal to a course of lectures from experts in science.

1115. Where do they get it?—From Mr. [illegible], agriculturist, and Mr. Gray, horticulturist, and myself. If I put it [illegible], for formerly I [illegible] the time to the pupils.

1116. What are the duties of these gentlemen?—Mr. [illegible] is the agriculturist, Mr. Gray is the horticulturist, and they are both men of enlightenment as regards their profession.

1117. Do they give lectures?—They give courses of lectures to the teachers when they are up.

1118. That is more in the practice of horticulture?—And also in the theory and practice of agriculture as far as they go.

1119. CHAIRMAN.—I see on the memorandum you have handed in at the bottom of a page these words: "These students do not take part in manual labour; but the course of instruction is mainly in the direction of explaining the principal management of the crops and live stock of the farm attached to the institution." Is it possible for a person who only goes for a course of lectures of six weeks, which of necessity cover a limited part of the year in which crops are growing, to be really instructed practically how to grow those crops. Take for example the turnip crop, the first thing you have to do is to dig or plough the ground, then you have to put in manure and then you have to put in the artificial manure in sowing, then you have to thin the crop and all that takes a considerable part of the year. Is it possible in six weeks to give such really practical instruction as will enable a person to do these things himself?—Yes, my lord, considering that those men have come from the agricultural classes, they will understand the lectures they hear, and be able to apply the knowledge that they get on the institution, better than might be expected, because as I say they are mainly from the agricultural classes.

1120. Then you say those persons come up with a considerable amount of knowledge to begin with, and it is to make their general knowledge more scientific?—And more accurate.

1121. That is what you aim at?—Yes.

1122. And if you had a person bred in town he would not have that general knowledge?—No, you could not expect it.

1123. Mr. REDINGTON.—None of the teachers come up for an eight months' course?—No, but a good many of the young men who have had the eight months' course have become teachers afterwards.

1124. What are the months during which the eight months' course lasts?—1st March to 30th September.

1125. CHAIRMAN.—What is the eight months' course?—It is for male agricultural pupils. When the Albert Institution, the present establishment, was started about 1851, a two years' course was given, but some reason or another that was set aside and short courses were established. When I came to the institution in 18[illegible] I found the courses were [illegible] months each. Just about that time it was thought advisable to develop dairy instruction at the Glasnevin Institution. I suggested that in the eight months of the year when the largest amount of the most useful agricultural practice might be had, there should be given in the male establishment a farming course, and that the winter months should be given to dairying instruction for females. There has been an effort to crowd into the institution more than ought to be done. Instead of having so much in one place it would be very much better I believe to have schools where the subjects would be dealt with separately.

1126. Mr. [illegible].—After the eight months' course is over for male pupils there are two courses for dairy pupils for the remaining four months of the year?—Yes, sir.

1127. From 1st November to 1st of March?—8th of November to 20th December, there is one course, and from 6th January to 28th of February there is another.

1128. Each course lasts six weeks?—Each course lasts six weeks.

1129. How much do the pupils pay?—They pay £5 for the six weeks.

1130. Of the students attending the eight months' course a certain number have free places?—There are twenty-four free places provided for students of the eight months' course, these places are obtained by competitive examination all over the country.

1131. If you wanted to have the teachers of the country practically instructed in agriculture what would you suggest as a more practical way of giving instruction than the six weeks' course?—I would suggest that the Albert Institution should be completely changed, that it should be made a large normal college, that the best talent that could be discovered should be attached to that establishment, and that the teachers as far as possible should pass through that normal school, for their agricultural, and, I may say, scientific courses.

1132. How long should the course last?—I think that it ought to last at least twelve months. I should like it to be a two years' course, but certainly not less than twelve months.

1133. Do you think that the present six weeks' course is of much value?—It has a certain amount of value, but not nearly so much as I should like. I should like to have a longer course of manual instruction there for teachers of schools.

1134. I think you stated that it was not of much value, from a practical point of view, as the teachers cannot be present during most of the operations of the farm?—It has a certain amount, but not very much I would say.

1135. In regard to scientific instruction, they only come in for a portion of the course given to others [illegible].

1136. Professor FITZGERALD.—I understand you agree with the late Dr. Sullivan, of Cork, who stated that the Glasnevin farm should be converted into an agricultural normal school for the technical training of the masters and mistresses of rural primary schools?—I do, I have had a great many conferences with Dr. Sullivan on this point.

1137. Do you think that all teachers should be trained at Glasnevin?—I think if it could be accomplished it would be very advisable.

1138. At least those for rural schools?—Those for rural schools.

1139. Then you would propose that the course they should go through for the whole year should be somewhat like the present eight months' course or somewhat analogous to it, except, I suppose, more of an educational character?—Excepting this, that if it were turned into a normal school for teachers I should say that while in your mind handicrafts might also be taught. There is everything at the institution that could be turned to this account very readily.

1140. Then you think the same school could be made an agricultural and a handicraft school?—I do.

1141. At present are agricultural experiments carried on by the teachers at the school. Do you think agricultural experiments could be carried on there?—We have got some very valuable experiments at the present time, and have had for a number of years. Each year we have a number of experiments at Glasnevin.

1142. Do you think it is of value to the pupils to see these experiments actually carried on?—I think of very great value.

1143. Is there any provision being made at the present time in the Queen's College, Belfast, for agricultural education?—I don't know whether the lectures are continued in Belfast; there is a professor attached, Dr. Hodges, but I don't think the lectures are going on.

1144. Would it be possible to utilise that in any way for our teachers?—I think it would; I think the Queen's Colleges might be utilised for teachers, but at the same time it is only fair to state that the attempt at the teaching of agriculture at the Queen's Colleges was a complete failure.

1145. Was it because the teaching was a failure or because the people would not use them?—I think the people would not use them advantageously, and I don't think that a desire for acquiring a knowledge of scientific agriculture existed at that time. About that time there was a considerable amount of feeling against what was called scientific farming.

1146. It was premature?—It was premature, I believe.

1147. The present scientific lectures that are given to teachers at Glasnevin, are they in any way practical as far as the teachers are concerned; do the pupils of the school there actually perform any experiments themselves?—Do you mean as regards science or on the farm?

1148. I mean as regards science. Of course farming experiments are very slow sort of things?—There is no attempt at experiments in chemistry or physics.

1149. Are there demonstration lectures?—Yes.

1150. Is the room suitable for demonstration lectures?—Well, it is scarcely suitable. I have been trying to get the Board of Works to give us proper accommodation, as, for instance, a gallery for lecture room, but they are rather slow about it.

1151. Then the teaching there is rather this, "If you do so and so such a thing will happen," without giving the pupils an opportunity of doing it themselves and seeing themselves what will happen?—The pupils have not an opportunity of doing it themselves; the experiments are performed before them in the lectures.

1152. Ought women teachers to be trained?—At the present time they are supposed to be instructed in agriculture.

1153. In agriculture?—At the present time the teaching of agriculture by females is optional. There are some schools where female teachers teach agriculture, and also some schools where female pupils are taught agriculture by masters.

1154. Do you think that before they taught, the women teachers ought to be trained?—I think so, they have, however, to pass an examination before being allowed to teach.

1155. Mr. [illegible].—Is there any other body at present in Ireland, except the National Board, competent to undertake the teaching of the pupils attending the Albert and Munster Farms?—Not at present.

1156. Is it not a fact that the managers of the Munster School have applied for a Charter for an extension of their system?—They have got a Charter.

1157. But they have applied for an extension of their lands for the purpose of teaching agriculture on a more extensive scale?—I believe they have applied for money to enable them to carry that out.

1158. Is it a fact that the lands attached to the Munster Farm are not properly adequate for the teaching of agriculture in that district?—I think the acquisition of more land would be very useful and a great deal might be done in a variety of subjects, planting and afforesting.

1159. The students that now come to the Albert Farm and to the Munster Farm, do they come with much or any previous knowledge of, say, drawing and science or handicraft?—In my examinations of those schools it is almost painful to see the total absence of the faculty of observation that those pupils show through want of such training before coming.

1160. Therefore if there was a better system of teaching those subjects in elementary schools the higher places such as the Munster and Albert Farms would be better able to carry on their work much more effectively?—Certainly.

1161. Do the teachers in the South of Ireland avail to any large extent of the Munster Farm?—We have had a good many attending at Glasnevin from the South of Ireland. Of course the proportion that has attended up to the present is very small indeed of the teachers throughout Ireland; they have been mainly men who were already in occupation of agricultural farms or school gardens or who intended to have farms or gardens connected with the agricultural department.

1162. What difficulties are there in the way of the teachers of the South of Ireland gaining the full benefits that are to be obtained at the Munster Farm?—That would require a reconstruction of the establishment. As regards Glasnevin there are no more difficulties in the South of Ireland than in the North, the privilege of attending at Glasnevin extends to the whole of Ireland.

1163. Is it that the teachers are rather careless themselves and don't care to take up the subject of agriculture?—Possibly that may account for it, a good many teachers have not the facilities for practical agriculture, they have not the land attached to their schools, neither for gardens nor for farms.

1164. Captain Shaw.—With regard to those six weeks' courses do they go on continuously throughout the year?—There are three of these courses commencing in May and ending about October.

1165. Following each other?—Following each other.

1166. Do you not consider that the agricultural operations which should be carried on from September to May are almost always the most important?—As I remarked already these men know a good deal of the practice of agriculture, and their coming to Glasnevin will be mainly with the object of being taught better systems or the reasons for what they have been doing.

Chairman.—I beg your pardon. With regard to the questions that are being put, I will just tell you the heads of Mr. Carroll's evidence, so that we may keep the subjects together. The first thing was the general matter, then the question of male agricultural students, then of dairying, then carrying, breeding and managing, then the dairying department for females, creamery managers, the Munster Dairy School, the Cannolstown Model School, then the agricultural schools and gardens, and the itinerant dairy instruction, and then some general questions bearing on agriculture.

Captain Shaw.—Then my questions would refer to a subject that will come afterwards.

1167. Mr. [illegible].—Pending the reconstruction of the Albert Model Farm into a normal school, have you any suggestions to offer how the existing state of things could be improved in favour of the teachers?—I don't see how the existing state of things can be improved to better account than is being done at the present time. I think everything is being done at the present time that can be done.

1168. Rev. Dr. [illegible].—With regard to the Model farms, do you know whether they have paid, or a success?—To what class of Model farms do you refer?

1169. Those that were established many years ago, and have been conducted on scientific principles?—Previously to 1879 the Model farms of the Commissioners did not pay; but I believe that too much was expected in that direction. If you ask a farmer who is making a very large profit by his present system to take in a lot of pupils into his farm, and change his system and farm for teaching purposes alone, I don't think it would be fair to ask that man to show a balance sheet with a large profit, to keep separate the teaching from the practical farm work.

1170. Is not that the main reason why up there and elsewhere scientific farming was not in favour with the country people?—Scientific farming is not in favour in any agricultural country that I know of, mainly because farmers who have gone in for scientific farming have as a very large extent been failures, but a scientific farmer who has a knowledge of farming, as

[illegible] Professor [illegible] Carroll, M.R.I.A.

a merchant has a knowledge of his business, will make money, but mere scientists and men who can write a great deal about farming have generally been failures in farming for profit.

1171. As a class they have failed, I know. I am sure we are all greatly pleased to learn that the number of females attending the class for dairying is increasing largely, I trust it will increase more and more. So far as your experience goes has that yet told on the quality of butter produced?—I have letters from several districts in Ireland testifying to the improved quality of the butter through the instruction of our schools.

Rev. Dr. Wilson.—There is nothing our country needs more than an improvement in that respect, we are much pleased to hear of any changes made by this instruction in dairying.

1172. Rev. Dr. Evans.—The students at Marlborough-street Training College go to Glasnevin?—Yes, sir.

1173. Male and female?—No, not the female.

1174. Is there no instruction which the female Queen's Scholars could profit by given at Glasnevin?—Oh, yes, there is, you will find details of this later on.

1175. Do the Queen's Scholars from Drumcondra go to Glasnevin?—No, they have a special agricultural teacher, and they have some land of their own, but if they wish to come we shall welcome them.

1176. Do the Queen's Scholars from Kildare-place go?—Yes.

1177. How many?—About thirty.

1178. How often do they come?—One day in each week.

1179. Are they taught in exactly the same way as the students from Marlborough street?—Exactly, except that they don't take up surveying.

Chairman.—That is a head we are coming to presently.

1180. Rev. Dr. Evans.—Do any of the Queen's Scholars from our Lady of Mercy go?—No, sir.

1181. Do any from De La Salle?—No.

1182. Is there anything in connection with De La Salle Training College to compensate for the advantages which the others have at Glasnevin?—Yes, the College at De La Salle has a nice little farm within about three miles of the city of Waterford where the students go, there is a very good teacher there, and I believe that a very useful system of teaching agriculture is practised at the De La Salle College.

1183. Have you any means of comparing the instruction in agriculture at De La Salle, with that at the Model farm?—Except from having seen De La Salle.

1184. And you believe what is done there is, shall I say, neither more in advance or behind what you do?—I don't wish to be supposed to be egotistical, but I think we do it better.

1185. You said there was a competitive examination by which those who come up from the country are admitted for instruction at Model farm?—Yes, sir.

1186. What is the character of the competitive examination, and where is it held?—The questions are set in general subjects of education. The last examination was held in this way; the Inspectors of schools set questions.

1187. You mean the Inspectors of National Schools?—Yes, sir; they were invited by the Chief of Inspection; centres were named in the country convenient to the Inspectors, and to the largest number of candidates; examinations were held at those centres on one day; the papers were then sent to the Education Office and marked by independent Inspectors.

1188. You mean by the office the Education Office, Marlborough street?—Yes.

1189. Do you have communications from those who have been trained after they go back to the country?—Yes, we are in frequent communication with them.

1190. Is it optional, or is there any system by which you require reports to be made to you?—May I ask you to explain what you want to get at, [illegible]

1191. Have you any regulations requiring those who have been taught at Glasnevin to report to you respecting the work they do after leaving?—No, we have not got such a system, but as I say correspondence is kept up between the officers and those young men, friendships have been formed, and correspondence is kept up.

1192. And you have ground to believe from that correspondence that good has accrued to the districts to which they have gone from the instruction they received?—I believe so as to themselves in the first instance, and if they show good results in themselves the districts should be benefited.

1193. You were asked a question about experimenting; you were very successful in your experiments in [illegible] spraying [illegible]?—Yes, sir.

1194. And much valuable information has emanated from Glasnevin in regard to spraying as a remedy for potato disease?—Not alone from Glasnevin, but from nearly all the agricultural schools, we have sent out material to the forty-six agricultural schools, and to the Munster Dairy School, and experiments in this direction were carried out at those schools.

1195. Lord Chief Baron.—I wanted just to ask you one question, and it is in reference, not to the Albert Institution, but to the generality of the ordinary National Schools throughout the country. Are you able to say whether there is in the generality of the ordinary National Schools in Ireland any efficient teaching in the elements of agriculture, either practical or scientific?—There has been a considerable improvement in the quality of the teaching in those schools. I have had a return made out of the results of 1890, 1891, 1892, as compared with 1893, 1894, 1895, and I find that a larger number of pupils have been presented for examination, and the percentage in the results of answering have largely increased. Comparing those two periods, in 1890 the percentage of passes was 56·8; in 1891, 61·5; in 1892, 61·3; in 1893, 60·9; in 1894, 63·4; in 1895, 65·9. The comparison in numbers, in 1890, 31,456 were presented; in 1894, 42,614 were presented. The fact that there is an increase in the percentage of passes, I think, shows that the quality of the teaching has been improved.

1196. Rev. Dr. Evans.—I want to ask Mr. Carroll does he know whether those who have been trained at the Model Farm have competed at local fruit and flower shows, and with what result?—Yes; there have been a good many of those cases. A good many of the teachers of school gardens and school farms have competed and taken prizes. I have just before my mind a case in the county Tyrone (Drumbeg) where the teacher takes off all the prizes. He grows new varieties of vegetables.

1197. Lord Chief Baron.—Now, Mr. Carroll, I wish you to take the best year in reference to agriculture. Do I understand that is the year 1895?—Do you mean for the teaching in the National Schools?

1198. The ordinary National Schools. Take the year in which you consider the teaching was the best and most extensive?—1895 appears to be the best year.

1199. In how many schools was agriculture taught in 1895?—It is a compulsory subject in all rural schools. There are very few urban schools take agriculture.

1200. Speaking roughly, can you say what is the number in average attendance in all the rural schools in Ireland?—That will be more a subject for the Money Inspectors. I have not to take cognisance of that, but I should say the attendance would be perhaps 60 per cent. of those on the rolls of the rural schools.

1201. Would you say there were 60,000 on the rolls?—Oh, more than that.

1202. I want to see how many students are supposed to be taught agriculture. Would you kindly approximate as near as you can in numbers to the students in rural schools?

Most Rev. Dr. Walsh.—I find the exact figures here in the report. The number presented for examination in agriculture in the year 1896 was 32,314; the number that passed was 22,717.

1203. Lord Chief Baron.—Surely there are a great many more students in rural schools than 32,314?—Yes, and a great many more taught agriculture, but those boys have not made the necessary attendances to enable them to be presented for examination in agriculture.—I should not like to venture on figures.

1204. I should say that a large number that are taught agriculture were not presented for examination in agriculture through not being qualified by 100 days' attendance.

1205. Professor Fitzgerald.—Is it only boys above the fourth class that are required to take agriculture?—Quite so, fourth class and above.

1206. Lord Chief Baron.—Could you form any approximation of the number that ought to present themselves in agriculture who in fact do not present themselves?—That is 32,314 ought to present themselves and have presented themselves; but in addition to that a very large number, half as many more, have been instructed in agriculture, but for a shorter period. Those that I have given are boys and girls that have made 100 attendances at the school.

1207. Now in your opinion are the generality of the National School teachers in rural schools throughout Ireland competent to teach the elements of agriculture?—The results of the papers will indicate something in that way. I must say that I think the teachers ought to be better informed in agriculture, and I have made out a comparison of the percentages of passes in England and Scotland as compared with Ireland, but in making these it is only fair that I should state that a better class of students are presented for examination in England and Scotland than are presented in Ireland. The passes in England with a very small number and of a higher class as regards their education of those presented; of 1,315 presented only seven were refused a pass. The percentage of passes in Scotland for 1895–96 was 86·6, in 1894–5, 87·1, but a much smaller percentage of school persons was presented in Scotland than in Ireland, and that will probably account for the difference. I believe that in Scotland the teachers of agriculture are better prepared than are our teachers.

1208. But the value of those will depend upon what is required for a pass?—Yes.

1209. Now I wish to bring you to this question, do you think that there are a substantial number of students of these schools in Ireland that get any real efficient knowledge in agriculture in the ordinary National Schools?—If you ask me if they get a useful knowledge, I should say yes.

1210. By a real or any efficient knowledge of agriculture?—I should like to have it explained whether that would mean that a boy of sixteen leaving school would be fit to take a farm and farm it.

1211. Oh, no?—If it is meant that he gets such a fair amount of knowledge as will enable him to farm better through the use of this knowledge, I believe that he does get a useful knowledge.

1212. Such a knowledge as will enable him when he gets a farm for himself to farm it efficiently and get as much profit out of it as he reasonably ought?—I believe that if the boys leaving schools in the sixth class were to put into practice the information that they get at the school they could farm their farms more efficiently and more profitably.

1213. Monsignor Molloy.—That information is taken entirely from books for the great bulk of the boys?—For the great bulk of the boys.

1214. Lord Chief Baron.—Have you ever seen boys examined in agriculture?—I have.

1215. And is it your opinion from what you yourself have seen that these boys acquire any real knowledge of practical agriculture?—I believe that they acquire a useful knowledge of agricultural subjects.

1216. How to what extent and of what nature?—I shall read the programme.

1217. I don't want the programme, I want in your own words what knowledge they really get, would they be able to know how to put in a crop, how to care that crop, and how to take out that crop and how to save that crop?—They will get a great deal of information that will enable them to do it better than their fathers did before them.

1218. Chairman.—Well, but Mr. Carroll, do you think the young farmers are better farmers than their fathers were?—I think the agriculture of Ireland has improved considerably.

Chairman.—I cannot say that is my experience.

1219. Rev. Dr. Walsh.—They would acquire such a knowledge of the various classes of soil as to know the best crop to put into it?—Yes, that is the subject of instruction.

1220. Professor Fitzgerald.—May I ask whether the percentage in Scotland is higher than in Ireland in agriculture?—In 1895–96 of 5,121 examined 4,048 passed, being a percentage of 80·6.

1221. And our percentage?—In 1895 was 68.

1222. Then of our children that were examined 68 per cent. passed, and in England of the children examined 99 per cent.?—I don't think it would be fair to compare the two, because I believe that those examined in Scotland were older than the children presented in Ireland.

1223. Was there any other reason do you think why the Scotch children should be able to answer better than the Irish ones?—From what I know of the Scotch system I believe that the teachers are better prepared for teaching agriculture.

1224. Then you think the teachers are not given a sufficient preparation by our present system of training teachers?—That I believe.

1225. Most Rev. Lord Plunket.—I only wish to ask how long the teaching of agriculture has been a compulsory subject in the National School to the same extent that it is now?—I should say from about 1877 or 1878.

1226. Most Rev. Dr. Walsh.—You propose that the teachers should be brought up to Glasnevin to be trained there?—That is what I should like.

1227. What would be the length of the course?—I should say at least twelve months.

1228. You are aware that twelve months is the length of the course of a teacher in an ordinary training college?—Quite so.

1229. Do you propose that a teacher should be trained twice, once in the ordinary training college, and once in Glasnevin?—I believe that an arrangement might be made by which the teachers in training could reside at Glasnevin, or make more use of it than they do at present.

1230. The teachers in the De La Salle College, Waterford, for instance?—At De La Salle they have a farm which they could increase very much the productivity.

1231. I thought your idea was that all the teachers were to be brought up to Glasnevin?—Not all to be brought to Glasnevin, my lord; those who had no other place to go to might go to Glasnevin.

1232. But they have a place to go to at De La Salle?—They have a place at De La Salle, and with a little arrangement it might be developed into a very useful place for teaching.

1233. Are you aware whether any assistance is given to the Brothers who have the management of De La Salle Training College for this useful department that they have got up there?—Well, I don't enter into the details of finance in any of the schools.

1234. The establishment at Glasnevin is not kept up out of the grant for the Training College at Marlborough-street?—No, my lord.

Feb. 2, 1898.

Professor Thomas Carroll, M.R.I.A.

Feb. 2, 1897.

Professor Thomas Carroll, M.R.I.A.

1235. There is a separate fund for that?—A separate fund for that.

1236. So that on that point there would not be an equality between the Training College at Waterford and the one at Marlborough-street, and those other Training Colleges in Dublin, as they have within reach an agricultural college provided by the State, whilst the Training College at Waterford has no agricultural college provided by the State?—That is so.

1237. And to that extent there is an inequality?—That is so.

1238. In your idea, all the teachers who have no other place to go to should come up to Glasnevin. How many could Glasnevin accommodate?—If Dr. Mulligan's idea was carried out, which I may say I adopt entirely, it would require a very large development to make Glasnevin what it ought to be as a normal training school.

1239. And this would be a great Training College under the Commissioners of National Education?—I should not like to——

1240. That is what you propose?—I propose it should be done under some arrangement.

1241. Are you aware that when it was attempted to train all the teachers of Ireland through one college under the Commissioners of National Education the result was that only a very small percentage of the teachers could be trained?—In agriculture?

1242. In anything?—I would rather confine myself to agriculture.

1243. You are aware that at present there is a number of training colleges in the country?—Yes.

1244. In our report I find these figures, that the number trained in all our training colleges taken together last year, 1895, was 840; the number of vacancies to be filled was 1050; so that we were 210 short of the demand with all these training colleges in existence. Would not that go to show that it would be utterly hopeless to set about training in agriculture unless we had a number of agricultural colleges through the country?—If I was to give expression to what I consider ought to be done——

1245. I thought you had done that?—Well, I did not expect to be asked so definitely to make suggestions; I supposed that I was to give evidence as to what is already in existence.

1246. So I understood also, but when I heard you making these suggestions, I wish to test your suggestions by the light thrown on them by these figures?—I should be glad, later on, if asked by the Commissioners.

1247. Then it may be better to reserve your opinion on that point until you have considered it. Now, in reference to the questions the Chief Baron has asked you about the teaching of agriculture in schools. I find the number who passed in the examinations last year was 52,000, and £12,000 was paid in result fees for this agricultural teaching, do you think that £12,000 was well spent?—I do, my lord.

1248. Are you frequently present at the examinations in agriculture in the schools?—Not very frequently. I have been at them.

1249. Who conducts those examinations?—The District Inspector.

1250. Well, here is an extract from a report of one of the Inspectors:—"The minimum expended on results fees for this branch in its present form would be far better devoted to fees for discipline, order, neatness, and so on. Agriculture is a disappointing branch, and I fail to see how any good can be done in it without practical instruction. The pupil's knowledge is purely theoretical, and not capable of being applied to any practical purpose." Seeing that statement made by an Inspector who has practical experience, are you still of opinion that the money spent in result fees is usefully spent?—Yes, my lord; and for this reason, that Inspector may have a taste for drawing, or for encouraging lace making, he may have a dislike for agriculture, or have a difficulty in examining it, and his sympathies may not be with it.

1251. Then I must give you another:—"If a child gets the necessary cue, he can easily continue for half a page without stopping. The meaning of difficult words is scarcely ever taught. . . . The results are rarely above mediocrity"?—I am afraid I must agree with that. I have been surprised in some cases to find boys repeat page after page of the book and know very little about the meaning.

1252. Now allow me to give you another:—"I examined in sixteen schools during the year, in but two of them did I find the pupils in possession of any useful grasp of the subject. It was adopted as an optional subject in three urban schools, and from what I saw of the consequences I should not be in favour of its extension"?—It appears to me that in that case the teaching was not properly regulated. If the Inspector found there was not efficient instruction in the urban schools, he could very soon have that matter settled by having agriculture withdrawn and attention given to other subjects.

1253. "Perhaps no more profitable subject could be found from the point of view of results fees, but many subjects more useful to the pupils are available." Are you aware there is a very high fee paid for this thing that goes on under the name of teaching agriculture?—I believe it is high.

1254. It is the highest fee given by the Board, higher than the fee given for subjects that are really taught in the school; is it not five shillings?—Four shillings to five shillings.

1255. What do you think of this from another Inspector: "A large part of this district is used as meadow and for agricultural purposes, the pupils who can glibly repeat the long list of grasses given in the book have no hesitation in saying that they never saw any specimens of them." We may take it for granted that there were specimens of these grasses in the fields all round that district?—Yes.

1256. Do you think there is any advantage in teaching agriculture in that way?—If you take the one subject—grasses. Take a grazing district, you would not expect that the teacher would teach only the matters pertaining to grazing; you must have the principles of agriculture taught.

1257. Is there any use in teaching long lists of the names of grasses when the children are unable to identify one of those grasses when they see them in the fields?—I say that is not efficient teaching.

1258. Is not that the teaching that goes on in our schools?—Not in all the schools.

1259. I have read the reports of five Inspectors, and I can assure you I could quote twenty such reports from this book showing that the teaching that goes on is of this same kind, and that the pupils are not able to identify in the fields the objects that they see the pictures of in the books. As far as that is the character of the teaching, do you think it worth keeping up?—I believe if the Inspectors themselves knew more of the subject you would have reports very different. It is just as difficult to examine in agriculture as it is to teach it, and unless a man has a fair amount of knowledge, and also a sympathy with it, he may form very erroneous opinions upon the subject.

1260. Then you don't take the testimony of the Inspectors as to what is actually going on in the schools. Is it not on the judgment of those gentlemen that £12,000 was paid last year in result fees?——

1261. Mr. Redmond.—You have nothing to do with the examinations of schools in theoretical agriculture?—No, sir.

1262. Monsignor Molloy.—There are 17 school farms in all Ireland?—Yes.

1263. How many school gardens are there?—About 65.

fit up such a dairy as would meet the requirements of the various classes, from the small farmer with three or four cows up to the factory; all the appliances necessary for each of these classes are provided.

1295. With regard to teaching surveying, levelling, and mapping, what have you to say about that?—We have got an efficient teacher, a man who has gone through the College of Science, and many of the young men who have been trained at Glasnevin have subsequently earned a great deal of money by surveying properties on their return to their homes.

1296. As regards the dairy department for females, will you tell us what is done under that head?—As I mentioned, two classes come up during the year; these young women are, according to the size of the class, divided into sections. In addition to practical dairying we have cookery and sewing classes, and the sections that are not at the dairying are at the cookery or sewing classes. These young women make notes of their lectures; these notes are examined and corrected by the teachers.

1297. Was some instruction given some time ago to the female students of the Marlborough-street Training College in connection with the dairy department at Glasnevin, that is the case at present?—Instruction in dairying was commenced some four years ago, but in consequence of the development of itinerant dairying we were obliged to discontinue for a few months. It is intended to carry it on, as I find the teachers in training are anxious to learn it, and I believe it will be very useful in the country.

1298. With regard to the creamery managers at Glasnevin, what have you to say about them?—These were some up to be prepared for employment in creameries.

1299. Monsignor Molloy.—There has been a misunderstanding with regard to the report of Mr. Downing; I will read the sentence preceding the sentence which I read. The marginal note is "school farms," and he says:—"My experience of National Schools with farms attached for the purpose of practical agricultural instruction is not favourable to them. The efficient management of a school, and the efficient management of a farm of any considerable extent by the same person, seem to be incompatible." The report then is unfavourable to farms of any considerable extent attached to a school for agricultural instruction?—Yes, to farms of any considerable extent.

1300. Rev. Dr. Evans.—Does the Model Farm pay its way?—As a farm it does; we can show a profit for many years of from £300 a year to £600, and it would be a very great shame if it did not, considering the markets we have so near.

1301. You were asked a little while ago who paid for the farm implements and appliances—would it be correct to say the farm paid for them itself?—The farm pays for all implements necessary for the farm; the Commissioners pay for all the implements necessary for education.

1302. Which are they?—If we had to fit up the dairy as a money-making dairy on a farm we could do it for £30 or £40; if we had to fit it up for an educational dairy we would lay out £250 or £300 on it, because we require a number of implements that would not be necessary for practical dairying but would for a teaching dairy.

1303. In the kind of dairy instruction you give at Glasnevin such as farmers' daughters might use in their own homes or in their own localities?—It is so; and I may say that if you give us the pleasure of your company some day during next week I shall show you that we have a real commercial dairy going on at present. We get the whole of the cream from a dairy proprietor in the county, and we supply his customers. The girls that are here at Glasnevin have to do all manipulation, and any faults that occur in the manufacture of the butter are reported to the owner.

1304. Quite so. I am prepared anywhere to testify that you produce butter fit for the Queen, but my point was, is the kind of instruction in producing this butter such as farmers' daughters could carry out in their own localities?—Yes. I may say at the end of the session, when examinations are held either for granting certificates or prizes, these girls are obliged to make the butter with the simplest appliances; they are not allowed to use any of the elaborate machinery for more extensive dairying.

1305. Professor FitzGerald.—Might I ask whether, in calculating the profit of Glasnevin, rent and interest on buildings and capital is deducted?—Rent is; but in consequence of the buildings being educational, interest on the actual building is not charged.

1306. But is there interest on buildings that might be required for a farm of that size deducted?—No, sir; but I may say the rent is about £4 an acre, and that is a very high rent.

1307. High for the neighbourhood of Dublin?—It is; in our neighbourhood lands of the same quality let at 60s. an acre.

1308. So that the excessive rent would more than pay for interest on the necessary buildings?—Quite so.

1309. Monsignor Molloy.—Can you form an idea of how many pupils of the agricultural class that have passed through Glasnevin are actually now engaged in agricultural pursuits in Ireland?—We are obliged to make frequent returns, but I cannot remember the numbers just at present.

1310. Perhaps you would let us have that return. Can you state your own general opinion as to how far they have been successful in agricultural pursuits since they left Glasnevin?—I have knowledge of a very large number doing very well.

1311. I understood you to say you have no exact record, but I wish to know your general opinion?—Quite so; I may say I was a pupil of Glasnevin myself.

1312. Mr. Redington.—I take these figures from our last report—taking Glasnevin and the Munster Farm together, there has been a net profit on the farm of £156, and the net cost of agricultural training has been £3,348; leaving the total net cost to the State of £3,192. Are those figures correct?—Those are correct.

1313. Most Rev. Dr. Walsh.—I should wish to put the same figures to you in a slightly different way. Separating the farm and the educational establishment—the college—I see it stated here that the cost of the maintenance of agricultural students and the salary of agriculturist, &c., is £3,618. That is the cost incurred by the State in 1893 for the education in Glasnevin?—Yes.

1314. Fees of pupils, £548?—Yes.

1315. Is there any other income to set off against the cost of maintenance of the educational establishment?—What is called the proportion of the profit on the farm would go against that.

1316. Am I right in saying that the whole profit on the farm is about £362; Farm produce, £2,741—is that correct? Then look a little further down on the page, £2,379, that is what goes out?—Yes.

1317. Therefore the profit on the farm is about £360. You say this is to be set off against the outlay of £3,618 for the cost of the establishment?—Yes.

1318. And with that exception the only other income is fees of pupils, £548, so we have about £900 to set off against an expenditure of £3,600?—Yes.

1319. In other words, the educational work done in that establishment cost the State £2,700?—Yes, that is quite right; but then take into account the numbers that passed through.

1320. Most Rev. Lord Plunket.—I have one question to ask—it is with regard to the information given to the teachers in training at Glasnevin. It is very clear I think that they acquire a great deal of valuable information; but there is a great distinction between acquiring information and acquiring a knowledge of the method of imparting that to others?—Quite so.

[illegible]

Feb. 6, 1898.

Professor Thomas Carroll, LL.D.

1352. And they had to be given up at a loss to the State of £100,000?—That is about it.

1353. Mr. Redington.—Had they not been given up—could not the management have been changed?—I believe if the management had been changed they could be very useful, and might be maintained in usefulness to the present day.

1354. Most Rev. Dr. Walsh.—Do you think local management is better than the management of the Commissioners?—I don't say that entirely.

1355. Take the facts: when those schools were worked by the Commissioners they were worked at a loss, and had to be given up, at a loss of £100,000. We have before us at the present moment a school at Cork that was not successful when it was under the management of the Commissioners, and is now successful under local management. Putting all those facts together, does it not show that local management is to be preferred in the interests of the State?—I quite believe that local management is absolutely essential; but I should not like to admit that the success of the Munster Dairy School is entirely owing to the local management.

1356. But this school is now a-going under the local management?—It is a-going under the co-operation of local management with the Commissioners of National Education.

1357. There is no difficulty whatever in having the co-operation of the Commissioners of Education with local management?—None whatever.

1358. How are the ordinary Training Colleges managed?—With perfect harmony.

1359. You know the College at Drumcondra, of which I am manager; there is no difficulty there about the co-operation of the Commissioners?—None.

1360. Therefore we may put that point about the co-operation of the Commissioners out of the question—we can have that whether a school is under the Commissioners' management or under local management?—Quite so.

1361. Then do you not think that the change of the management from the Commissioners to the local committee had something to do with the success of the Cork school?—I quite admit local management is essential to success.

1362. There is no local management at Glasnevin?—I should like to see it—I have often asked for it.

1363. You think that local management is essential to the successful working of the Albert Model Farm at Glasnevin?—I don't particularize; I say local management would be essential to the development of agricultural education in Ireland.

1364. Why should the establishment at Glasnevin stand on a different footing from the establishment, for instance, at Drumcondra?—I think it is admitted that the management of the Albert Model Farm——

1365. Will you allow me for a moment. I don't like to hear the word "admitted," I want only to get the facts?—Quite so; I may say as a fact that the management at Glasnevin is satisfactory—the results from Glasnevin are satisfactory at present.

1366. Do you think they would be more satisfactory if there was local management instead of the management of the Commissioners?—I don't think it would be in the case of Glasnevin.

1367. But everywhere besides Glasnevin, through the rest of Ireland, local management works better than the management of the Commissioners?—I believe it would be essential to development.

1368. Everywhere else, but not there?—I don't go as far as that.

1369. Mr. Redington.—At the time the Commissioners were forced to sell those Model Farms, was it not optional with the Government to have altered the management of them, and transferred them to local bodies?—I should say it would have been competent.

1370. In your opinion would it not have been better?—It would have been better under the circumstances then existing.

1371. Therefore there was no necessity to surrender them at a loss?—No. Of course it is well understood that the cause of the surrender was the pressure brought by the Treasury.

1372. Professor FitzGerald.—Do you agree with Dr. Sullivan in this—that "the chief causes of the failure of these schools"—that is, the old agricultural schools—"were, first, the state of the land tenure; secondly, they were centralised institutions having no local connections, and consequently were not in touch with the farmers; thirdly, the majority of the farmers did not understand the value of scientific farming; fourthly, the buildings, cattle, and methods of farming did not in general offer examples worthy of following"?—I agree with that generally; I say that centralisation had a good deal to do with it; farming from Marlborough-street was not the way to conduct these institutions. Then there was also Treasury interference.

1373. Then you would agree with the conclusion of his report:—"The management should always be in the hands of local authorities, subject to careful and competent government inspection and rigid audit"?—I believe that a system largely on those lines might be devised to work satisfactorily.

1374. Mr. Harrington.—With regard to the local management of the Munster Dairy School, has it not been the desire of the people who have conducted that establishment with such great success that they should practically have the management of the institution in their own hands almost entirely?—I think it is.

1375. Chairman.—Now, have you any remark to make with regard to the Ravenhill Model School Garden?—A very interesting experiment was made there, that I think would be deserving of development in other Model Schools where there were facilities. There is a very large garden attached to the school—and about seven years ago a portion of this garden was cut off in plots; each of the pupil teachers had one of these plots to cultivate under the direction of the gardener; he found the seeds and implements himself, and the crop was taken by the head master at market prices. Very good results came from that. I examined the pupil teachers and found that they got a good deal of practical information in the working of these gardens.

1376. Monsignor Molloy.—The Munster School is an agricultural school as well as a dairy school?—Yes.

1377. Do you think it would be possible to make it more efficient and successful as an agricultural school?—I don't think it would, and keep the dairy department in its present state; you cannot have the two seasons together.

1378. Have you not both at Glasnevin?—Not at the same time.

1379. But you have both in the institution at different times; is that impossible in Cork?—They have the same system at Cork, but the dairy sessions are much longer than at Glasnevin; the governors of the dairy school objected to the short period given to the instruction of young men, and they propose to take a farm at some distance from the school, and have this developed as a large agricultural school—a very worthy object.

1380. Then, in your opinion, it would be desirable to have a separate building for agricultural students?—I quite think so.

1381. But might both be under the same management?—Both might be under the same local management.

1382. Do you think if that difficulty were got over, it would be possible to convert the agricultural school at Cork into a successful agricultural school as well as a successful dairy school?—If you reduce the length of time.

1883. Ch., no; I contemplate that it means an extension, so it is put it is a position to do both works?—The institution might, but you would require separate buildings.

1884. Would you consider that desirable?—I think it would be very desirable. I may add that for the present year the whole of the places at the Munster Dairy School are applied for, and a number of applications have come in for the year 1898.

1885. Am I right in supposing that the local committee approve applicants and [illegible]?—Very.

1886. And are [illegible] they would [illegible] if they could do it?—Yes.

1887. Rev. Dr. Evans.—About the giving up of these Model Farms: was there any application from the localities where these farms are situate, to the Commissioners or to the Treasury to have them continued?—I have a knowledge of an application coming from Cork; I was not sufficiently long connected with the establishment to know whether in other cases there were applications.

1888. Might it not be that it was the want of local interest in these farms which led the Treasury to seek their abandonment?—I am not aware.

Chairman.—There is a meeting the Commissioners have to attend, and therefore we must stop your evidence now, and ask you to come back on the next day we meet.

The Commission then adjourned the taking of evidence.

Feb. 6, 1897. Professor Thomas Carroll, M.R.I.A.

FOURTH PUBLIC SITTING.—FRIDAY, FEBRUARY 19th, 1897, AT 2 P.M.,

Feb. 19, 1897.

At the Antient Concert Rooms, Dublin.

Present:—The Right Hon. the Earl of Belmore, K.C.M.G., in the Chair; His Grace the Most Rev. William J. Walsh, D.D.; The Right Hon. C. T. Redington, M.A.; His Honour Judge Shaw, Q.C.; The Right Rev. Monsignor Molloy, D.D., D.SC.; Rev. Henry Evans, D.D.; Rev. Hamilton Wilson, M.D.; Stanley Harrington, Esq., M.A.; W. R. J. Molloy, Esq.; Captain T. B. Shaw, and J. Struthers, Esq., M.A.;

with J. D. Daly, Esq., M.A., Secretary.

Professor Thomas Carroll, M.R.I.A., Agricultural Superintendent, Albert Farm, Glasnevin, further examined.

Professor Thomas Carroll, M.R.I.A.

1889. Chairman.—With regard to Agricultural Schools and School Gardens; how many of them are in connection with the Agricultural Department?—At the present time, my lord, there are two Agricultural Training Establishments—one at Glasnevin and the other at Cork; there are forty-seven School Farms distributed over the country; there are eighty-two School Gardens, six schools in which dairying is taught, and eight schools in which poultry management is taught, and three schools in which bee management is taught.

1890. Were any of these schools formerly under local management, and if so, was that management efficient?—There were, I think, somewhere about a dozen schools under local management; these declined by degrees, and at the present time very few of these schools are now in connection with the Agricultural Department of the Commissioners. The management of these schools was in all respects similar to the management of the ordinary National Schools, with similar rights of directing and management.

1891. And was it effective on the whole?—For some time these schools were very effective; but I think, from the Farm Commissioners' Reports and my own observation, a good deal of difficulty arose—it may be called agrarian difficulty—misunderstandings as to the objects of the schools. Farmers thought that these schools were in some cases established by landlords for the purpose of increasing the value of land, and a good many other difficulties of that class were noticeable.

1892. And after that do you think they ceased to be as effective?—They ceased to be as effective; in fact pupils were not sent to them. I have known cases also where the school teachers were rather lax in their management, waiting for rent settlements. I think agrarian difficulty at the time had a great deal to do with the decline of these schools.

1893. Then I understand from that answer that these teachers were themselves farmers?—Generally they were teachers farming these school farms as their own. They were given a grant by the Commissioners for the agricultural instruction of the pupils. I have had a map prepared, my lord, showing the position of the different classes of schools in the country (produced).

1894. Monsignor Molloy.—Are there copies of this map that we could get?—If you wish, I could have one made for you—this is made specially.

1895. Most Rev. Dr. Walsh.—It is an ordinary travelling map of Ireland, marked with the places of the schools?—Yes.

1896. Chairman.—Will you describe the system of instruction in these agricultural schools and school gardens?—In all cases the teachers of the schools instruct the pupils on the farms; in the greater number of the schools there are what are called industrial agricultural classes established at the present time. There are 32 out of the 47 schools in which these industrial classes are established. In these schools where the industrial classes are established the Commissioners pay the pupils at the rate of 2d. per hour for work done on the farm for the teacher. There are what are called agricultural monitors who supervise this work. I shall hand in the rules in respect of this industrial department. In addition to the work on the farm by these boys, they are obliged to keep notebooks, and I consider the keeping of these notebooks one of the best features of the system. I will hand in a blank copy of the notebook having an example sheet, explaining how the boys should copy it. The notebook has the time of the work, the time engaged at work, the nature of the work, remarks on the weather, and notes made by the boy of various matters of agricultural interest in the district. At the end of the book is a weekly account in which he is obliged to keep the time he works and the cash that he receives. This is in some cases now used as a literary exercise in composition, and where that is done the result has been very satisfactory. I may state that these schools have also what we call the literary part of agriculture, or what is known as Part I. I examine on the practical part, take the pupils on to the farm and examine them upon what they are taught upon the farm, and I examine their notebooks to see they are properly kept.

1397. Do you go about the country for that purpose?—I go about the country; it takes very nearly half my time to go over these schools.

1398. Mr. [illegible].—You inspect the school

pay; in fact I was enabled, through th[illegible] of many of these farms, to prepare a [illegible] return as to what was called the c[illegible] it was a most telling matter—in fact it [illegible]

[illegible] Professor Thomas Carroll, [illegible]

1427. Mr. Strickland.—When I was referring to say the ordinary school with school gardens attached? —There the pupils are employed, and, in almost all cases, work in the garden for half an hour; this half hour may be either taken at playtime or after school hours.

1428. Do all the pupils of the higher classes take part in this work?—That is the regulation.

1429. But as a matter of fact?—They do, of course; at some times I would not say there would be more work to be done than at other times, but as a matter of fact they do take part in the work.

1430. Mr. Redington.—No pupils under the fourth class take part in it?—Oh, no; you mentioned the higher classes.

Mr. Strickland.—Yes, from the fourth up.

1431. Of pupils who are—[illegible] who attend the industrial classes you refer to regularly attending the ordinary school?—Oh, yes; they are pupils of the ordinary school.

1432. How many hours each week does each pupil give to it?—Three hours I may say, and recently a change has been made which appears to work more satisfactorily. Instead of taking an odd half hour during the week, Saturday—which is an off day—is given to the industrial class; and I may also say that I have it in my mind to have a portion of the farm given up to these boys, so that they shall do the whole of the work of this plot, and I hope that by having this work done in a superior manner—for instance, the deep cultivation of the soil, and a good deal of work that I need not detail, will show that better crops can be raised by good cultivation—I hope that the industrial classes may be thus made more useful.

1433. Then do you consider it a good plan to have a separate teaching in the theory of agriculture from the teacher in practical work?—I don't see any objection to it. I may say that occasionally when a discrepancy or difference has arisen between my examination of the practice and the corresponding in theory, my attention has been called to it at the office, and I am obliged to take cognisance of it; but I find it is rare that my examination and the examinations of the Inspectors generally accord.

1434. Are they taught the general scientific principles which underlie any improvement which you may expect in agriculture?—I may say that up to the present a good deal of fault was found with the text-book. I believe the present text-book will meet that difficulty. There is more attempt made to bring principles into the text-book at present in use than was the case in the old text-book.

1435. Do you think the training which a boy who has reached the fourth standard has got is sufficient to enable him to comprehend those principles if they were taught to him?—I quite think so. You would be rather astonished if you were to examine some of these country Irish schools. I lived in England for some years myself, and was the manager of two schools. The Inspector told me he would always tell the Irish boys from their sharpness in picking up information. I quite think, with suitable books, that the boys of the fourth class can comprehend the elementary science of agriculture, a subject that in practice they have before their minds every day.

1436. Mr. Ridgeway.—Do you find any difficulty in [illegible] [illegible] of the agricultural farms [illegible] time much larger than at present?—Nearly double the number. I found, I think, about ninety on the list, but many of these were only useful as affording examples of work to be avoided.

1437. Would you think it desirable to have the work of the school garden examined by a practical man like you, as the school Inspector?—I quite think that would be almost necessary—at least for a time. I believe that the Inspectors, from what I know of them, would very soon qualify themselves to examine the practical work of the school garden, but they do require a little training and encouragement.

1438. How many of these [illegible] teachers that you refer to would you think necessary?—I like to have small beginnings. I should say if three men were appointed it would be a very great help and very useful; then, as the project was found to be successful, let the number be increased.

1439. Mr. Harrington.—Was it owing to the withdrawal of Treasury grants that certain agricultural schools under local management failed?—Not, for the ordinary agricultural schools. The grants withdrawn by the Treasury were for schools that were under the sole management of the Commissioners. They were schools that correspond pretty well now to the ordinary agricultural schools, excepting that they were supposed to be looked after better by their managers.

1440. Do you find from experience that the teaching of practical agricultural work in these School Farms interferes with the ordinary literary work for the boys?—There are very few of the schools to which farms are attached where bad literary results are to be found—and I make it a point to look into the Inspector's examination roll very generally at these schools—and I don't see that there is very much fault to be found with the literary work of these schools. I may say that I don't consider at all that the knowledge of agriculture or practical farming will unfit a man to be a literary teacher; in fact, I should think that an accomplished agriculturist ought to be a good literary teacher.

1441. Are these School Farms considered models of good farming in the districts in which they are situated?—The large farms that I have in my mind now are certainly model farms.

1442. But as a matter of fact do the farmers come round and get information from these farms that are supposed to be conducted on scientific principles?—I have heard of cases where that was done; I may also tell you that the old hard-and-fast line of following a distinct system has brought a great deal of discredit on these schools. For example, a teacher is required to carry out a rotation that was considered the proper thing for the district—that was the opinion of one man, and possibly he was not quite correct. A uniform system for farming universally I hold to be quite a mistake, and at the present time the same rotation system for the whole country is not carried out at the agricultural schools.

1443. But then these School Farms are not at all as perfect as you should like to see them, I take it?—No; I should like to see them more perfect. I may say that since the increase in the result fees, granted some time ago, there has been a very great improvement in the management of these farms.

would be quite possible and extremely useful. I brought before the Commissioners some time ago an illustration of how teachers might cultivate an interest in such matters in their pupils.

1450. How old are the boys in these classes?—From 11 to 15 or 16.

1451. Where do they come from?—The immediate neighbourhood of the school.

1452. Then each school is only supplied by the boys from its own immediate district, and only educates the boys in its own immediate district?—Quite so.

1453. Then the boys in the school are never over 16—in fact the education is primary education?—When the boys pass the second stage of sixth class they are not eligible for the payment of fees either.

1454. Do you think it is in general necessary for a teacher to have a farm of his own in order to have opportunities for practical illustration of his own agricultural lessons?—In some cases it would not be necessary, but I think it is in all cases desirable; because a teacher, if he did his work properly, would do upon his farm what he could not get permission to have done on other farms.

1455. Would not a comparatively small plot be sufficient for these things?—Yes, I believe that.

1456. I see here, for instance, in your own book on practical farming, there are a number of things which are stated—"If you take a seed, a bean, or a grain of wheat. It is to all appearance lifeless, but if split and you will find it is made up of different parts. If you take the bean or grain of wheat that has begun to grow, and keep it out of the ground for sometime, you will find it for sometime is green, but after a little while it withers and dies. You thus see that plants require food." Are these practically illustrated for children in schools?—I am very sorry to say they are not, but I hope they will be. I hope they will get ideas from the book that they may carry out in their instruction.

1457. Then you think it would be desirable to give them some scientific training?—It has been the desire of my life that they should get a little education in that direction.

1458. Would it not be well to introduce some experimental work into the farms?—Yes; that is done to a fair extent. I have had manures sent to those school farms to have experiments carried out. I have sent potatoes and seeds. A few years ago I had the idea that the haricot bean would be useful for introducing into poor districts so as to improve the diet of the people, and I had a large quantity sent to those schools, and the teachers got them.

1459. Don't you think that would be likely to make our future farmers more willing to make experiments for themselves?—I think it would.

1460. Is not that a great want in our present farming?—I think it is a great want.

1461. Do you think the instruction given in our schools has tended to make farmers more willing to make experiments?—I scarcely think it has.

1462. Then you think our present agricultural teaching has produced very little effect?—I think it might be improved.

1463. But you think it has produced some effect?—I am certain it has produced some effect, and I would like to go back to my evidence of the other day, and [illegible]

1464. Chairman.—A rural school?—I think the teacher, if he had five acres, could do a good deal towards the teaching of practical work.

1465. Monsignor Molloy.—Would you think five acres about the best typical size?—I think so.

1466. I think you have told us already that you think it desirable to extend very largely the system of teaching agriculture in the schools?—Yes.

1467. In such an extension how would you propose that the farms should be provided?—At present I understand the farms are provided by the school-masters?—Yes.

1468. Do you think that would be the best system to follow in extending this kind of teaching?—There is power at the present time for acquiring land that could be put into force.

1469. Chairman.—Acquiring by whom?—By the school managers. You will find that at the end of the rules and regulations.

Most Rev. Dr. Walsh.—There was a provision inserted for this in a Bill that the Government brought in last year.

1470. Mr. Redington.—Do you mean compulsory acquisition?—Not by which means you [illegible] for the acquisition of lands.

1471. Monsignor Molloy.—I wanted rather to get your opinion as to how it can be best effected, whether it would be desirable for the Commissioners to provide the farm or for the manager, or, as at present, the schoolmaster?—I think that would be a most difficult matter to arrange. The difficulty of getting land in that way is at the present time very serious. I don't see how the Commissioners could do it. If they could do it I believe that would be the best way, because they would be possessed of the situation as regards the quality of the work performed. But the only way I see at present is to take advantage of places where the teachers have farms.

1472. Do you think that would be the most practical way?—That would be the most practical at present; but if the Commissioners could acquire farms, I think that would be the best.

1473. Do you think the method of the school-master providing the farm would allow of the system being very widely extended?—I think it would.

1474. At present the total number of school farms is 47, and I suppose the number of schools in rural districts for boys would be something about 3,000 or upwards?—About that.

1475. And therefore the actual number of school farms is insignificant compared to the possibility of extension?—Quite so; but all the National Schools need not have them. I believe with these schools dotted about over the country, say at a radius of five or six miles, they would effect a great deal of good.

1476. Then you think that an extension would be very desirable even though it would not be carried out everywhere; if it could be carried out in certain localities it would beneficially affect the whole neighbourhood around?—I quite believe that.

1477. Professor FitzGerald.—Would you confine it to the 4th, 5th, and 6th class for boys?—I think so.

1478. Would you despoil the schools in the neighbourhood for these schools?—No; this would be [illegible] who has the school, or that it should be given by itinerant teachers?—It must necessarily be given by the teacher who teaches the school, but I believe that teacher could be improved by itinerant teachers; and that is one of the things that would be the most important duty of the itinerant teacher.

1481. Then you would advise to have the itinerant teachers not for teaching the schools but for teaching the schoolmasters?—Exactly.

1482. Mr. [illegible].—What is the minimum size of a school garden?—About a rood, but that has been exceeded.

1483. Do you know whether the Inspectors have time to pay incidental visits to those school gardens at other times than at the yearly examination?—I may say I know very little of the time of the Inspectors, but I think they are required to pay incidental visits, and do look at those school gardens.

1484. Do you think it essential that there should be visits paid at other times than at the annual examination?—I quite think so; the [illegible] those [illegible] visits are paid, the better.

1485. Monsignor Molloy.—With reference to the itinerant teachers, do you think it would be possible to combine their function of teaching the schoolmasters with the function of agricultural inspectors?—I think that could be done.

1486. Most Rev. Dr. Walsh.—I don't fully understand the distinction between agricultural schools and school gardens; kindly explain what an agricultural school is?—An agricultural school is a school in which practical agriculture is supposed to be taught. There are forms giving information about this which I shall put in.

1487. But I should prefer to have it on the notes. What is meant by an agricultural school as distinct from an ordinary school?—An agricultural school is a school to which a farm is attached, and on which the boys are given the practical instruction. Upon this farm live stock of various kinds are to be found.

1488. Then the difference between an agricultural school and an ordinary school consists in this—that there is a farm attached to the school in the one case and not in the other?—And that the teacher gets a good result fee for teaching practical work on the farm.

1489. But as regards the school itself to which the farm is attached, is there any substantial difference between these agricultural schools and ordinary schools?—No difference, except that practical agriculture is taught in the agricultural school and theoretical agriculture in the rural schools.

1490. And it is only theoretical agriculture in the ordinary schools?—Yes; and the literary side of the school is the same in both cases.

1491. Well, then, as to the school gardens?—School gardens correspond with school farms. They are on a smaller scale. They are not required to have live stock, and that is the only difference.

1492. Is this the state of the case; for I think it would make it much plainer if it could be stated in this form. In reference to agricultural teaching, our schools are of three classes; first, ordinary schools, in which theoretical agriculture is taught?—In the rural schools.

1493. But agriculture is also taught in the city schools?—It is not compulsory; it is optional.

1494. That makes no difference in the case. Optional or compulsory, the thing goes on. Even in Dublin a few of Sir [illegible] may be marked for what is called agriculture, merely learning things out of books. Coming back, then, to the point, I ask you is this the division, that our schools in reference to this teaching of agriculture are of three classes; first, schools in which theoretical agriculture is taught, and only theoretical?—Yes.

1495. Secondly, schools in which practical agriculture is taught, these being again of two classes, schools to which school farms are attached, and schools to which school gardens are attached?—That is so.

1496. What is the difference between a school farm and a school garden?—A school farm is a larger piece of ground than the school garden; the school farm has crops grown upon it that are not grown in the school garden. The school garden is supposed to have a greater variety of vegetables and flowers than the school farm.

1497. It is a difference mainly in size?—And in cultivation.

1498. And the difference in cultivation results from the difference in size?—Quite so.

1499. Is this system of school gardens and school farms on the increase, or on the decrease in Ireland?—The system of school gardens is on the increase; and there is beginning to be an increase in the case of school farms.

1500. But there has been a great falling off in the number of school farms in Ireland?—There has been a great falling off.

1501. Well, at all events, a falling off in number: What was the cause?—The Commissioners considered that the [illegible]

1502. I want to make sure of the facts first. There is a falling off?—There is a falling off.

1503. In the abstract of evidence that you have given us, you speak of schools under local management—schools in connection with the agricultural department under local management,—and then you speak of the cause of the failure of those schools under local management, now what does that local management consist in?—It is exactly similar to the present management of ordinary National schools.

1504. What other kind of management is there in reference to these agricultural establishments as distinct from local management?—As the matter stands no difference. In former times, at schools under local management a fee of £[illegible] was given to keep each [illegible] owned by the [illegible] [illegible].

1505. I want to know the two kinds of management, that you seek to distinguish?—The management, so far as I can make out, is the same.

1506. This was to your point in speaking about schools under local management, as having failed?—Assuming a fact.

1507. But is there any other kind of management except local management in those agricultural schools?—These schools were mainly got up by [illegible] [illegible]

1508. What schools are you now speaking of?—The schools that were in old times under local management.

1509. I want to know first is there any other kind of school except those under local management?—If your Grace would allow me to explain.

1510. Your explanation will be thrown away upon me unless I know what it is that you are explaining. You have spoken of schools under local management; I am asking simply for information. I want to get before my mind your different kinds of management. What kind of management is there distinct from local management?—Does your Grace allude to——

1511. I don't allude to anything; I am asking a question. Is there any other kind of management than local management, and, if so, what is it?—The local management will follow in this way——

1512. I am not asking you how anything will follow. I want to know is there any other kind of management than local management?—The Commissioners have something to do with the management.

1513. They have something to do with the management of every National school in Ireland, yet those schools are under local management. Is there any other kind of agricultural management in Ireland except local management?—Except Glasnevin and Cork.

1514. Those are the only two exceptions?—Yes.

1515. And there is there a mixture of local management with the management of the Commissioners—that is only of [illegible] [illegible]?—Yes, in respect of the Cork School.

[illegible] Professor Thomas Carroll, M.R.I.A.

1516. You have said that the schools under local management failed owing to some misunderstanding; people thought they were got up in the interests of landlords to raise the value of land?—That opinion prevailed.

1517. Does that apply to all the agricultural schools in Ireland?—Not at the present time.

1518. But those schools are under local management?—A different sort of local management.

1519. What are the different kinds of local management?—I will tell you; those schools alluded to there were brought into connection with the agricultural department of the Commissioners of National Education by enthusiastic proprietors of property. I have one in my mind near Castlebellingham, Tyrone.

1520. What you speak of in your evidence as schools under local management—do your remarks apply to all the schools under local management, or only to particular schools?—Particular schools started some years ago.

1521. Then you did not intend to convey by this statement you put before the Commissioners that the schools that were under local management failed, and the schools that were under some other kind of management, distinct from local, did not fail?—No, my lord.

1522. I must say I inferred from your statement that you did, but I am glad to have evidence on that information. Now the teachers of these agricultural schools must be qualified—what is the qualification?—The procedure as to recognising them will explain that. Application is sent to the Commissioners for what are called grants to support these agricultural schools. This application is sent on to me, to report upon the school and the school teacher. I go to the school and see whether the accommodation is suitable, and whether the school teacher is capable of teaching agriculture. I report to the Commissioners, and on my report the grant is made or withheld.

1523. How do you satisfy yourself of that; is it not by putting him through a written examination?—No, my lord.

1524. By observing his actual capacity?—Quite so, and by conversation and putting questions.

1525. You don't hold a written examination?—I do not for them.

1526. You spoke of these school farms as paying their way. When you speak of a farm paying, do you take into account the question of the maintenance of the farmer and his family?—No. If I were asked to value a farm, I would not endeavour to find out what that farm would produce for the maintenance of the farmer merely.

1527. Take two farms in the country, one is a farm attached to a school, the other is the farm of some neighbouring farmer. The neighbouring man's farm is not supposed to pay unless it enables him to live and bring up his family. Would you consider that a school farm paid if it merely gave a balance of 5*l.* at the end of the year?—It depends upon what was required of the farm.

1528. Would you consider that it paid?—I would consider that it paid as a farm, but if that farm were used for experimental purposes——

1529. When you speak of farms as paying is that the sort of paying you have in mind?—No, my lord.

1530. Do they keep accounts of these school farms?—Yes.

1531. As a rule, what would be the profit per acre?—It varies considerably, from possibly 5*s.* to 2*l.* or 3*l.*

1532. The work on those farms is done to some extent by the pupils?—Yes, to a limited extent.

1533. Are the pupils paid for that?—Where the industrial class system is taken up they are paid.

1534. Well, where it is not?—They are not paid.

1535. So the labour is so far gratuitous?—Yes.

1536. Well, is it not much easier for a farm worked under these circumstances to pay than for a farm worked by an ordinary farmer?—Having had a good deal of experience of unskilled labour I would say that I give very little credit for such labour.

1537. Well, now, another question about the inspection. You discharge the duty of inspector for this important department of work in connection with the National system of education in Ireland?—Yes, my lord.

1538. Are you paid at the same rate of salary as the inspectors who do the work of literary inspecting; you are not, I believe?—Well, I think it is about the same as the District Inspectors.

1539. But a District Inspector may rise to be a Head Inspector?—He may.

1540. You have no such prospect of advance in your department?—I am sorry to say I have not.

1541. Therefore, so far as encouragement is given to this department through the payment of inspectors, agriculture is at a suitable disadvantage?—As far as the inspectors are concerned I suppose it is.

1542. You examine the pupils as well as the teachers?—I examine all the pupils in the two stages of 5th and the two stages of 6th class.

1543. Do you examine them according to a regular programme?—Yes, there is a programme provided for the examination.

1544. That is not held in writing, your examination?—No, my lord.

1545. Are results fees paid on your examination?—The agricultural results fees, yes.

1546. Can you tell me about the amount of those fees? I see mention of "Scale of payment for practical proficiency of pupils as tested on the school farm"?—I think you will find that the school garden comes below that. Section 2 is what I examine on (practically).

1547. Well, now, 5th class for "A pass in knowledge of the crops grown on the farm and of the means of raising them, &c." How is that knowledge tested?—The boys are taken out to the farm and taken to the crops. I take them and examine them as to their knowledge of how the land is prepared for that crop, the time it should be harvested, and the quality of the crop.

1548. And you don't examine them on mere book-work?—I don't examine them on book-work, but the programmes are made up somewhat in harmony.

1549. But the result fee that is paid for the mere book-work is just the same as the result fee for the practical work?—Yes, that is so. Some time ago results fees on the farm were much less than for the book.

1550. Have you happened to see a letter that was written by Professor Fitzgerald on this question of agricultural instruction in the schools recently, within the last year or two?—Oh, yes.

1551. Well, now, without going into particular matters of detail, did you not consider that a very valuable letter?—I did; I consider it a very useful letter.

I trust we can have that letter put in.

1552. CHAIRMAN.—There is one subject I should like to put you a question on, arising out of Judge Shaw's examination, and that was with regard to teaching pupils in the agricultural schools how to value cattle. As I understand you to say the school farms are small, and therefore naturally there cannot be much cattle on them. By what system do they teach the pupils to arrive at the value of cattle and test their knowledge afterwards?—There is no attempt in the ordinary agricultural schools to teach such principles. The idea is that they will get information of that kind from their parents, who are engaged in rearing, buying and selling of stock; but it would be a difficult thing to introduce that subject practically.

1553. You would agree with me that to be a good judge of cattle you would want practical experience in buying and selling cattle?—Yes, and that point is dealt with in the new agricultural class book.

[illegible] 20, 1887. Professor Thomas Carroll, [illegible].

1554. There is another question which does not arise out of anything said yet, but it is an important one, and that is with regard to the weeds that grow all over Ireland, particularly in the grass fields. Are there any pains taken to teach the people the necessity that exists for destroying weeds?—There is a practical way of dealing with that question. If the farm is not in a clean condition the fees are either reduced or withheld altogether, and of course the teacher has to keep the farm clean, and in doing so he shows the pupils how to do it.

1555. The other day you gave us some evidence about the [illegible] Model School. That school is under the supervision of a head teacher?—Yes, my lord, he has the garden.

1556. And he has a grass field adjoining the garden (I have to pass it very frequently) in which I have seen weeds flourishing?—You may [illegible], but that is under a literary inspector. About two months ago I gave the teacher a little of my mind for that neglect.

1557. Most Rev. Dr. Walsh.—Is not that the place you praised so much to me?—Oh, yes; it was the system. I think his lordship, the Chairman, will admit that the garden is very well cultivated.

1558. Chairman.—There is one other point with regard to the difficulty of acquiring school farms. I suppose that arises from the very varying tenures on which schools are held. Sometimes a school is on the land of a tenant and sometimes not?—That must be a difficulty.

1559. And unless the manager, as is sometimes the case, is a tenant farmer there would be a great difficulty about acquiring the land?—A very great difficulty, that is the difficulty about the extension of the system.

1560. Most Rev. Dr. Walsh.—Just one question, as Lord Belmore asked you about the weeds, you said, in the case that his lordship referred to, that the weeds were in a grass field adjoining the school, have you ever seen a weed flourishing in a school garden?—I have heard of them.

1561. Does it surprise you to hear that the most flourishing collection of weeds I ever saw was in a school farm?—The local inspector should look after that.

1562. Mr. [illegible].—You are aware that there are compulsory powers for the acquisition of a teacher's residence and that the site has been defined to be a quarter of an acre. Are you aware that a Bill was brought in by the Government last year to extend that to an acre?—Yes, I saw the Bill.

1563. Do you think that would be advantageous to promote the study of gardening?—I think it would be very advantageous.

1564. Chairman.—Could that be extended, if Parliament chose to do it, to five acres, to make a school farm?—That would depend on the Bill brought in.

1565. That would be practically the only way of introducing it by providing a farm in connexion with a teacher's residence?—Quite so, but as I understand some of the Commissioners would like to see even small portions of land attached.

1566. Most Rev. Dr. Walsh.—The rule is that the school farm should contain not less than three acres?—Yes.

1567. Chairman.—[illegible]

it would appear that the [illegible] of this instruction is increasing very much. I may also add that the dairy classes of the dairy schools have to a large extent been filled in consequence of the interest taken by farmers where this instruction is being given, and I should like to see this instruction given largely in the schools in districts where the inspectors go.

1568. Is there evidence of the good effect of this itinerant instruction?—I have frequently had letters testifying to the improvement in butter made.

1569. Would you particularise as regards the improvement whether the persons who have been instructed became instructors themselves?—I have had instances in the county Antrim, where the price of butter has been increased by 3d. a lb. From the county Clare, which they were not noted for making very good butter, some Limerick merchants have expressed very satisfactorily at improvement [illegible] in consequence of teaching, and several additional pupils have come to the schools. I have here a printed report on the work of one of the itinerant instructors during the last year, I shall put that in.

1570. In what way could there be an improvement effected in this class of instruction?—By increasing the facilities at National schools, and allowing more freedom in the purchasing of materials, a great difficulty arises about getting sufficient materials for practical teaching. I should like to see more land given at these schools so that the persons attending could with their own hands work under the direction of the instructors, at the present time that is almost impossible owing to the want of funds.

1571. Is dairy management taught as an extra branch in National schools?—Yes, but this is at the present time mainly confined to Convent schools.

1572. Will you describe the methods pursued in those schools?—These Convent schools are inspected to find out whether they have the appliances suitable for teaching, and whether there is a teacher in them capable of giving instruction; on my report the school is recognised and the subject is taught and paid for as an extra branch.

1573. Are there advantages from the teaching of dairy management under the results system?—I have not had knowledge of much, but my opinion is that these girls when they are [illegible], when they go to their homes will be able to exercise a very large influence with their mothers and sisters in improving their dairy produce.

1574. Is poultry management as practical instruction introduced into schools under the Board?—Yes.

1575. Will you describe the methods?—Poultry management is taught as an extra branch. It has not made the progress I should like, mainly in consequence of the difficulty of getting appliances and accommodation for the poultry, but I believe there is at the present time an inclination to increase this branch at schools, and I believe that an increase in the fees for dairying, poultry, and bee-keeping would do a great deal to increase these branches.

1576. Is there much bee-keeping?—Only three at present, but it appears to me that the keeping of bees will be increased by being recognised as an extra branch in schools.

1577. Rev. Dr. Evans.—I think you said, Mr. [illegible]

Feb. 20, 1896. — Professor Thomas Carroll, M.R.I.A.

1582. Rev. Dr. Wilson.—Do you think there is anything more important for Ireland than that the number should be increased from three to fifty of these institutions?—I think it would be extremely useful. I may say that not until recently has there been any great desire, it has been with very great difficulty that the system has been introduced in the country. In Cork and Kerry it was very uphill work to get this taken up by the farmers, but it seems to have taken hold now, and I think it will grow.

1583. Mr. Struthers.—Are these classes held in schools always?—Not always in schools, sometimes in large buildings attached to the farms.

1584. In that case they are attended by whom?—Farmers' wives and daughters.

1585. And when they are held in schools by whom are they attended?—By the same class as in other places, and in addition by the older girls of the school.

1586. Of what age?—Girls from thirteen to sixteen or seventeen.

1587. They will have already passed the 6th standard?—The 5th or 6th.

1588. Would this kind of instruction not be more effectually given in evening classes to pupils who wanted it?—As a rule they are held after school hours, not during school hours, that would be against the rules.

1589. But not immediately after the school hours?—Well, almost immediately, the children go home to have something to eat before the class commences.

1590. Mr. [illegible].—Did not the dairy instructors visit farm houses in the neighbourhood of the towns they were sent to, that is, they did not confine themselves to the particular town, but visited farm houses and gave instruction there also?—Oh, yes, in almost all cases in addition, the teaching is at a rural place, not in towns but almost invariably in the country. In addition to teaching at these centres, they visit and advise farmers who may require their services.

1591. In all cases are there not local committees established to co-operate with them?—That is the rule, and I find in Clare that the clergymen of all denominations, and a good many of the landed proprietors, but the clergy in particular, have in all cases given most valuable support.

1592. One of the earliest instances, if I mistake not, was Ennistymon, where Colonel Burgess was the chairman: was not that a great success?—A remarkable success.

1593. And within a comparatively short time the price for butter was increased?—Within a few weeks the price was increased very much, but the most striking case was in Rathkeale?, where the young lady spent some months, the prices there were increased considerably.

1594. Mr. [illegible].—Do you consider teaching in these subjects, dairying, poultry keeping, and bee-keeping comes under primary instruction?—I am afraid that is rather a delicate question to give an opinion on. I don't see why a great educational department might not have a department for industrial work as well as for primary education. I don't see why it should not supply a great want.

1595. Mr. Struthers.—Is there an agricultural department in Ireland?—Oh, no, that is what is hoped for; the agricultural department I refer to is the agricultural department of the National Board.

1596. Professor FitzGerald.—Has there not been a Bill promised to be introduced into Parliament this Session for the purpose of creating an agricultural department for Ireland?—I have heard that stated.

1597. Monsignor Molloy.—Is dairy work taught only at Convent schools, and not at other National schools?—At Convent schools principally. There are one or two applications for ordinary National schools where the wives of the teachers have been at Glasnevin for a course of teaching, and there has been an application to take these up.

1598. When it is taught, what is about the age of the children to whom it is taught?—The rules for the other branches apply; the age will be fifteen or sixteen.

1599. Most Rev. Dr. Walsh.—You said that before a school is taken into connection for the purpose of dairy instruction, the Inspector must be satisfied that the school has sufficient dairy appliances?—Yes, my lord.

1600. At whose expense are these provided?—At the expense of the school authorities.

1601. Not at all out of the education grant?—No. I may add one of the points I had asked here to recommend for an extension of the dairy instruction at schools, is help for providing apparatus.

1602. For the present we are dealing only with the actual state of the case?—The case is, that all the appliances and the cost of the training of the teacher has to be found by the school at which dairying is taught.

1603. Well, dairying is taught at Glasnevin, is it not?—Yes.

1604. At whose expense are the appliances provided there?—The estimate provides the appliances.

1605. That is, they are paid for out of the public taxes?—That is so.

1606. But that is not so in the ordinary schools through the country?—No; the only payment to those schools is the results fees.

1607. No provision is made for the appliances; and without appliances dairy instruction cannot be put up at all, and therefore there cannot be results fees?—Yes.

1608. And, therefore, the school is met by the initial difficulty that there cannot be dairy instruction?—Not without the appliances.

1609. You say in the Convent schools that difficulty is got over. How is that?—By the Nuns providing it from their own resources.

1610. Professor FitzGerald.—Would the results fees that are earned in a large school pay a good interest on the money spent in providing the appliances?—Well, barely; the fee is five shillings a pupil, and if there were twenty girls examined—I don't think there are as many as that generally—that would give £5. To fit up a dairy and train a teacher and provide apparatus, it ought to cost over £100.

1611. Most Rev. Dr. Walsh.—Take that point in another light. Suppose that it did pay the interest on the capital, would there be anything left for the [illegible] teacher except the salary for ordinary school work—in other words, would there be anything for the trouble the teacher took in teaching the dairy instruction?—Not in that branch.

1612. So the teachers would have first to lay out their money in getting up these appliances, and the only return would be a sort of interest on their money, then they would have the labour of teaching, and have nothing for their trouble?—That would be about it. I would like to see some further encouragement given to them.

1613. To what extent is the dairy teaching in Glasnevin connected with the work of dairy teaching in the National schools of Ireland?—I don't see that there is any connection excepting that the young women are trained at Glasnevin. I don't know whether any of them are school teachers, but we have had a good many trained at Glasnevin who have gone to Convent schools as teachers.

1614. Are you aware there is a rule—say in Kildare-place, Drumcondra, or Baggot-street—that before a candidate can be admitted to a training college he must sign a declaration that he intends bona fide to teach in a National school in Ireland, or in some other specified way to devote himself to the work of teaching in the public service—is there any such declaration required for the admission of a person to get the benefit of the Glasnevin establishment in dairy instruction?—No, there is not, but the Glasnevin establishment is intended for the agricultural classes generally, and not specially for teachers.

Mr. J. P. MORAN, Teacher of Drawing in Marlborough-street Training College, examined.

[illegible]
Mr. J. P. Moran.

1615. CHAIRMAN.—Will you tell us what position you hold in connection with National Education?—I teach drawing in the Training College in Marlborough-street to the male and female Queen's Scholars, and I superintend the teaching of drawing by the regular staff in the nine schools, both male and female.

1616. Which nine schools?—The nine schools that are in the Central Model school and the infant school. That makes nine in reality, but with the latter I have nothing to do; and I also teach a special class of pupils, both male and female—that is, two classes selected from these nine [illegible].

1617. To begin with the Queen's Scholars in Marlborough-street, will you tell us their number, and about their knowledge of drawing on arrival?—They are usually about 100 on each side—sometimes 105, sometimes more. This year we have on the female side 114, something unusual. Their knowledge of drawing is very limited on arrival as a rule, with the exception of some ten or fifteen on each side, who may have certificates. Some arrive with certificates, but the majority of them with entire ignorance of drawing.

1618. What sort of certificates?—The Board's certificates in drawing. Then on arrival they are examined with the object of drawing them at the proper standard, according to their capacity which varies. Some have a slight previous knowledge, and others have absolutely none. Their knowledge on arrival has been somewhat higher within the last few years. It has gone up rather than otherwise.

1619. Is the drawing that they have a knowledge of generally confined to drawing from the flat?—Yes, as a rule. Those who have certificates may have done some model drawing.

1620. Will you explain what is meant by the term "improvement in standard" in your memorandum?—I mean that seven or eight years ago there were fewer students had received instruction of any kind, so much so that I got them to write on their first examination paper whether they had been taught or not. That is what I meant, that the number who have been taught has increased very considerably within the last few years.

1621. What do you say about the general instruction and individual teaching?—They get general instruction to begin with as to the methods they are to employ in doing their work, the class collectively, and [illegible] each student is taught individually.

1622. Perhaps you will tell us something about the method of drawing?—Collective teaching gives them an idea of the general principles that are to be adopted in copying their examples, and individually each example is marked by conspicuous lines showing the construction of the design and how that construction is to be reproduced—how the design is to be accurately and intelligently copied; they do that for a considerable time. We are speaking now of drawing from the examples, the very elementary part of the work. Then when they have a certain facility in copying actual size without measuring, ruling, or any mechanical means, these examples have to be drawn on a larger scale.

1623. What time is spent at freehand?—They have three hours a week, and those three hours are devoted to freehand until the month of July.

1624. Will you just tell me exactly what you understand by freehand?—Freehand drawing from the flat, the most elementary form.

1625. You mean drawing without a ruler?—Certainly, without any mechanical means whatever—copying a flat copy and example.

1626. Freehand drawing would include drawing from objects?—Certainly, to make it fuller I should say—freehand drawing from the flat as distinct from freehand drawing from the round, or model drawing.

1627. Now, will you tell us something about the second year's work of first year's students and what they do?—As a rule they pass in the freehand at the first examination in July, that gives them their certificate—they get their 60 per cent., which entitles them to a first freehand drawing and model result fees. Their second year is devoted to model drawing or drawing from the round and familiar objects, in which they also endeavour at the following July to get another 60 per cent., and what would correspond in reality to a second certificate, which I believe is not recognised as a separate certificate by the Board; however there is a record kept of this second examination.

1628. Do they learn something about geometry and perspective?—Yes; they learn something of perspective before they begin model drawing to teach them the principles of vision.

1629. What is the programme of first year's Queen's scholars?—As a rule, if they have not a certificate on arrival they are put to drawing from the flat, as being the more elementary, and more likely that they would be required to teach in their classes.

1630. What have you to say about model lessons and the opportunity afforded of utilising them under supervision in the practising schools?—The model lessons are given at frequent intervals to a number of fifteen or twenty boys from the different classes in the hearing and presence of the Queen's scholars; the design set before them is drawn largely on the blackboard and explained to these pupils as the work progresses. The Queen's scholars take notes of this method and make marginal sketches of the several stages in the progress of the work, so that they may when called upon to do so teach a similar lesson. The pupils' exercises are corrected by me in the hearing of the Queen's scholars, so that they may have this experience as to how pupils' work should be corrected. This lesson lasts as a rule from thirty to forty minutes, and is what I would call practical teaching.

1631. What do you mean by criticism lessons?—Criticism lessons are given during the last few months of the year amongst the Queen's scholars themselves. I call upon one of them to give a lesson to an imaginary class, say of 5th, 6th, or 4th class, with a suitable design, which he is required to draw, and to explain the method by which it should be reproduced. He gives us the best of his ability a complete lesson. Then each of the Queen's scholars is called upon in turn to supply what in his opinion may have been omitted, and so on all round the class. And when all have finished, if anything has been omitted by the entire number, I supply the omission, and make whatever general observations on the results of the lesson I may think necessary. And this is what I know as practical training.

1632. Have you anything to say about the teaching of pupils by the regular staff under your supervision?—That was a change that was made in 1899 or 1890, when it became possible to earn results fees for the subject of drawing. It was very necessary, I assumed, as the number to be taught was too large for one man. It divided the labour, and gave the teachers an opportunity of earning result fees by teaching drawing. Many of them, I believe, had not taught before, though they had certificates. However, with the slight help that I was able to give them, the change has done well.

1633. Have you control over the books and charts used?—Yes; when the teaching was transferred to the regular staff I had to inform them of the books necessary to carry out the Commissioners' programme, what books were the most suitable, and after a while I was able to induce them to use charts, which are preferable to drawing from books, as it prevents entirely any measuring or tricks.

1634. You mean by charts, charts on the wall?—Yes, large diagrams held at a distance.

1635. And you give suggestions whenever necessary to the teaching staff as to keeping the standard up to the Commissioners' programme?—Yes, because it is sometimes difficult to get the classes to do the exercise of the required standard. Then also during this supervision I have the Queen's scholars under my notice, and they get the opportunity of teaching these pupils. At the same time it gives them some confidence in the very difficult subject of teaching drawing—difficult because there is no text-book, and there they may very definite idea of teaching drawing except what they learn from their teachers.

1636. Will you tell us something about the other drawing classes of boys and girls, which are also taught by you, as to the frequency and the selection of pupils?—The special drawing classes of boys and girls had their origin with a small class I commenced in the girls' school on my appointment. I found that some of the girls showed a talent for drawing, and drawing from the flat was not, as I thought, the best method of teaching them advanced drawing. I began to make them draw from models and familiar objects. That took long, and the Commissioners instituted a similar class for the boys, and they added other subjects—geometrical drawing and elementary design. These classes are now taught both on the boys' side and the girls' side, and the pupils are selected from the different classes who show particular aptitude for drawing.

1637. I don't quite follow you in that observation. What do you mean by the selection of pupils? Are they pupils who are being trained for teachers or pupils in some of the schools in Dublin who wish to learn drawing?—No; I am speaking of the pupils in the Central Model Schools, the only pupils I have to deal with, whom I see at work in the several schools.

1638. You are not speaking of the Marlborough-street Training College?—No.

1639. I want to know whether the children you are speaking of now are young persons being trained to be teachers?—No; they are the ordinary day scholars.

1640. Judge Shaw.—You mean you select those who have a particular aptitude for drawing, and put them in the particular class?—Yes.

1641. Out of all the classes you select those and put them into a particular class?—Yes.

Professor Fitzgerald.—There are two schools at Marlborough-street.

1642. Chairman.—Is the attendance good?—On the girls' side it is very satisfactory; it is not quite so satisfactory on the boys' side, as I fancy they have a good deal of algebra, book-keeping, and several other subjects to attend to—in fact it is very difficult to get a proper number in the class. As well as the model drawing, I should have mentioned that they are taught practical geometry and elementary design, of course of a very elementary nature, as they have very little time for it, only one hour in the fortnight; but the practical geometry I think to be a very useful part of elementary manual training, inasmuch as it trains their hands to work with the compass and ruler with great clearness and accuracy, and they are furthermore called upon to do these problems on the blackboard, when they have to use a large compass and a large T-square, so that they have double practice with their hands. This is manual training of an elementary kind.

1643. Rev. Dr. Evans.—There are Queen's scholars who come in for one year's course?—Yes.

1644. Have you anything to do with them?—With all. I examine all, and if the one year's scholars have a certificate they devote their time to study the literary subjects as their programme is a heavy one.

1645. In your opinion do the teachers that come for one year's course of training acquire a fairly sufficient knowledge of the theory of drawing and some facility in the practice of it during the one year?—Certainly; they only get that instruction in case they have not got a certificate, and the great majority of those do at the end of the year obtain a certificate.

1646. Have you noticed any marked difference in regard to aptitude or capacity for drawing between the male and female teachers who come for one year's training?—Well, I never looked at it in that light. I found, I may say, as a general thing, that there is more taste or aptitude for drawing perhaps on the female side; it is more after their own lines of thought, I think, than that of young men from the country who have never even seen a drawing book.

1647. As to the Queen's scholars who come for a two years' course—do you know that pupil teachers form a considerable proportion of them?—Yes, I understand they do, and monitors too.

1648. Do you find that the pupil teachers and monitors are better prepared in drawing than the other Queen's scholars?—I have never gone into the question as to whether they were pupil teachers or monitors. I teach them just as they come to me, and it is no part of my duty to inquire into their status previous to their coming to Marlborough-street.

1649. But as regards those who enter upon a course of instruction in drawing, do you find any considerable difference in the Queen's scholars that come in for the two years' course?—Well, one year's men are more experienced, they are older as a rule, and some do have had some experience in teaching, which the others have not.

1650. We are at the two years' course now; and I want to know if you observe any difference between the pupil teachers and the other Queen's scholars who were not pupil teachers and who were not monitors?—I have never been able to form an opinion. I have never inquired into their position when they came into my class; they all come in on an equal footing to learn drawing, and that is all I know of their position.

1651. Well, the pupil teachers were engaged in Model schools, and it is to be presumed they were taught drawing to some extent?—On more than one occasion I asked those from Model schools who were present to raise their hands, then amongst those who had been taught drawing—and in some cases I found a few who were not taught, as I had been given to understand that all coming from Model schools have been taught; this only occurred on a few occasions in the last two or three years and as I say, I found they mostly had been taught, but they were very few, four or five.

1652. My object is to ascertain whether or not drawing is efficiently taught in Model schools, and what evidence your experience affords on that subject.—I have [illegible] you the idea as well as I can, that I am unable to distinguish between those coming from Model Schools, except in some particular cases; but as a general rule, I may say my experience is, drawing is very much a go-as-you-please subject. A great many of them do a lot of work, very hard work, but absolutely innocent of method as a rule.

1653. Judge Shaw.—Is drawing compulsory on all Queen's scholars, both male and female?—Since I have taught in the schools for the last 3½ years, every student who had not a certificate was put to draw without exception.

1654. What proportion of Queen's scholars, at the end of their term of training, are, in your opinion, fit to teach drawing?—We have done pretty well, so far as certificates go; it has varied very strangely, the teaching has remained the same, but the results of the examination have varied wonderfully. I have must figures back as you asked that question—we got one year 158 certificates, other years 108 and 125.

1655. You are not giving us the number that are actually under instruction?—Always the same number under instruction. I was saying to give you an idea of the number of certificates out of the 250 Queen's scholars each year. One year I say we had 78 certificates for Male Queen's Scholars and 60 for Female, that was the largest number; a very short time since, only 74 and 30 Male and Female respectively, in 1884, more unsuccessful.

1656. Do you find that a number of these teachers who are in training are entirely unfitted even to learn drawing?—I don't say that; I think every intelligent person, everyone who has come there, is able to learn drawing.

1657. And so much?—After a year or two's training they have mastered a method by which they can get their study put on at the examination and if they have not forgotten that method they should be certainly in a position to teach elementary drawing.

1658. Do you think everyone who gets a certificate is qualified by a teacher to teach drawing to children in a school?—More or less; there are different degrees of capacity for teaching—there are those who can draw very well, and who perhaps may not be able to impart that knowledge; there are those who can draw fairly and can impart it very well.

1659. You say you teach drawing in the Model schools on the ordinary day subjects?—Only a special class.

1660. Who teaches the others who are not in the special class?—The regular staff—the teachers of the special schools.

1661. Drawing is not compulsory there?—Well, I understand it is—I don't think it is stated—but it is certainly the wish of the Commissioners, and as far as it is possible it is compulsory with the exception perhaps of two classes, which is rather unfortunate.

1662. At which stage do you commence drawing, teaching drawing to children in the school?—The third book, third class or standard. It is in the third or second book that drawing is not taught, unless the pupil has gone through these stages of the kindergarten.

1663. Then he or she has been taught drawing in the first or second; in the kindergarten drawing is a part of teaching in the first and second class?—Yes.

1664. What is the general age at which a boy or girl is in the third class?—About nine they leave the kindergarten.

1665. And you consider that quite early enough to commence with?—Not at all. I would like to see the drawing continuous from kindergarten to the sixth; from the first to the last. There is a break unfortunately in the class where a pupil leaves the kindergarten before he goes to the third book, and that interval is lost, two years sometimes.

1666. You think then that drawing ought to be a part of the course from the beginning to the end?—Certainly; just as writing or anything else.

1667. Can you tell me what amount of time is given in the case of an ordinary day school?—Two hours a week.

1668. At what times is that given; is it two whole hours on two days of the week or four half hours?—Sometimes it is four half hours and sometimes two separate hours; but never two successive hours.

1669. Do you think that is sufficient for drawing?—We must be satisfied with it, considering the number of subjects in the programme. It is very fair, I think, considering what has to be taught; but, of course, it is not all that might be given to it.

1670. You say the attendance in the case of drawing is indifferent?—In the special drawing class.

1671. In the ordinary classes do you know how the boys attend there?—They are there the whole week, and they must do drawing when they are present in the school. In the special drawing class they have to come out to the drawing school, a room set apart for drawing; they have to leave their schools, and that necessitates a different arrangement, and in that way their attendance at the special drawing is not what it might be.

1672. When you take a boy or girl into your special drawing class is not he an also compelled to attend drawing in that class?—As far as I can compel them they are compelled to.

1673. Is there any difference in the compulsion they are under?—I have no authority so far as that goes.

1674. You have no authority to compel a boy to come to your class after you have drafted him into it?—No. I can report him for being absent, and I have done so frequently; complain to the master of the school to which he belongs, but I do frequently see the boy in many cases will be at another branch of study, for which credit fees are given. These are not exempt from the special drawing.

1675. At what stage do you commence to teach them from the model?—I don't teach them from the flat at all in the special drawing class. I teach model and geometrical drawing.

1676. Then when you take children into your class you consider they have got a good training in drawing from the flat?—They have passed their examination, and I inquire into their knowledge of other subjects so as not to bring them with a dead knowledge of arithmetic or reading, for instance.

1677. Could you give us an idea of what proportion of teachers at the end of two years' training who are entirely incompetent to teach any drawing?—Even those who have not got their certificates have had the same instruction as those who get certificates. They have learned the method and could impart it. Though they could not draw up to 60 per cent. they may have got 50 per cent.

1678. Do you think a man who knows how drawing is to be done is capable of teaching others although he cannot do it himself?—Yes, but as he has learned the method to do it for no matter your or more for a second year, I think he is certainly qualified to give instruction in elementary outline to small boys.

1679. Is every teacher who passes through the Training College more or less qualified to teach drawing in your opinion?—I believe myself he is.

1680. And quite sufficiently to teach drawing to his own pupils to a certain extent?—He could certainly make a very creditable attempt, because he has the method marked for him by very conspicuous lines on each of his books, and those are the very books used by pupils, and he has there the instruction in extenso. His memory as to how he is to impart it to his pupils.

1681. Then I take it, in your opinion, if the Commissioners made drawing a compulsory subject every trained teacher would be competent to teach the subject?—I would like to say he was capable of teaching up to the 5th class anyway, because in 6th class they demand more subjects, different model drawing and shading.

1682. At least for drawing from the flat you think they would be competent to teach?—I think it would be very desirable they should be made do so, even though they have not the excellence.

1683. Mr. Stevenson.—Some teachers leave the Training College after one year's training?—Quite so.

1684. Some after two?—That is so.

1685. What about the proportion of those two classes?—The number of one year's students varies very much, sometimes ten on each side and sometimes twenty or twenty-five; this year we had twenty-eight.

1686. How many leave a second year's course?—They vary from 100 to twenty. Those we have at the end of the first year have received instruction in freehand drawing from the flat only, unless they have a certificate in freehand drawing, and then I put them to a second year's course of model drawing and perspective.

1687. You speak of some of them having certificates when they come; where do they obtain those certificates?—In the country.

1688. From whom?—From the Commissioners.

1689. From the Inspectors?—I don't know anything about that, they are examined and come up with a certificate.

1690. You have seen the certificates?—Oh, yes, I make a point of seeing their certificate to make sure of it.

1691. You don't know who it is granted by?—The inspectors' names are at the bottom, and it is simply mentioned in the certificate that they are qualified to teach drawing, which is a little vague because in some cases they have sent in drawings in one or three different subjects.

1692. Take those who leave at the end of the first year who have not taken drawing along with the second year's students, they have only had a course of freehand from the flat?—Yes, unless as I said they came in with a certificate.

1693. Had those were taught with second year's students?—No; they are taught in their own division, but in special subjects.

1694. But those who have not special certificates only get freehand drawing from the flat?—Yes.

1695. Of those who fail, to get a certificate?—Yes.

1696. But they have all had instruction and would be competent in your opinion to teach freehand drawing from the flat?—Yes.

1697. But nothing else?—No.

1698. Is there anything else but freehand drawing from the flat taught in day schools?—By the regular staff, no.

1699. Captain Shaw.—Who is it who holds the examination of these students at the end of the year?—There is an examiner named at the head of the paper, and that is the only information I have on that point. Presumably about [illegible] with [illegible] inspectors.

1700. What is the style of the examination in freehand?—It is, as a rule, a difficult example from the flat, which is to be drawn on a larger scale, and for the most part they are selected from the South Kensington books, for 2nd grade freehand drawing, rather difficult for eight months' practice.

1701. Are they judged by the inspectors and marked by them?—So I understand.

1702. Then the examination in model drawing?—It is carried on in the same manner by the inspector. They set up a group of models, and in the paper that is sent round there are instructions what the group is to consist of. That is set before the students by the superintending inspector of the examinations. He places these models in exact accordance with the written instructions, and I believe there is a drawing sent as well, so as to have the examination as nearly as possible uniform all over the country.

1703. Then as regards the examination in geometry and perspective?—Questions are set each year, but to my knowledge they very seldom take up those subjects, for this reason, that eight months is quite short enough time to learn freehand, then for the next eight months to learn model drawing and elementary perspective. Geometry and perspective form special subjects, and if they take up those subjects alone, and even get 100 per cent. they would have failed. They all learn perspective before they learn model drawing. They confine themselves to getting a certificate of their knowledge of model drawing alone, though they do know elementary perspective.

1704. As regards geometry, is that plane geometry?—Yes, and solid geometry, too, but very few of them, for the reason I stated, take that up.

1705. Then as regards the model lessons, how often would each student have an opportunity of seeing a model lesson?—He gets at least one opportunity of seeing each class taught—third, fourth, fifth, and sixth class.

1706. During his two years?—One year.

1707. He sees six lessons?—During the two years he would have them over again.

1708. That is he would see twelve lessons?—Twelve model lessons. The criticism lessons are an arrangement of my own, purely and simply. We have some six at the end of the year, three or four for freehand and three for model drawing.

1709. There is no practical examination of the teachers in the method of teaching?—No.

1710. They are not required to draw on the blackboard?—No; the only means of showing their knowledge of proper method is their drawing on their examination when their method shows in their work.

1711. What is the object of the special drawing class?—To give the boys and girls who have a special aptitude for drawing an opportunity of developing that taste.

1712. That is an opportunity they will only get in the Model schools?—I don't know whether it exists elsewhere but certainly there is a very considerable opportunity in the Model schools, and it is very frequently availed of and sought after by the girls, and some of the boys never miss a lesson.

1713. Mr. [illegible].—You are aware that in the case of the ordinary pupils drawing commences in the third class?—Yes.

1714. Would you be in favour of commencing earlier?—As I have already said, I would have it continuous from the kindergarten to the highest class.

1715. The indispensability of the kindergarten?—Certainly.

1716. In what class would you begin?—As soon as a boy can hold a pencil I would put him to draw something straight, something simple.

1717. Professor Fitzgerald.—With regard to drawing to scale. Is that taught in the practising schools?—Not anywhere I know of; it is no part of my programme.

1718. Is it taught to the Queen's Scholars?—No.

1719. A teacher can get a certificate in drawing for freehand independent of any knowledge or acquaintance with geometrical drawing?—Quite so, by reaching the standard of 60 per cent.

1720. Do you think that drawing to scale should be taught?—Most decidedly.

1721. Teachers, you say, come up having certificates. Those are the Board's certificates. Do any teachers come having the Science and Art certificates?—Very few indeed; perhaps one or two in the year. Some years not even one having the Science and Art certificate, which is recognised by the Board, and of course places them in a position to study some other branch. That is the Second Grade Science and Art.

1722. In teaching drawing to children is it not necessary they should begin drawing from copies before they begin drawing from models?—Not absolutely necessary. There was a time, and I dare say it is done still, for I have used them myself, where the models were actual pieces of wire instead of lines on a flat piece of paper. In that case they drew directly from these models from the commencement. Is that what you mean?

1723. I did not know that there was that method of making lines for them. It is drawing from a copy practically?—These models take the form of squares, triangles and circles.

1724. They are flat models?—Yes, but they are not always in the same plane. The circle can be made an ellipse by foreshortening.

1725. That is a method by which drawing can be taught without drawing from a flat copy?—Yes, a very expensive one. We had to have the apparatus for those models made in London.

1726. When you talk of drawing to actual size and then on a larger scale, do they draw on a larger scale by eye?—By eye always.

1727. They don't do it by machinery?—[illegible]

1728. The question was asked here with reference to some of the other subjects as to whether it would be possible to teach drawing by a single drawing master from a centre having a large number of schools going him to the neighbouring district, and it was objected that there would be a difficulty on account of the small number of schools that one teacher could manage. How many schools could one teacher teach?—I have no knowledge whatever of the position of the schools throughout the country. I am confined mostly to Marlborough-street, but if it is more or less possible to spread the knowledge in that way than any other manner it would be highly desirable.

1729. How many schools would a peripatetic teacher efficiently teach?—It would be a matter of arithmetical calculation, I fancy.

1730. How many hours ought he to devote to each school per week?—It would not make much difference to the teacher the number of pupils present at the lesson if he used the black board. He could give the general instruction, and if he were aided by the teacher of the school, who would see that the instructions were carried out, he could teach a large number indeed.

1731. If the teacher went once a week to a school do you think it would be a great assistance?—One hour a week would be a great assistance.

1732. A skilled teacher might do three schools a day for five days; that would be fifteen schools?—Yes, but that is very rough. I am not in a position to make any such calculation.

1733. You think one hour's work for a peripatetic teacher to go to each school may be a great assistance to the teacher in getting it properly taught?—I am sure it would. He would get more insight into the method of teaching to begin with.

1734. You think that any person of moderate ability could be taught drawing?—I have always proved it to be so as I was examining.

1735. It does not require an artist to teach it?—No; furthermore, it was thought there was a knack and that few shown at drawing from the round, that any one might draw from the flat, but when it came to represent an object from the round it required a special talent, that I always deny.

1736. The special talent is so universal?—They do it with different ability, but I believe it can be taught to any intelligent person.

1737. Mr. [illegible].—Do you approve of 50 per cent. as a standard for a certificate in drawing?—Not if the object was to increase the teaching of drawing, I certainly think it should not be so high.

1738. What percentage do you think should be the minimum for a certificate?—I think that under this new arrangement where 50 per cent. is required for a pass that this ought to qualify a teacher to teach up to the 6th standard; that is an idea of my own.

1739. Would you require any proof of the teacher's power of imparting his knowledge of drawing other than his ability to copy examples put before him?—He is present at those lessons at which both the method is explained, and he has, under the supervision of the master, the opportunity of putting those lessons into practice. He can get a certificate from hand work and copying accurately and [illegible] anything put before him, and then they do it a matter of luck.

1740. Is that sufficient to make him a good teacher of drawing?—Certainly not.

1741. There should be some proof that he is able to impart that knowledge?—Certainly, a case came under my knowledge this year, I asked a teacher how he got his certificate, and it turned out that by some mixing the examination paper for one year got into his district, and he got and copied that year after year until it turned up again and he got his certificate.

1742. Most Rev. Dr. Walsh.—You are aware that the percentage required for a certificate to qualify a teacher in drawing is very much higher than the percentage required in ordinary school subjects?—Yes.

[illegible]
Mr. J. F. Moore.

1743. Twenty per cent. will qualify a person to teach in a National school in geography, grammar, arithmetic, or book-keeping, provided he gets 30 per cent. on the aggregate of marks; you are aware of that?—Yes, my lord.

1744. Are you aware of this, that in order to teach drawing he must get 60 per cent. in drawing, in addition to getting 30 per cent. all round?—I am, indeed.

1745. Do you think that a reasonable arrangement?—I do not, my lord.

1746. You don't consider that the present system of giving certificates gives us real security that the persons who get them are qualified to teach?—I can only answer that by what comes under my own notice.

1747. In the case you have described, a certificate was given to that ingenious teacher who kept working away the years at an old examination paper?—Yes; he showed great perseverance in his application.

1748. That sort of thing may go on under the existing system?—I know it is going on.

1749. Then you don't consider our present system a very efficient one for testing the fitness of teachers to teach drawing?—No, but it is the best.

1750. Suppose you found a teacher who proved by his work that he was able to teach drawing, don't you think that he would have a better claim to a certificate than a man who got a certificate on that extraordinary system you have described?—Certainly.

1751. The man that is able to teach, as shown by his results, is related [illegible], and results that are given, to the man who got qualified under this extraordinary system?—I would give results first to him who could show results.

1752. Now, as to another point, about your own work in Marlborough-street. You told of some class of pupils who came to you there that you came to the conclusion that drawing is a good disciplinary subject, and that those who draw seem to be superior as to rule or principle. To what class of pupils, or teachers, did that observation refer?—Mostly to the Queen's Scholars, who were come up from the country schools for the first and second year's training.

1753. Does it apply generally to those who come up from the country for two years' training?—Yes; I would not say so much in those one year's students of the higher division. They have some experience of teaching and some [illegible] of method. Whether it comes to them naturally I don't know, but those seem to be more [illegible] about their work.

1754. It is true to a large extent of the pupils that come up to you in Marlborough-street that drawing, as they learned it, appears to be a great disciplinary subject?—Very much, except those from cities like Belfast and Cork.

1755. You teach drawing in Marlborough-street both to the Queen's Scholars and to the ordinary pupils?—I teach only special classes in model and geometrical drawing.

1756. Therefore you teach them in none of them?—Yes, my lord.

1757. Are you a certificated teacher under the National Board?—I never drew in a National school in my life.

1758. So you are allowed to teach in the Model school although you have not a certificate. A teacher would not be recognised as a teacher in an ordinary National school if he has not got a certificate?—Yes, and there is the hardship.

1759. It seems to me more than a hardship—it is an absurdity. You spoke of two classes of Queen's Scholars. Some of these come up for one year's teaching, and some for two?—Yes.

1759. Those that come for one year's training are already teachers of National schools?—Yes.

1760. A person who is not a teacher in a National school, and comes up to the Training College, must come for a two-years' course?—Yes; I know nothing of their course. That is my impression.

1761. You spoke of your class of pupils in the schools as being a picked class. The boys and girls in the department of drawing are picked out?—Yes.

1762. Then they have the advantage of a special teacher specially paid by the Board?—Yes.

1763. Do you know whether there is anything like that in any other National school in the country?—I have not any knowledge of it. I don't know of anything outside my own school.

1764. ... as it exists in the Model school. There is a special teacher paid there. In the departments of drawing taught by the ordinary teachers?—Freehand drawing is taught by the ordinary staff, but then they are not expected to do first-class work.

1765. The teachers in the Model school in Marlborough-street are not expected to do first-class work in their department?—They are only called upon to teach drawing from the flat examples.

1766. And the higher class work is handed over to be done by you?—Yes.

1767. And you are paid a special salary for doing that?—I am paid the same salary as I was paid when I had the entire teaching of all the pupils in the several schools.

1768. You said the pupils you have there are not very regular in their attendance?—The boys are not as regular as might be desired.

1769. Although they are the picked boys of the place?—Yes.

1770. The boys for whose teaching a special teacher is paid by the State. Who picks them out?—I do.

1771. That is, you go round and pick out the most promising pupils?—With the concurrence of the teacher; I consult whether the boy is backward in his essential subjects.

1772. But they are not picked out by ordinary inspectors, but by you as an expert in this department?—Yes.

1773. And although they have shown a special efficiency in drawing in their own schools and are picked out by yourself, as specially promising pupils, they seem to lose all interest in the subject when they get into your school, and don't attend regularly?—Very often. They have to go to another school, and that is a drawback, and I think there is no interest in keeping them at their other work, and then there are no funds here for special drawing.

1774. So in this Central Model school of the National Education Board there are capitation fees for ordinary low-class drawing and no results fees for high-class drawing?—None; I have not any capitation from the Board, and that would account for it.

1775. Though you are quite as good a teacher, to say the least, as some of the people who have certificates?—I ought to get certificates.

1776. Yet, under the present system, your teaching of drawing is not recognised as a thing that would entitle you to get results fees; but if you had gone up for years copying from an old form until it began again in ten or twelve years, you would get a certificate that would entitle you to get results fees?—Yes.

1777. Professor FITZGERALD.—Has the President of the Royal Hibernian Academy got a certificate from the Board to teach drawing?—No, nor I don't think Sir Thomas Farrell or Leonardo da Vinci ever got them.

1778. Mr. [illegible].—I take it that before you were appointed, you gave some proof of your competency as a professor of drawing?—Yes, I had been teaching drawing elsewhere, and had a proof in the results of the [illegible] as well as given a proof of a certain capacity in art.

1779. Had you exhibited in the Royal Hibernian Academy?—Yes, and in the Salon.

Most Rev. Dr. WALSH.—In other words, you had proved your fitness, not by passing an examination and getting a certificate, but by good work done in your own department.

1780. Mr. [illegible].—How do you select those pupils for the special class?—I ask the teacher in those classes who would desire to come to the special class, and if a pupil expresses the desire, the teacher with his desire I am very glad to attend to him. I then select those who seem to me to have an aptitude or taste for drawing.

1781. Some of the boys you select might be unwilling to come?—Yes, and are very often; they do not wish to go to the class, afraid of missing a new subject.

1782. Would it not be important to find the reason?—I can easily give you the reason; they at first [illegible] have the chance to study at night, [illegible] they may require to learn book-keeping, or algebra, or some other subject in which they have a direct interest.

The Commission adjourned to next morning.

FIFTH PUBLIC SITTING.—SATURDAY, FEBRUARY 20, 1897, AT 11 O'CLOCK A.M.

Feb. 20, 1897.

At the Antient Concert Rooms, Dublin.

PRESENT:—The Right Hon. the EARL OF BELMORE, G.C.M.G., in the Chair; His Grace the Most Rev. WILLIAM J. WALSH, D.D.; The Right Hon. C. T. REDINGTON, M.A.; His Honour Judge SHAW, Q.C.; The Right Rev. Monsignor MOLLOY, D.D., D.Sc.; Rev. HENRY EVANS, D.D.; Rev. HAMILTON WILSON, LL.D.; Professor G. F. FITZGERALD, F.T.C.D.; STANLEY HARRINGTON, Esq., J.P.; W. R. J. MOLLOY, Esq.; Captain T. B. SHAW; and J. STRUTHERS, Esq., LL.D.,

with J. D. DALY, Esq., B.A., Secretary.

Mr. JOHN COOKE, M.A., Professor, Church of Ireland Training College, Kildare-place, examined.

Mr. John Cooke, M.A.

1784. CHAIRMAN.—Will you tell the Commission what office you hold in connection with the Church of Ireland Training College?—I am a Professor in the Church of Ireland Training College.

1785. In carrying out the duties of your office what do you do?—My time is divided between English and drawing, about one-third of my time is given to the teaching of drawing to the students under training.

1786. And will you tell us about the course that is taught?—The course covers freehand, model, geometrical, and perspective drawing.

1787. What time is given to it?—To the men two hours a week, to the women, three.

1788. How long does a lesson continue at a time?—One full hour.

1789. Will you tell us about the power of [illegible]?—Of the students who enter I find that about eighty per cent. of them have never learned drawing, and they have to begin at the very beginning, in fact almost at kindergarten work, straight lines, and at the end of the first year a small percentage are able to pass, the remainder have to pass it in the second year.

1790. About what percentage?—Well, my Lord, I could hardly say, about 20 to 25 per cent. pass in the first year, the standard being high, as you are aware. At the end of the second year, I have taken an average of the last seven years, about 80 per cent. passed. Of those under training the remainder of course have been taught thoroughly.

1791. You said 80 per cent. passed; what remainder did you allude to?—The remainder who have not passed.

1792. But they have been taught?—They have been taught thoroughly.

1793. Although they have not been taught up to the standard?—Yes, and I concur with Mr. Molloy when he said that he considered these students were capable of teaching elementary freehand and drawing well.

1794. MR. MOLLOY.—That is the remaining 20 per cent.?—Yes.

1795. CHAIRMAN.—Then as regards the South Kensington examinations?—The South Kensington standard is higher than that of the Board, and the time of the year, as a rule, in your place, the examination occurring in May or April, is rather inconvenient, very few of the students go in for the South Kensington examinations. I generally have some, however, who pass of them, as I think it is very advisable that they should have all the certificates they can get, particularly those of the high standard of South Kensington.

1796. Will you tell us about the new programme for Training Colleges?—The new programme for Training Colleges has made it now compulsory for all students to be taught drawing, and every student is expected to pass in one subject at the end of each year.

1797. MOST REV. DR. WALSH.—Do you mean in one branch of drawing?—Yes, your Grace, the result will be I think a lowering, inevitably of the standard of drawing, for the very large majority.

1798. CHAIRMAN.—Lowering?—I don't quite follow that.—I will explain, my Lord. For instance a student passing at the end of the first year on 60 per cent.; you see clearly in this that the majority will not be able to rise to the high standard of 60 per cent., that is if I am to take my past experience as a guide. The second year they would have to take up freehand, geometrical, model or perspective, and there would also be low standard.

1799. MOST REV. DR. WALSH.—That means that they would have to take up another branch of this subject?—Yes, the result will be that you will have I think for the majority a low standard in two subjects, instead of, as in the past, a high standard at least in one.

1800. CHAIRMAN.—What would you suggest yourself to avoid that?—What I suggest myself is to make drawing compulsory, as it has always been in Kildare-place Training College for every candidate, and retain the certificate which will be a better guarantee for those who have it that they have been well trained, and well grounded, and that, when possible a second course in one of the branches, such as model or geometrical drawing should be taught in addition.

1801. Do you mean in the first year?—In the second year.

1802. Will you tell us about the course of instruction in schools?—Of course, my Lord, I have no practical experience of that in National Board Schools, except what has come under my notice in those that I, unofficially, have paid to schools from time to time, and looked at the drawing in those schools. There is no connection between the teaching of drawing in Kildare-place College and the schools as was explained yesterday in reference to Marlborough-street, that is, there is no work done by the students, under my instruction, in the schools.

1803. You only instruct teachers?—Only the teachers. I have seen the course pursued in schools, and those that I have visited I don't consider had reached at all a high standard; and the reason, I think, is due to the fact that the time is very limited. I don't think that half an hour is at all sufficient for a drawing lesson, two half hours in the week for the subject.

1804. Would it improve matters to have one hour?—One hour is much better than two half hours, but I would like to see two hours a week for drawing.

1805. What copies are used?—The copies that are generally used were the old Vere Foster, which were poor, these have been much improved in recent years by Messrs. Blackie. Of course the teacher can choose any, but these being issued under the Board's approval they are more generally used than any other. But I made a suggestion in my memorandum to you, I think, that for Irish schools we should have some copies of

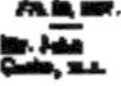

peculiarly Irish design, it has a beauty of its own, which is unique and has never been surpassed in my mind, and I think a series of those would be very useful to those children who afterwards take a technical line of life, such as illuminating, or leatherwork, or fretwork, or wood carving, and so on.

1806. What do you say about kindergarten?—The kindergarten drawing is taught in many of our schools, and in those that I have visited—I am not quite sure whether the general—tablets have been drawn up as examples. I think the kindergarten tablet and copies should be used, and I know one or two pieces of design that are exceedingly pretty, beautiful in design and richly coloured, and these would be most interesting to a child, as the colour appeals to the child much more than black lines. Then the coloured chalk is only allowed to be used in Third Class in kindergarten. I would put the coloured chalk into an infant's hands at the very beginning as it would be more interesting with [illegible] the coloured chalk appeals to the eye with much better results than plain black lines.

1807. What do you say about the more advanced training of Queen's Scholars?—That is a subject I have given a good deal of thought and attention to. I am most anxious to see the drawing taught far more efficiently in our schools than it is, and far more time given to it. I may mention that of those students who come under my notice, those that have been trained in [illegible] Schools were much better and more efficiently taught than the average student from other schools. In our Colleges when we get a student entered with a good qualification in drawing, say one or two certificates, it would be well to pick those students out and see if they could not get, while under training, more efficient teaching; some subject might be dropped and more time given to the drawing in order that the Commissioners might have at their hand a more highly qualified set of teachers than they can possibly get under the present system. In Kildare-street I see no reason, with some arrangement come to by the authorities of the Training College, why two or three hours a week should not be given in the drawing school which is at their very door; the same might be done perhaps with the students at the Central School, Marlborough-street, and at Baggot-street. But supposing that could not be done you have in your Model Schools, or in other city schools, a number of teachers who qualify under them, and I say that it would be no hardship to students who had learned drawing, and had been pretty fairly qualified, during their two years course, to attend for six months or a year, two or three times a week, the night classes in the School of Art. The Commissioners could, of course, have lists of those students who have taken higher certificates, and it should be in their interest to see that those students got into large schools where drawing is made a very necessary subject, or rather a prominent subject in the teaching.

1808. How far would students in the School of Art advance in the art of drawing?—They can advance to the Art Teacher's Certificate, or the Art Master's Certificate.

1809. Do they get such training as would teach them to become artists?—They would have to be years there to do that, but I mean that they should attend only to get a higher qualification for teaching purposes.

1810. You don't anticipate that the persons you are alluding to should go so far as that?—Oh, dear, no, but they would get more efficient teaching in the Schools of Art for three or four hours a week, than they can possibly get in the large mixed classes we have in the Training Colleges.

1811. What do you say about the poor results of the present system and their principal causes?—What I mean by the poor results are the results that come under my notice, namely the large number of students who have never learned drawing, and of those who have learned a large proportion have been badly taught. The only reasons I can assign for that are,—first that the time given to the subject is too short at present; secondly, that the teachers of these pupils are inefficient, and I am unaware whether I can assign any other cause. Those two are the main ones to my mind.

1812. Most Rev. Dr. Walsh.—Only about eighty per cent. of the teachers in training, of those under your care, succeed in getting the certificate of the Board; do you consider that the present standard for the certificate is too high?—Much too high to make drawing compulsory.

1813. You can tell the Commissioners what the percentage is that is required for getting a certificate?—Sixty per cent.

1814. That is a far higher percentage than is required for teaching any of the ordinary subjects?—Oh, much higher.

1815. Do you think there is any reason for maintaining a much higher standard in the case of drawing than in the case of the other subjects?—I see no reason.

1816. Do you think the standard should be at all higher in the case of drawing than in the case of ordinary subjects?—Well, as an optional subject, one can draw a marked distinction somehow between an optional subject and a compulsory one; drawing has been looked upon more as an accomplishment than anything else, and I suppose that is the reason.

1817. Suppose it was to be made a compulsory subject?—You must drop the high qualification, it would be most unfair.

1818. Your idea is that the same percentage should qualify a teacher for a certificate to teach drawing that qualifies for a certificate to teach arithmetic?—Yes.

1819. You spoke about the Board's new programme. I understand you to say that it will have an injurious effect on the drawing department, I did not quite follow your explanation?—What I mean, your Grace, is this, that retaining the certificate of sixty per cent., which is a high one, a student who only gets one certificate, and a large number of them only get one, must have been raised pretty high in freehand. Now seeing that the overwhelming majority have never been taught drawing coming in, and taking my experience for the last seven or ten years, I think they will not be able to reach anything like a high standard because they are compelled to take two branches.

1820. Why do you say that?—The new programme seems to enforce every student to pass in one branch in each of the two years.

1821. Allow me to read this for you. There are three columns in the programme, the first gives the course for entrance to the Training College, "drawing, freehand or mechanical," fifty marks assigned in each case. What does that mean?—That they can take either freehand or mechanical.

1822. Suppose they take freehand, let us keep to that. Column two gives us the course at the end of the first year in the Training College. "Freehand, or object or outline, or mechanical," fifty marks in each case. What does that mean in the case of a person who has taken freehand for entrance?—That in mechanical or model they must secure twenty per cent. at the end of the first year.

1823. This has to be cleared up. I understand your statement to be that under the working of this programme it would be necessary for a person who had taken freehand the first year to take up one of the other branches in the second year?—Yes.

1824. Is that prescribed in the programme, it may be, but I don't know of anything in the programme that indicates it; take the programme and show us what you refer to?—We shall find, I think, that of those who enter, taking freehand or mechanical as compulsory for entrance, then most of the students will take the mechanical, that is the geometrical drawing, that I know from experience of recent years, that the students will not take up freehand to any great extent.

1825. Let us keep to one point at a time: first, take the case of a person who misses the [illegible] drawing, is there anything to hinder him from going on with freehand for the first year and second year, anything in that programme?—No, nothing to hinder that.

1826. The reason I asked you the question was because I understood you to say that there was [illegible].

1827. Now as to another point. You do not teach in the practising school at Kildare-place?—No, no.

1828. Can you tell us what provision is made for the teaching of drawing in the practising school there?—I am sure it is a very efficient provision, but just to explain the nature of it—I made inquiries and I find that a large number of the children come in the mornings and get an extra half hour, and there two half hours the week.

1829. I don't mean the time so much as the provision for teaching: is there provided by the Commissioners of National Education a special teacher of drawing for the benefit of the children attending the Kildare-place School?—There is no special teacher.

1830. You are aware that there is in Marlborough-street?—I am aware there is in Marlborough-street.

1831. Your own teaching in this department is confined altogether to the Training College?—Yes.

1832. You spoke of the time given to drawing there: One hour a week is the present arrangement?—One half hour a week is the present.

1833. Do you think it a better arrangement to have two hours a week or half an hour every day?—Two hours a week would be better.

1834. You spoke of the poor results of the present system; you are speaking of the system as worked in the ordinary National Schools of the country. Do you consider that a large number of the students who come in the Kildare-place College have been badly taught?—Very badly taught, at least who have been taught.

1835. And you think that part of the explanation is that the teachers are not efficient teachers?—Not efficient teachers.

1836. May I ask you to assume that all these teachers have qualified by the Board's certificate on the present high standard of [illegible]?—I would not like to hazard an opinion on that.

1837. Well, it is likely they have, if they are teaching in the schools?—Yes.

1838. No remuneration can be paid by the Board unless the teachers have a certificate?—That is my reading of the rules.

1839. So then, if these teachers are getting results they have a certificate. Do you think our system of examination is a good means of securing the efficiency of teachers of drawing, putting candidates to copy things out of a copybook on examination paper, and requiring them to get 60 per cent.; does it ensure good teachers of drawing?—In drawing I think examining better might be done.

1840. Do you think a better test of the fitness of a teacher to teach drawing would be some observation of his methods of teaching. You understand what I mean?—I don't think I do, quite.

1841. Compare the two methods of selecting a teacher, one putting him down at a desk and asking him to copy something, and perhaps to answer some questions about drawing, the other method would be asking some competent observer to see how he teaches drawing in his school: which of these two ways would you consider most likely to secure efficient teachers of drawing for us?—I find it very hard to answer that question.

1842. Do you think the first method is a good method?—It is an easy method; I don't think it is the best.

1843. What do you think a better method?—A better method would be to make examination in part, and the report of the teacher of drawing in the Colleges should go largely towards granting a full certificate.

1844. Well, for the teachers who cannot have the benefit of training, and the immense majority cannot?—I am afraid you must leave matters pretty much as they are. [illegible] Mr. John Sparkes, [illegible]

1845. You don't think you could get a better set of teachers by having some skilled expert upon their methods of teaching?—Is it of those who are already teaching in schools?

1846. Suppose a man says: "I wish to teach drawing in my school," what he has to do at present is to study it up in some way and come up for examination; would it not be better if the Board were to send either you or some competent person to see if that man knows how to teach drawing, getting his class before him and seeing how he teaches them?—If he showed me good results I would not have the slightest hesitation in granting a certificate.

1847. Do you not think that a better plan than the present system of examination?—I think it is much better: there are many teachers of forty or fifty years of age, and it would be a hardship to ask them to go in for an examination in drawing.

1848. You spoke of the teachers that come up to your Training College from different schools; you said that those who came from the Model Schools are the best prepared?—Yes, as far as my inquiries, which were not exhaustive.

1849. From what class of schools do the pupils come to you, from the Model Schools, I suppose?—Yes.

1850. Others from?—The ordinary National Schools throughout the country.

1851. Of course the pupils come to **you from the** Convent Schools?—No.

1852. So that your experience gives you no means of judging that the children in the Model Schools are better taught than those in the Convent Schools?—No, I have no means of judging of that at all.

1853. Mr. Richardson.—Why is it a hardship to a man of a certain age to be examined in drawing? Do you know what the examination consists of?—I do.

1854. Merely copying a model?—I look upon it as a hardship on a man who is some years teaching to have to go in for any examination, say a man from thirty-five to forty or fifty. If drawing is compulsory I think it would be hard to ask him to go in for an examination if he teaches well.

1855. If he teaches drawing ought he not to be able to draw?—A man might teach drawing well and at the same time not be able to make 60 per cent.

1856. Your point was that he ought not to be examined at all?—I think if he teaches well, he ought not to be examined at all. I would give him a certificate.

1857. The examination being merely to copy a model?—Yes.

1858. How can he teach drawing well without being able to draw himself? Has he not to show on the blackboard how things are done?—Yes, the blackboard enters into teaching, and I can only answer that by saying that I have seen very good writing coming from National Schools under teachers whose writing was what I would call villainous. I have actually seen that.

1859. Would it be a great hardship to ask a teacher who teaches writing to write?—No.

1860. Then why is it a hardship to ask a teacher who teaches drawing to draw?—Well, I am speaking personally, that if I had to go and take something up which I considered myself well qualified to do, I would consider it somehow or other a hardship to have to go and stand an examination in it.

1861. The word "examination" means rather alarming, but when the examination reduces itself to making a copy, which he ought to be doing every day of his life, why is it a hardship?—Perhaps hardship is a strong word, it is more a sentimental attitude I take up on the subject than anything else.

1862. You are aware that the minimum percentage for teachers in arithmetic is 60 per cent.?—Yes.

1863. Do you think that is a sufficient percentage on which to grant a certificate in drawing?—Well, I would put it this way, I would let them pass in drawing, I would grant the certificate, but I would not give it to a student who qualified under 20 per cent., just as you have graduates in honour and ordinary passes. I would look upon a certificate as a kind of diploma; a man who secured 20 per cent. I would consider it a pass and let him teach, the other would be no honour.

1864. If he got 30 per cent. you would allow him to teach?—Yes.

1865. You have fully considered what the percentage should be and that is your deliberate opinion?—Yes.

1866. Professor FITZGERALD.—How many do more than mere freehand?—Yes. In model, which is a separate advanced course, the percentage in the Training College for the last seven years has been about 75 per cent. of those who entered and got certificates in model.

1867. In addition to the other?—In addition to the other.

1868. Do any of them do drawing to scale?—The principle of scale drawing is the only thing that I can teach them, just simply to teach them the principle on which it depends, when increasing them in making an object smaller or enlarging it; but I think it is a pity that time and so on does not admit of it.

1869. Would it be better then to have a lower standard in some of the other things and to require the drawing to remain?—Yes; I think if something could be dropped out and more time given to drawing. If the Commissioners are desirous of making drawing a thorough thing in our schools that it shall permeate the whole of the system of teaching, you would give more time to it.

1870. I see in the Science and Art Syllabus they begin using rulers in Standard No. 1?—Yes.

1871. Do you think that is desirable?—I think it is very desirable that the use of instruments should enter into the teaching as early as possible.

1872. Why do you think that the candidates would in general prefer mechanical drawing as entrance?—I think it would be easier for the large majority of teachers to learn the elements of geometrical drawing than to learn freehand. I think it is easier to get seventy per cent. of a result in geometrical drawing than even in freehand.

1873. Do you think it would be desirable to compel a man then at entrance to take freehand?—Speaking personally I would much rather they came in on mechanical than freehand, on account of the bad way and manner in which they have been taught freehand. I would much rather begin with them de novo.

1874. Would it be better then to have an arrangement something like the Science and Art Department certificate, in which they are required to pass in both at entrance?—Well, in order to get a certificate of the Science and Art Department you have to pass in both and model.

1875. Do you think it would be better for us to require teachers at entrance to pass in something like this, the 5th Standard of the Science and Art?—I don't think you would get it done.

1876. With our present machinery?—No, I don't think so.

1877. But you think it would be desirable if we could get it done?—Oh, yes, most decidedly.

1878. You said that they would enter on mechanical drawing?—It is likely.

1879. Do you think it would be likely that they would take up freehand in the second year?—That is what I would wish.

1880. You would try and get candidates that had entered on mechanical drawing to take up freehand?—Yes, and have model them for the third year.

1881. So that the teachers might go out in the three?—Yes, it would be a very good plan.

1882. Instead of allowing them, as in this new programme, to keep on the mechanical during the whole course?—During the whole course; at present it is allowed.

1883. In the new programme you said that you thought that there would be a low standard in two instead of a high standard in one?—Yes.

1884. Do you modify your view on that or do you think the candidates as a matter of fact would stick to one all through?—It would be very hard to tell what the result would be.

1885. You think on account of the certificates?—Yes.

1886. If a certificate were not necessary for drawing in the schools, do you think they would stick to one all through, if it was no advantage to them to get two certificates?—I am not quite certain whether I take your question clearly.

1887. If it were not necessary for a teacher to get a certificate in both freehand and mechanical drawing in order to teach whichever he liked in the schools, then would he change from one to another during his college course?—I don't think so.

1888. Then you think that whatever one they entered in they would go on with?—I think the authorities in the Training College would not allow it. I would not allow it.

1889. Even though the Board's Syllabus allowed it?—Yes, my desire is to get them qualified in three, if possible; at present I get as many as I can qualified in two. I keep it more or less.

1890. Most Rev. Dr. WALSH.—That is, of course, because the Board has left that course open to you?—Yes.

1891. Professor FITZGERALD.—Do you think it would be desirable that the teachers should be compelled to attain some standard in drawing, that is the trained ones?—Certainly.

1892. To what extent do you think it would be possible to develop, throughout, the art side of drawing?—I think in very, very few cases; we had one notable example in Marlborough-street, a girl who took a scholarship in South Kensington, and was in her year there. I suppose in the whole of the Board's service there is not another girl so competent as her.

1893. Then, she had a special qualification?—Yes, she entered with the full teacher's certificate into the Training College, she went to South Kensington for a year, and obtained a medal in design, and she is now teaching under the Board. I am not aware whether her powers of drawing are taken notice of, but I think they ought to be.

1894. Then, you do not think it would be desirable for us to go beyond freehand and object shading, as the development of the art side of drawing?—I don't think so.

1895. Mr. HARRINGTON.—Of course you are aware that the difficulty of introducing drawing into the schools is owing to the fact that teachers are not competent to teach it?—In a great majority of cases.

1896. If the Commissioners wanted to introduce drawing compulsorily into those schools where there are not teachers available, how would you get over that difficulty with regard to instructing the teachers of existing schools sufficiently to enable them to teach drawing to the pupils?—In that case I think the Board would have to avail themselves of the services of a certain number of itinerant teachers to go round, and give a series of lessons to teachers, and try and train them up.

1897. Do you think that itinerant teachers going round in that way, and visiting the schools, say once a week, or at particular times, would be sufficient, after a given period, to enable the teachers themselves to teach, without their having to come to some Training School?—It is quite possible; it would be very hard to say; but I think that an intelligent teacher, having seen a great man at work, and been shown proper methods, ought to be able to carry that out with certain results.

Feb. 20, 1897. Mr. John Clarke, M.A.

1898. What time do you think an Assistant teacher ought to devote to that method?—I have not given this subject any consideration, and would not like to hazard an opinion on it.

1899. In places where there are Schools of Art, such as Belfast and Cork, what time do you think country teachers ought to spend at drawing in order to qualify them for teaching, would once a week be sufficient?—I don't think so, with two or three evenings a week for six months they should certainly be able to teach elementary drawing.

1900. Would you suggest that in places where Schools of Art are available within easy reach of teachers that would be a better system for such persons to learn than by being taught by [illegible] teachers?—Much better; and I think the Board ought to enforce it in the large schools; I am speaking now of making drawing compulsory. The Board should enforce on those teachers, who are living in Dublin, Belfast, Cork and Limerick, where Schools of Art exist, and good schools, that they should put in at least a six months' course, two or three lessons a week. I don't think that would be a hardship, and their expenses should be paid, if necessary.

1901. Mr. Molloy.—Are you aware that under the existing regulations connected with schools, there is nothing to prevent the authorities sending the teachers from Kildare-place to the School of Art for any purpose?—I don't think there is any difficulty, except a modification of the time-table to their case.

1902. There is an analogous case, perhaps you are not aware, that in Drumcondra the students come to the University College, Stephen's Green, and attend special instruction there?—I was not aware of this, and that being so, there is no reason why the other should not be done.

Most Rev. Dr. Walsh.—That is only in Natural Philosophy.

1903. Mr. Molloy.—Is it not likely then under the revised programme, students on entering College will have acquired some mechanical drawing in the first instance, in view of the fact that now for the first time mensuration is a separate and obligatory subject?—It is very likely.

1904. Then your proposal is that in the first year of the two years' course you would devote yourself to freehand, and complete the course at the end of the second year?—Yes, with model.

1905. What arrangement would you make in the case of teachers who only come in for one year?—In that case I think freehand should be the subject that should be taken up on account of its use for blackboard illustration, and, so on, and geometrical drawing, if it is to be taught. I don't think any man that has learned any Euclid would find any hardship in learning geometrical drawing, and the girls, I think, could also acquire it.

1906. What time would you recommend as the period for instruction in drawing in the college; you found fault with the existing arrangement of two hours?—Well, for the purpose of a pass, if the Board don't require anything more from the teacher, two hours a week is a proved sufficient, but if they are desirous of still higher qualifications in drawing two hours would not be sufficient.

1907. But that is a matter altogether in the hands of the college authorities. They can set down twenty hours if they think proper; there is no interference with them on that subject?—Oh, no.

1908. Once or twice you referred exclusively to the percentage for a certificate being 50. Are you aware that there is a percentage of 50 in the case of any student or any teacher throughout the country who takes up two branches of drawing at the same time?—Yes, I am aware of that.

Most Rev. Dr. Walsh.—It is important to keep that in mind; it is not merely 50 per cent.; if two branches are taken, it would be, say, 60 per cent. between the two, but 50 per cent. in each.

Professor Fitzgerald.—It might be 60 and 40.

1909. Mr. Molloy.—The 50 won't pass, there would be two 25's, and on that account the time fixed for the examination is a period of three hours, so as to admit of students taking all these or any one of the three?—Yes; while speaking of that might I express my opinion that the subject being compulsory I don't think that an hour would be sufficient time to give to any one of the three subjects in the July examination; the time ought to be enlarged, at least one and a half hours.

1910. I think you mentioned that you would be content with a percentage of 50 in the drawing?—Yes.

1911. That is the same as for the ordinary subjects, such as arithmetic, but you would like in the case of a certificate in drawing, to have a higher percentage?—Yes.

1912. Would you advocate a higher percentage also for arithmetic?—I would leave that to the Professor of Mathematics.

1913. Professor Fitzgerald.—Would you give a certificate in English literature; do you think there ought to be a certificate in English literature given as well as a pass? Would it be an encouragement?—Well, I don't know; they are taking to it very well at present.

1914. Mr. Molloy.—You mentioned that you would like to see in connection with the Board's ordinary schools drawing copies of Irish designs?—Yes.

1915. Perhaps you are not aware that they are already in existence on the Board's list for the past fifteen years?—I have not seen them.

1916. There are patterns from the Book of Kells produced by Marcus Ward, of Belfast?—I have never seen them, strange to say.

1917. I believe the class of teachers under you was inspected by a representative from the Science and Art Department?—Yes.

1918. Kindly let us know what his report was?—The only report, or rather the result of the report, whatever it was, was this—I am not qualified as an Art Teacher or an Art Master which would be necessary to earn grants here under the South Kensington Department—whatever representations he made in London, the Department granted to the college that so long as I was there result fees might be earned by the students, which I thought was complimentary to me.

1919. And that was done without subjecting you to any special examination?—Without subjecting me to any examination whatever.

1920. It was done exclusively on witnessing the result of your teaching in drawing?—Yes.

1921. Would you be disposed to generalise on that throughout the country?—If an inspector went around and visited these schools and found successful teaching going on, whether the teacher had a certificate or not, I would give him the same compliment as was paid to me.

1922. I know that the action of the South Kensington Department was regarded as a very special compliment to you and was generally looked on as highly deserved. You mentioned a while ago about kindergarten. I think you have devoted some attention to that?—Yes, considerable attention.

1923. Up to what class would you continue that instruction?—From the main infant to the entire course.

1924. And in connection with kindergarten would you carry on instruction in drawing?—Most decidedly, from the earliest period.

1925. Instead of as at present commencing with the third class?—I think that is a mistake to omit it in class one and two.

1926. Captain Shaw.—There is a practising school attached to Kildare-street Training College?—Yes.

1927. Do I understand from you that no model lessons in drawing are given in that school?—None.

Feb. 22, 1897. Mr. John Cooke, B.A.

1928. It is not used for instructing pupils of the Training Colleges in drawing?—No, it is not.

1929. Who is responsible for framing the course which the students go through at the Training College in drawing?—The Board.

1930. They don't lay down what they are to do from day to day?—No, the programme is arranged by the College authorities.

1931. CHAIRMAN.—Who are the College authorities in Kildare-street?—The Board; and of course the staff arrange a time table of that kind, and it is approved of by the Board.

1932. Most Rev. Dr. WALSH.—You mean the special Board of Governors of that Training College, not the Board of National Education?—Not the Board of National Education.

Monsignor MOLLOY.—The Training College in Kildare-street is under a scheme prepared by the Educational Endowments Commission; and the Board of Governors is now a corporate body.

1933. Captain SHAW.—But the particular instruction, which is given within those hours, you arrange that yourself?—I arrange that myself.

1934. Can you give a course which you consider satisfactory for training teachers in drawing, or would you alter it. If you had not to make those students gain a certificate at the end of each year, would you go through the same course as you do now?—I would slightly modify it; if my hands were free I would give far more blackboard work than I do at present. The fact of my having to train teachers to pass at sixty per cent. ties me down to a certain course of work from which there is no relief. If my hands were free I would give the students more practice in blackboard work, which I consider essential to their powers as teachers, not only in drawing, but in everything else, illustrating geography for instance.

1935. How much blackboard instruction do they get at present?—Very little, except with the more advanced students; I give them a little practice from time to time.

1936. Some of them might get no practice at all?—Some of them have no time for it.

1937. You recommend that teachers who show an aptitude for drawing should gain special training in the Training Colleges?—I mean that the Training Colleges might afford facilities towards getting it in the School of Art.

1938. If they devoted more time to drawing than to other subjects that might give them a bias one way in their schools?—It might.

1939. But you think they would be useful for the position of itinerant teachers, or taking classes for other teachers of the district?—My idea was, that getting a high standard in those or their subjects they would be qualified for large schools where drawing was made a prominent subject, in towns particularly.

1940. Or might organise for a group of schools?—Quite so.

1941. If you were sent round to examine a teacher and give him a certificate, you would not give him one unless he could show moderate proficiency on the blackboard?—No.

1942. As to the question of a man of forty, is it not much more difficult for a man of forty who has not been drawing to train his hand to make a finished

1943. Do you think the students who come in Kildare-street are more backward in drawing than the students who come to Marlborough-street?—That I could not say, but judging from Mr. Morris's remarks I think we are about the same.

1944. You said that supposing drawing were made compulsory in the schools the teachers might be trained to be able to teach drawing in large towns by attending schools of art?—Yes.

1945. These provisions of itinerant teachers would only apply to rural districts?—Yes, those in large towns could very well do that.

1946. Would an itinerant teacher take a district and group the teachers of this particular district, and bring them all together to a particular centre for the teacher of drawing, he would not need to go to each school and teach each individual teacher?—I am afraid he would have to, rather than bring a number of teachers together, he would work it better by visiting the schools say for a few months in rotation, and then let the teacher see the way he went to work.

1947. He would teach drawing himself?—Do you mean?—Teach drawing himself; give a number of lessons and the teacher would be better able to carry that out than by getting a number of lessons himself.

1948. Then you would not advocate the combination of training in a centre in each district and bringing the teachers together on a particular morning of the week or two evenings of the week?—That taken with the other would be an excellent plan.

1949. And he would go around the schools in the daytime?—Yes.

1950. CHAIRMAN.—Would not that come to the same thing as Judge Shaw is putting to you—bringing the teachers together?—I thought it was an alternative scheme.

1951. Judge SHAW.—I understand Mr. Cooke would advocate a combination of the two?—Yes.

1952. CHAIRMAN.—If you brought the teachers to one centre, you could bring thirty or forty teachers there, whereas if they went round the schools they could only perhaps take five or six schools in the time given to each district?—Yes; but I think it desirable that the teachers should see a good man at work.

1953. Why could not the teacher see it in a centre with thirty or forty teachers present as well as in his own school?—He would see him at work with perhaps a class of boys taken in.

1954. Judge SHAW.—There would be no difficulty in a teacher teaching in the evening—one of these itinerant teachers—teaching in the evening a number of school teachers, and in the day going round through the schools and showing the practical work of instruction?—Yes.

1955. CHAIRMAN.—Would you let the pupils of the schools have the benefit of that?—Quite so.

1956. Monsignor MOLLOY.—I think I understood your idea to be that the itinerant teacher should go to the school himself and teach there, and set up a good system, which the schoolmaster would see, and so learn how the thing could be well done?—It would be very desirable.

1957. And in connection with that, schools might be established to which schoolmasters might come and get formal lessons?—Yes.

Jan. 28, 1898. Mr. John [illegible], esq.

1865. Drawing should be as necessary to him as writing?—His writing permeates the whole work of his day.

1866. Mr. Molloy.—Are you acquainted with the Board's present system of organisation by special teachers. You are aware that there are organising teachers under the National Board at present?—I was not aware.

1867. Well there are, and the position is this, they go to the particular locality for a week or a fortnight, they visit certain schools or within a radius of three miles, and on Saturdays they assemble all the teachers within that same area or outside it, if convenient to the teachers, to receive instructions from them in a broad and general way on methods of teaching. Do you think a development of that would be appropriate for the subject of drawing?—Decidedly.

1868. It would be the examination Judge Shaw speaks of?—Yes.

1869. That has been in force since 1893 in Primary schools?—I did not know.

1870. Monsignor Molloy.—Do you think could these itinerant teachers of drawing act also as inspectors of schools in the matter of drawing; there would be a certain economy in using them for both purposes?—There would; they might act as inspectors; of course I don't know what the qualifications of inspectors are at present, or why they should be superseded by these men.

1871. Well, that raises a question on which I would like to have your opinion. Do you think a special inspector of drawing would be more efficient for that purpose than an inspector who would inspect the schools as part of his ordinary work?—I think a specialist is more desirable and more efficient and better qualified to judge.

1872. Judge Shaw.—Who examines in drawing at present?—The inspector who examines in reading and writing and so on.

1873. The same inspector?—Yes.

1874. Monsignor Molloy.—You told your hands were tied in the training of teachers in Kildare-street by the necessity of reaching a standard of sixty per cent.?—Yes.

1875. You would prefer a system in which the standard would be lower?—It admitted great freedom in many ways.

1876. And you think that such freedom would contribute to more efficient teaching?—It entirely depends. I would not like to hazard an opinion, considering we are only at the beginning, in the first year of this programme.

1877. We should then most, this possibly is it [illegible] that a lower standard would contribute to a more efficient teaching?—Not necessarily. I don't like a lower standard. That arises out of the question of Captain Shaw, he raised the question about black-board work. Take half a dozen teachers who are possibly well up in freehand, and I am certain would pass on the seventy per cent. I would have more freedom in bringing these students to the blackboard also, if I was kicking at sixty per cent.

1878. Then for a thoroughly good teacher who would use his freedom for the benefit of the school a lower standard would enable him to bring good students to a higher degree of excellence?—Yes.

Miss Prendergast, Directress of Needlework under the Board of National Education, examined.

Miss Prendergast.

1879. Chairman.—What position do you hold in connexion with the Training College in Marlborough-street?—Directress of Needlework.

1880. Will you tell us what position there is for teaching needlework?—The first is the ordinary programme for plain needlework which every pupil in second class and upwards must be taught for an hour daily according to the rules of the Board, a progressive graduated according to the capacity of the children. They learn so much yearly, and practise what they have learned in previous years, and by the time they have reached sixth class they ought to have acquired a knowledge of all the stitches that are used in ordinary plain needlework, have learned how to mend garments, to knit, to cut out these articles, and to make, as a rule, four.

1881. What is the alternative scheme?—It was introduced with a view to bringing into the hands of girls a much more extended course of needlework than could be taught by the ordinary programme; there are a great many branches, but some of them are ones that could be very seldom taught in a school, rather out of the reach of schools.

1882. Give us an example of those that are not useful or ordinary at school?—Ecclesiastical embroidery in gold and silver is a branch that is out of the ordinary capacity. A branch which is not useful is flower making, it is practically out of the thing; and I think nobody has looked upon it with much favour; but the ordinary branches, such as dressmaking and the making of fine underclothing, are very useful where they can be well taught.

1883. Is dressmaking an extra?—There is also dressmaking as an extra, supposed to be a more advanced kind than that taught in the Sixth Class; that would be a very useful branch if the power of teaching it were confined to older girls than are taught at present.

1884. Would not that be teaching a trade?—I don't think so. I think it is meant for their own use, to teach them to be able to make their own working dresses, and to repair and so forth in a more intelligent manner than that may have been made for them by more skilled persons.

1885. Will you tell us now what are the industrial departments, such as lace making?—Those are schools in which a special grant of money is made to a special teacher who has charge of a class consisting, one may say, of three elements—the pupils of the school who have passed twice in Sixth Class, and for whose industrial education a fee is no longer paid; the monitresses of the school who have also passed twice in Sixth Class, and who are on the same plane as regards fees; and extern girls who are generally ex-pupils.

1886. Are those schools generally in towns?—Generally in towns, and more mostly in towns of a certain size; they are not so often in very large towns as in moderate-sized ones and rather small ones.

1887. Not in very large towns?—Not so large, and not so useful there, because there are other positions for work; there girls go to factories and workshops, whereas in the smaller country towns they are very glad to get a course in which they are taught work and get the opportunities of earning.

1888. Does that apply to Convent schools and Model schools?—Principally Convent schools have those industrial departments, but there are a few Ordinary schools and one Model school.

1889. Which Model school is that?—The Central Model School in Marlborough-street.

1890. What do they teach besides lace making?—A great number of various things. Dressmaking is very commonly taught, making fine underclothing, shirts; vestment-making is taught in several departments and the making of other ecclesiastical garments, and Mountmellick embroidery, drawn thread work, knitting and crochet is almost universal; of course a great many articles are made in these subjects.

1891. I suppose worsted work is never taught?—I am sorry to say, my lord, that it occasionally is—it is very ugly. You perhaps mean stitching on canvas?

1892. I mean what used to be much more the fashion than it is now?—Yes, it still survives.

by the pupils

National school
work mistress?
think it is dis-

I want to know
... the
that is in the

weaving expenses are ..., and so what remains goes for wages to the girls.

2014. Have you seen any of the webs that are woven?—Oh, yes.

2015. And do you consider the product is good?—Very good; I have bought produce of the looms and found them quite satisfactory, and there are very few weaving departments which have any difficulty in disposing of their linen. As a rule they can sell it quite easily.

2016. Rev. Dr. Evans.—Do the Commissioners supply the materials to the girls for this industrial programme?—No, the only provision that has ever been made to assist in that way was the Board's stores where materials were sold at wholesale prices.

2017. You refer to the materials mentioned in this list I hold in my hand—you are acquainted with it?—I think so; I am, I think, acquainted with this.

2018. Do you think the materials mentioned in this list are sufficient for the work that you superintend in the schools?—In an ordinary way I think they are.

[illegible] in [illegible] in this class?—Yes, I thought it was very creditable [illegible]; it was the first [illegible] they had ever thoroughly [illegible].

2028. Rev. Dr. [illegible].—Is the teaching in needlework popular with the girls?—It depends a good deal upon the teacher. If the teacher have good knowledge of her work, and, what we may call a fitness for it, [illegible] is, she generally [illegible] to make her pupils [illegible]; if she feels it a [illegible] they feel it dull too.

2029. They are desirous to learn it?—Not always; particularly in [illegible] it is very difficult to induce them to take an interest—it takes a very good and active teacher there to push them forward. I was in a large city school recently, and I had various complaints about the [illegible] of the children—that they took no interest in their work.

2030. As to the weaving industry, is that increasing?—It has a great deal increased; it is not a thing that can be treated in a [illegible] because of the cost of the [illegible], but it has done very well in the eight schools which have taken it. Of course the [illegible] all cost a good deal of money; the Commissioners generally require about seven looms to start.

2031. [illegible].—About what would [illegible] would that represent?—Some of them can be bought, I think, for about £5, and other large heavy looms cost £8 to £9.

2032. Then it would take about £50 at any rate to start?—I think so; there is also warp [illegible] and a [illegible] required for drawing the threads into lengths, and there are wheels for winding.

2033. Mr. [illegible].—You say there is a workmistress where there is an average attendance of twenty girls?—Yes.

2034. If there is an average attendance of ten or twelve girls under a mistress, there is no needlework taught at all?—No; there is no needlework taught in that case.

2035. The girls receive no instruction whatever in needlework?—No. I once had a question raised me by a lady whose brother was manager [illegible] two small schools at a distance of about three miles apart; she asked would it be possible for a workmistress to be appointed to conduct the needlework of both schools, as the average of girls attending both would reach twenty, and I put the question to the Commissioners, and heard it was not possible as the rules did not provide for it.

2036. Have you any idea of how many schools there may be in the country with an average attendance of less than twenty girls?—No; I don't think I know that.

2037. Do you think it is a considerable number? Leaving apart the number, you think it is important that girls in a school under a master should be taught needlework even if they are less than twenty?—I do think so if it could be managed.

2038. It would be extremely important to have some provision by which these girls should be taught needlework?—I think the proposal for a workmistress to be shared between the two schools would be very reasonable if it could be managed.

2039. When a workmistress is employed does she give instruction in anything but needlework?—No; she has no other business.

2040. She is generally a person who could read and write sufficiently, she has some literary education?—She has some, but I don't think she would be capable of teaching anything literary, in some cases.

2041. She could teach the alphabet and elementary subjects?—I cannot say about that. I write to workmistresses sometimes because there are flaws in their work, not serious enough to make me feel they ought to be rejected, but yet one would wish the girls to be taught more perfectly that particular subject, and in that case I write after the candidate has been passed to let her know what was amiss and give her a pattern of a more perfect article, whatever it may be; and the letters I receive in return are sometimes very well expressed and written; these are generally from ex-monitresses who are almost teachers, and waiting the [illegible] until they get a school; and some I receive are very indifferently expressed, with mistakes in spelling and so forth, and I think they belong to those who have never attended school much, but have learned needlework and are capable of teaching it.

2042. But many of these workmistresses are ex-monitors?—I think a good many of them; I generally [illegible] the information on the envelope—"Monitress at such a school."

2043. They could easily take charge of the literary training of the infants in a small school of this kind taught by a master?—Ex-monitresses, I should think, would be capable.

2044. Would it not be very desirable in those small schools that some person should teach needlework to the girls?—I should think it would.

2045. And would it not be very desirable, all things considered, that she should relieve the master of some of the work of the junior classes if she is capable of doing it?—That is going a little out of my province, because it is dealing with literary matters in which, of course, I am not interested in the slightest degree.

2046. Then about the teaching of dressmaking and [illegible], and so on, that is taught in primary schools?—There is very little dressmaking taught in the sixth class; it is almost entirely in industrial departments; a great deal of the best [illegible] in Ireland is made in the industrial departments.

2047. These industrial departments are not primary schools?—They are; the department is attached to the school; it does not carry on any literary work; it is attended by pupils who have literary instruction in the school; the industrial department is a workroom in which work is taught.

2048. Do you think that such subjects as dressmaking and [illegible] are proper subjects for instruction in elementary schools for pupils who have not completed their literary education up to a sufficient standard?—I think dressmaking is often taken up too early; dressmaking in our schools generally taken up at too early an age.

2049. At what age do you think it should be taken up?—From thirteen to fourteen. The children can be taught in first stage of Fifth Class. I think they are too young to profit by instruction at that age, but the teacher naturally thinks that when they reach Sixth class they may go away altogether, and the golden age must be secured.

2050. Would it be possible to have dressmaking and [illegible] taught in evening schools?—I think so.

2051. Which might be attended by pupils who have finished their ordinary literary education?—I think so.

2052. I understand one difficulty about the teaching of needlework is the difficulty of obtaining material?—Yes, that is a great difficulty.

2053. Who supplies the material at present?—The parents are supposed to supply it, but the teachers often complain that the parents don't supply it.

2054. If the parents don't supply the work are the children taught?—They are occupied in sewing the same stitches over and over again on little pieces of calico; of course they cannot advance in the same way as if their parents did supply them with materials.

2055. They don't make garments as the other children?—The teacher is obliged to show a garment from each girl in the school, but I don't know if it is possible to be exceedingly strict if she has to supply the material herself.

2056. If the material was supplied by the manager of the school, would there be any difficulty in getting it sold as garments after it has been made up?—I have been told by teachers that there is a difficulty.

2057. I have asked, because we find in schools in Edinburgh that there is no difficulty on that point?—Irish parents are different; they don't seem to take the same interest in the manual instruction of girls.

Dr. [illegible] Miss Fowler [illegible]

[illegible]

Miss Prendergast.

2058. Monsignor MOLLOY.—Is it that they would rather buy clothes in a shop? Yes, readymade, very often.

2059. Rev. Dr. EVANS.—You will see on that pink paper that you have before you that the Commissioners send out samples to the schools where they are asked for?—Yes.

2060. You mentioned that parents wish to have the opportunity of choosing themselves?—Yes.

2061. Now, do not the Commissioners provide for that by offering to send out samples to the schools which can be brought home by the pupils, so that these parents can see them and choose?—These samples have to be returned within a week, and I don't think it would be very wise to allow them to be taken to the children's homes in case they might never appear again.

2062. What then is the object of sending them out for a week?—For the teacher's choice.

2063. Not the parents?—No, I think, the parents, but the parents I think would very generally intimate that they were not ready to purchase at that time. In a few schools which manage the matter very well, each girl of the senior class is provided with a page of a little passbook in which her name is entered and the amount of money which the calico or other material which the teacher supplies to her will cost, and she then brings two or three pence weekly, as I suppose her mother gives it to her, until the price of the article is cleared away. That answers very well in a school where the alternative scheme is thoroughly successful, such as the Kenmare Convent; there is a quantity of work done there and done very well, and with perfect satisfaction apparently to both sides.

2064. Mr. STRUTHERS.—How many hours a week is needlework usually taught?—Five hours—one hour a day. Saturday is not a day of obligation.

2065. No school teacher gives less than five hours if she takes it up at all?—It is an obligation to take it up—the teacher is obliged to teach it.

2066. For five hours a week?—Yes; she possibly might evade that sometimes, but she is never supposed to do so.

2067. You think a girl would not get a satisfactory instruction with less than five hours a week?—I know when less than five hours a week was given to the subject it was unsatisfactorily taught.

2068. Supposing two hours of that time was given to instruct the children in drawing, do you think the time would be lost to needlework?—Lost to needlework, I think it would be.

2069. You think the instruction in drawing would not help needlework?—It may assist in cutting out, but the actual needlework—sewing—it would not help. I should not like to see any time taken from the needlework at present because it is not perfect as it stands, and if there were less time given to it I suppose it would be more imperfect.

2070. Captain SHAW.—With reference to the appointment of workmistresses, who has the appointment of them?—The manager of the school appoints workmistresses and notifies the Secretary of the Board; then there are instructions issued to the Inspector of the district to examine the workmistress, she executes specimens in his presence which he encloses in an envelope made for the purpose, and sends to me to examine. I report on the efficiency, and according to my report the Board informs the manager whether she is recognised or not.

2071. As regards the inspection of the school in needlework, how is that carried out?—The Inspectors have the general inspection, I, being only one, could not undertake it.

2072. Are the Inspectors generally proficient in needlework?—I think they generally understand more of the theory than the practice.

2073. Mr. STRUTHERS.—They can tell good work from bad work?—I think they generally can, and I know some have, in a way I have very much admired, tried to make themselves thoroughly understand it.

2074. Captain SHAW.—Do you think the Inspectors are capable of giving advice as altering the methods of instruction in needlework as a rule?—I don't know that they could give what you would call very practical advice, but they sometimes can. I have an Inspector in my mind whose district improved immensely in its work during his residence there; I think he must have been able to discriminate very well between good and bad, when he could raise the standard so much as that.

2075. Would you prefer to see any other system of inspection for needlework than the present one?—I suppose it would be more perfect to have a staff of women inspectors, but that would be a very large question and a large expenditure.

2076. Do you think the teaching of needlework has much effect on the clothing of the children throughout the country?—When it is well taught it has.

2077. In most country districts do the children wear the garments such as are made in the schools?—When their parents are sensible they do give them the materials, and they then do wear school-made garments which are more lasting and more satisfactory. But, of course, if parents like to buy things ready-made and won't give the materials to the children they cannot have them to wear.

2078. Monsignor MOLLOY.—Are the parents generally sensible?—I am afraid not, at least the teachers give me the impression that they don't find them always sensible.

2079. Captain SHAW.—I think there is a sort of universal garment worn in Ireland by both boys and girls, do you think that has been displaced at all—a sort of overall?—A gown do you mean? I very seldom meet with it. I think the ordinary clothes of civilisation now are penetrating very far.

2080. Mr. MOLLOY.—Commencing with the pupils' programme, you are aware that results fees are only paid from second class upwards?—Yes.

2081. Would you not think it desirable that the children in infant classes and also first class, both of which are very numerously attended, should also get instruction in elementary needlework?—I think it would be very well indeed if the first class did get instruction. I am not so sure about the infants—they are getting some training in kindergarten for one thing. The first class children are about seven and I think that is young enough.

2082. You were asked a question about dressmaking—is not the expression "dressmaking" too ambitious a term for what takes place; in our schools it is not used in the sense of professional dressmaking?—Still it is making a dress in the literal sense of the word.

2083. In connection with the alternative scheme which came into operation in 1869, have you noticed whether or not any improvement has taken place in needlework instruction throughout the schools; do they now give more time to needlework than under the old system?—When the alternative scheme was well taught I thought the results were very good, but there were schools in which I noticed that teachers only wished to find a way of getting through the work of the subject; the easiest thing that could be found, generally, was selected to teach, and the thing that required the smallest amount of material, material being the trouble; but that is not always the most useful thing for children to learn.

2084. You mentioned a while ago that under that scheme ecclesiastical embroidery was included; is not that branch very exceptional and rare? Would you not rather confine that scheme to such subjects as No. 1, girls' underclothing, knitting of jerseys, caps, repairing, &c., was not the alternative scheme virtually confined to those essential matters?—Principally—these were the principal subjects I have met with; but I have found useless ones taught—artificial flower-making in paper I did not think was very desirable.

2085. It would be desirable to omit that subject?—I think so.

She watched him at his operations until she learned how, and in a couple of years he proved out to be quite unsatisfactory, not steady enough, and he was dismissed, and she took his place, but she has received no salary. [illegible] Miss Prender-gast.

2101. Mr. Mahaffy.—Mr. Hamilton asked you a question about whole mixed schools attended by boys and girls; if the average were sufficient, would there not be a female industrial teacher, and would she not be responsible for [illegible] an appointment?—Yes, if the average were sufficient.

2102. Then that would limit the number of schools [illegible] in which industrial education is possible [illegible] owing to the few girls attending them?—I continually meet with girls in schools who have been taught [illegible] perhaps they were in second stage of fifth class, occasionally by a monitor; they have then to begin the industrial education from the beginning when they reach the work.

2103. Is it not a fact that sometimes local aid supplements the salary of the Board, and that a special teacher of needlework is employed where the attendance of girls would not warrant the National Board by Treasury Regulations in paying a salary?—I think that is the case in schools which are under the Church Education Committee.

2104. In connection with primary National schools I have before my mind [illegible] school at [illegible]?—Yes, [illegible]; they occasionally do.

2105. With regard to the lace, and that requisition sheet you have before you, it was stated by previous witnesses that the elementary teachers desired more variety than they had in lace; also that [illegible] only one application is made in the year from certain schools for school requisites; is it desirable to [illegible] the needlework depôt here in Dublin?—I think the depôt itself is obviously desirable.

2106. But would it be able to be worked on in such a manner that the teachers would be satisfied with the materials. Of late there is less [illegible] no grant for the buying of fresh materials, and those that remain are generally the remains of former times, so that I have had complaints in schools about the quality of the materials supplied of late.

2107. Do you think the female teachers would prefer having their own selection of calico, flannel, and muslin?—They are perfectly at liberty to go to the neighbouring towns; they are not obliged to have it from here.

2108. You are aware, of course, that under the new programme, in which you have [illegible] largely in the way of suggesting, more time has been devoted to needlework. Is not the programme also extended by the introduction of additional items for the various classes and hence that more will be taught than heretofore?—A little, not a large amount; but the plain needlework programme is very heavy in want of variety. I did not see the last programme.

2109. Are you not aware that [illegible] will henceforth constitute an important item of the female teachers' examination?—Yes; I am perfectly aware of that, and very glad of it.

2110. Mr. Hamilton.—With regard to this weaving, do you really think that that is properly within the functions of primary education; in other words, do you think it is of any educational value to the children in the primary school?—I think it is, in a sense; it is giving them a weapon with which they may avail themselves later on in the battle of life.

2111. Is it not really teaching them a trade?—I suppose, in a sense, it may be called a trade, but in the same sense would you not say that handiwork was the rudiments of carpentry?

2112. Do other girls besides the pupils in ordinary National schools attend these weaving classes?—Yes, extern pupils, generally ex-pupils.

2113. Is not the bulk of the weaving done by those outsiders?—The great bulk of the material sold is woven by these girls; the pupils come from the school merely to learn, and join, as they wish, or not, afterwards.

Feb. 21, 1887. Miss [illegible].

2114. Notwithstanding that there is a good deal of outside help in those classes where weaving is taught, is this weaving carried on profitably by them in addition?—They are self-supporting. All that is wanted is a certain sum to start with, because of the preliminary expense and what is called the working capital, and then the weaving department supports itself.

2115. Mr. [illegible].—Self-supporting if you include the teacher's time?—They pay the teachers; they don't go to the expense of the school.

2116. You have them in view in making the school self-supporting?—What I mean is they are not obliged to ask help from outside sources.

2117. Mr. [illegible].—Is it not very difficult for those schools where weaving is taught to compete with the machinery made goods?—No, they don't find it very hard.

2118. With regard to lace-making, is not that a very severe test on the eyes of young children?—I don't think it is, if they take ordinary care of their eyes and don't work by bad light; everybody knows that any work, careful work, done by the eyes by a bad light is injurious; I suppose even drawing would injure the eyes.

2119. But as a general rule it is done under favourable circumstances?—It is; the rooms in which it is taught are large and lightsome.

2120. Monsignor Molloy.—And not to work too long at a time, is not that an important element?—I don't think they work too long; they generally break up at a fairly early hour.

2121. What length do they work at lace-work at a time?—Four hours is the longest time I know, and I think there is a break in the middle of that for luncheon and a little rest. I have seen women of over sixty years of age still working fine lace, which I think is a proof that it cannot injure the eyes.

2122. It may be quite safe for a woman of mature years, and very injurious to children?—The children generally don't begin under fourteen years of age. I have seen a few as young as twelve, but generally about fourteen is the age and if as I say they take ordinary care of the eyes it does not injure them. Some of these old lace-makers tell me they were working from childhood, from infancy.

2123. Mr. [illegible].—As a matter of fact have you ever come across a case in which lace-making has injured the eyes of the children?—No, I have not.

2124. With regard to those local authorities, would it not be a desirable thing to have attached to the various schools throughout the country ladies' committees who would encourage the pupils and teachers in this needlework programme, or would it cause too great interference; in some cases this system of a ladies' committee has been very successful?—I think perhaps it is more successful in the form of exhibitions or competitions. I think what you might call perhaps committees interfering in the way of visiting the school, and so forth, might be a little resented by the teachers; they might think they were being spied upon, but occasional visits might be a different matter.

2125. Professor Fitzgerald.—Speaking about the garments the children make in the schools, if a person were to buy a garment would they buy a garment made in the same kind of way as the ones made in the school?—Yes; the garments are shirts, pinafores, articles of underclothing; they were chosen carefully as being what one might call necessary garments.

2126. And they are the same kind of garment as is worn in that district?—There is a small district where there is that flannel gown, and I should think that perhaps the inspector does not ask to see the garments there; otherwise, they are garments in common use.

2127. Would it not be quite as possible for a master to teach girls needlework as for an inspector to inspect?—Oh, no; I don't think so.

2128. Why should not masters teach needlework?—I know of one master who professed to teach his needlework, but I [illegible] he did not do it [illegible].

2129. You don't think there is any serious difficulty in a master learning needlework?—If he has been brought up in early life as a tailor he may be competent.

2130. If he had manual instruction in his youth, would he not be able to do it?—If he has gone through a regular course of needlework.

2131. Would it not be well that boys should learn needlework?—I have always thought it would be well if they learned kindergarten, to sew on a button and do a little rough darning.

2132. Why should they not learn more than that?—Because I don't think they would put their learning to use except for sewing a button or darning stockings.

2133. But darning a stocking is very difficult?—Not very difficult.

2134. It is as difficult as knitting?—But what use would they make of knitting?

2135. You seem to think simple darning is very easy?—Some of the work they do—plaiting of paper stripes—is very like darning and would make them to learn darning.

2136. I was very anxious at one time, and tried to get the Board to enforce needlework on the boys as well as the girls. I know I learned it myself and asked a little infant boy a few times whether he would like to learn it—he was [illegible].

2137. Most Rev. Dr. Walsh.—Do you know that we pay results fees for teaching what is called agriculture to girls?—I have not anything to do with agriculture.

2138. On the same principle we might pay results fees for teaching needlework to boys?

2139. Professor Fitzgerald.—It would be good manual employment for them. It has been represented to us by one of the Head Inspectors that one of the reasons the alternative scheme was not popular was because two hours needlework a day was rather too much; do you think two hours needlework a day for girls is too long to keep them at it?—No, I don't think so; they should have [illegible] varieties of needlework in that time.

2140. He thought it would be desirable to introduce some other manual occupation for them besides needlework for the second part of the day; do you think there would be any other kind of manual instruction that would be useful for girls, housework, and so on, washing—anything else?—Those things are not so easily managed in a school.

2141. You cannot think of any other subject that could be introduced?—You would turn the school topsy-turvy if you insisted on washing in out when the other children were learning lessons.

2142. This is for sixth class girls and they might wash it out after school hours?—A great many would be very much insulted if asked to do it.

2143. I meant was there any other subject that could be introduced instead of needlework, if two hours was too much?—My branch of course is only needlework. Cookery is an excellent thing, but I should have nothing to do with that besides considering it was excellent. Besides there are so many kinds of needlework useful for a girl that I have never come to the conclusion that she was over-weighted because she had two hours.

2144. Then the objection to the alternative scheme was, in your view, the difficulty of getting materials?—Yes; and also some of the teachers trained, perhaps, fifteen or twenty years ago had not given much attention to it, and they felt unhappy at having to teach what they had never very much learned.

2145. Don't people prefer patronising a shopkeeper in a country town who is a friend of theirs?—Yes, generally for ready-made articles.

2146. Monsignor Molloy.—I think you said the children don't take a great interest in needlework?—That only applies in certain places; city children are less interested than children in country towns and villages.

ground the peasantry, there is a great deal of amusement [illegible], and it seems to influence the minds of [illegible] great objection [illegible] anything.

2147. Have you any experience whether children who have been taught needlework at school have it in demand afterwards?—Yes; teachers have told me that they have had letters from former pupils who have gone to America; they have been trained in the [illegible] schools, first there, and afterwards principally in the industrial department, and they have written to their sisters telling them to take every advantage of the instruction in the school in needlework, saying they were making a livelihood by it in America, and that it was [illegible] for them to [illegible] so as to [illegible] among the [illegible], which seemed to be [illegible].

2148. For those who went to America it was very [illegible]?—Yes; I [illegible] girls who were taught the sewing machine, being able to go into workshops and earn at once. I have known very good situations as [illegible] got by girls who were able to show that they could take care of the [illegible] of children.

2149. With regard to those who go home and remain with their own families, do they turn their knowledge to account?—According to the disposition of the girl; if she is industrious she will be a treasure at home.

2150. I should like to know are many of them [illegible]. The [illegible] in school, and those who are not [illegible], that does not give us any light?—My impression is that good training in needlework helps to elevate a girl's character, and that she is more likely to be sensible after she has received it.

2151. Are the children at school taught to do needlework on their old clothing?—Not so often as I should wish; the mistress is sometimes perhaps rather shy of introducing it [illegible] that they require to be patched.

2152. One of the difficulties of teaching dressmaking is the difficulty of getting materials, but in the case of patching old clothes material seems to be very abundant in this country?—It is only too abundant.

2153. Do you think it would be desirable to extend the teaching of needlework somewhat in the direction of repairing and patching old clothes?—That is a question it is a little difficult to decide upon, because in Ireland people are rather ashamed of being poor, and they would rather that people did not [illegible] to notice the fact that they wanted to have their clothes mended.

2154. It would be less noticeable if they were painted?—You may remember that Sheridan defined [illegible] as "[illegible] poverty."

2155. Mr. Redington.—You are aware that a workmistress is appointed where there is an average of twenty girls in a school?—Yes.

2156. In counting that average, infants and first class girls are included?—Yes.

2157. No needlework is taught to infants and first class girls?—No.

2158. And the proportion of infants and first class girls in the whole number in the school may be taken at about one-third or a little more. Assuming that it would reduce the average of girls for which a workmistress is appointed to something like thirty?—That is very often the case I believe.

2159. Then a workmistress is only appointed in schools which have not got an average sufficient for a female assistant?—Yes.

2160. I don't know whether you are familiar with the last report. There are [illegible] schools in operation; of these [illegible] are for boys only, and the remainder [illegible] have female teachers, either principals or assistants, [illegible] have workmistresses, and there are only [illegible] mixed schools over, where there might be a deficient instruction in needlework. As to the alternative scheme for the sixth class, I think that the proportion of pupils examined in the sixth class is about 6 per cent. of the total number examined in the school; and as the alternative scheme only applies to the sixth class, it follows that for the great mass of girls it is not of any great use?—No.

2161. Do you think it could be improved, and made more attractive?—Yes, I think it could; I think it could be rendered [illegible] by omitting a good many branches.

2162. First of all, how much time is given to needlework and industrial pursuits under the alternative scheme?—Two hours a day is the minimum.

2163. Have you heard it said that that is too much time to give to those subjects?—Yes, I have heard it said in some schools.

2164. Have you heard it said that it leads to [illegible] among the girls?—Yes.

2165. What would you think of reducing the number of industrial subjects from two to one, in addition to needlework?—I think that would work very well in many cases where [illegible]; these subjects are considered too many to provide material for, and take up too much of the girls' time.

2166. Perhaps you may not be aware that the wishing of the Inspectors is rather in that direction?—And the restriction of arithmetic, because parents are dissatisfied generally that [illegible].

2167. So, if arithmetic took the place of one of the industrial subjects, it would make the alternative scheme more popular?—Much more popular.

2168. You are aware that it is only carried out in about one-third of the schools in which it might be introduced?—Yes.

2169. Therefore it would be desirable to modify it so as to make it more popular in the country?—I think so.

2170. Do you find much complaint as to the cost of the materials?—It is not exactly the cost, but the fact that the parents are unwilling apparently to give any materials at all.

2171. Has the teacher then to supply the materials?—The teacher in that case supplies them herself, or else [illegible] them in some way; it is a [illegible], and it is not the very poor parents who will not supply stuff—that is the puzzling thing. The very poor parents, if [illegible], will be [illegible], but well-to-do parents frequently neglect and even refuse to send materials.

2172. Are well-to-do parents in favour of having their children taught this alternative scheme?—Yes, as a rule; they prefer entirely literary instruction.

2173. I suppose they [illegible] their children for other situations, like that of telegraph clerks?—And assistants in shops and various things of that kind.

2174. Would you reduce the number of special industries that may be taken up?—Yes, I would reduce them to seven or eight.

2175. Could you put in a revised scheme, making suggestions as to how you would modify the alternative scheme, so as to make it more popular and to meet the objections you have heard expressed towards it?—I will try.

2176. Most Rev. Dr. Walsh.—Have you heard it objected against this alternative scheme, that it is work rather for the workroom than for the school?—Yes, I have heard that.

2177. Do you think that it is work rather for the workroom than for the school?—I hardly think so, your Grace, because if a girl is to learn anything useful about needlework, school is the only place in which she has a chance of learning it.

2178. But the needlework she learns under this alternative scheme is part of needlework she would learn if she were serving her apprenticeship to a trade?—No; except in some cases.

2179. But in some cases?—In some cases I suppose if she learned a fair amount of dressmaking she

Feb. 18, 1897.
—
Miss Prendergast.

might learn the same if she went as an apprentice to a dressmaker.

2180. I think you said that girls who went to America wrote back, recommending their friends and relations to take up this alternative scheme, as a means of securing employment in America?—Yes.

2181. And one of the things you mentioned was that they were able to pass into employment at once without serving an apprenticeship?—Yes.

2182. Does not that go to show that the work done in the schools under the alternative scheme is really learning a trade?—Well, knitting and crochet are two of the things which can be made very useful as a means of livelihood in America, and I don't know that there is anything that would be called an apprenticeship to serve to them.

2183. Did you not mention that in America the girls who have learned this alternative scheme are able to get employment without serving an apprenticeship; are we not to infer that if they had not learned under the alternative scheme they would have to serve an apprenticeship?—They would probably have to give their services for some time to whatever workroom would take them in, without payment.

2184. But under this scheme they can go in at once and get paid for their work?—If they have sufficient manual dexterity to make themselves useful at once.

2185. Then in the labour market it puts them on a footing with people who have been taught the trade in the ordinary trade workshop?—They would start perhaps on the same footing as a girl who had served her apprenticeship for some time.

2186. And to that extent the school is made to do the work of the workshops?—To a certain extent, yes.

2187. In reference to the question of this alternative scheme you said you would be for reducing the number of special industries at present connected to it—how many special industries are comprised in it at present I think seventeen.

2188. And you would be for reducing it to seven or eight?—Eight.

2189. Practically that seems to be all that exists in the country in actual operation. Let me call your attention to the last report of the Board. There is a list there of the subjects in which examinations have been actually held, and in which pupils have passed, and I suppose have got results fees. Kindly tell the Commissioners how many subjects are mentioned there?—There are fourteen, and other kinds of cottage industries, which might be several.

2190. I see that in one of these departments, "gold and silver lace work," there were only two girls examined in all Ireland?—I should not have thought there would have been so many.

2191. Then it would not be very much loss to the education of the country if that department was dispensed with?—No, my view is would not.

2192. You know something of the working of the schools in Marlborough-street—the Model Schools?—Yes.

2193. Is not embroidery of a very high and artistic kind taught there?—Yes, in the special industrial department.

2194. You have not told us anything of that. Kindly explain what the special industrial department of the Model School, Marlborough-street, is?—A special teacher is appointed at a special salary.

2195. Do you know is there anything like that in Ireland elsewhere, a special teacher paid by the Commissioners in addition to the ordinary staff of the school, for teaching this high-class needlework?—Yes; there are fifty-eight of those departments with special teachers paid.

2196. For teaching this high-class needlework?—Not for art needlework.

2197. Then I ask is there anything in Ireland corresponding to this special arrangement in the Model School at Marlborough-street?—No, there is not anything like that.

2198. Who is the instructor of that special department?—Mrs. Staddart is the industrial teacher.

2199. How many pupils does she instruct in this high-class work?—She has a very large number. About 130 I believe, on her roll, but she is unable to instruct that number daily; I don't think her daily number exceeds thirty.

2200. Does she teach there for the whole day?—During the school day, from ten to three.

2201. She was a specially trained teacher in this high-class needlework?—Yes.

2202. In one of the reports I see it mentioned that she teaches "embroidery on silk or linen with silver or gold thread, and wrought into choice patterns." Can you state from your own knowledge whether that is the kind of instruction that goes on in this special class of needlework in the Model School at Marlborough-street?—Yes.

2203. And that is what is paid for by the State for teaching needlework to these children?—Yes, and Mountmellick embroidery, which is a simpler kind of work, but the teaching is not confined to the children.

2204. Who else learn it?—The students of the Training College also have a share of her instruction.

2205. But I am speaking only of the Model schools—in those schools no one is taught but the pupils?—Only the present pupils of sixth class.

2206. Well, the children who are attending that school have this advantage specially provided for them which is not provided for the children of any other school in Ireland, having a special teacher paid for them by the State out of the public taxes?—It is exactly the same elsewhere.

2207. Professor FitzGerald.—Is there not an industrial department in Castlebar?—Yes, for teaching lacemaking.

2208. And is not the teacher paid out of the public funds?—Yes; and in Youghal Convent the teacher is paid for the teaching of Irish point, and in Kenmare Convent one of the Sisters is paid for teaching Irish point.

2209. Most Rev. Dr. Walsh.—Can you state what they are paid?—The Sisters in the Convents—the salary is usually £25 a year.

2210. Are you aware that the salary of this lady in Marlborough-street is £48 a year?—I know she has a larger salary; so has the teacher in the Baggot-street Convent; in the large city schools it was thought the work would be more onerous.

2211. Is the salary in Baggot-street paid for teaching, not ordinary needlework, but high-class embroidery?—In Baggot-street there is not very specially high embroidery taught; it is not at all of so fine a character as that taught at the Central Model School; but there is dressmaking taught as well.

2212. You don't look upon dressmaking as trade work in the ordinary sense?—No, pure Grace, I don't, because it is not intended to be made a trade; it is intended for the girls' own private use.

2213. They make their own dresses, the students in the Training College?—Yes; each makes a dress for herself that she may know how to teach the practical sewing to her pupils afterwards.

2214. They each make one dress?—They have not time to make any more.

2215. We may consider needlework as the chief industrial work of this department that you are connected with?—Yes.

2216. That is the work that is done on the largest scale. Do you think that this department of our system has worked satisfactorily?—I think a very great advance has been made in it during the last seven years.

2217. Then things must have been dreadfully bad seven years ago. Do you think they are satisfactory at present?—I don't think they will be entirely satisfactory until the fruit of the late revision of the rules regarding the examination of the teachers and monitors can be seen.

Feb. 23, 1897.

Miss Prendergast.

2218. I wish to call your attention to some passages that occur in your report, and I am quite sure you concur now in what you have written: "That it is still possible for teachers to pass into the Board's service, or continue in it, utterly ignorant of the branches of needlework which they are by rule required to teach." Is that so?—It was until the last revision of the rules. In future I hope it will not possibly be the case.

2219. I am only asking how things stand at present. This is your latest published report?—So long as the marks for needlework continue not to form part of the marks for classification, the teachers will not give the proper amount of attention to the thorough learning of that branch.

2220. You say, "There are exceptions to every rule, and they gleam out like gems among the rubbish in the form of finely worked and finished specimens which it is a pleasure to examine." Then finely finished work is an exception?—It has been up to this.

2221. "The hopelessly faulty productions of candidates, whose ambition seems to rise no higher than the acquisition of the art of cobbling, are common." Is that the actual state of things in our schools?—It has been unfortunately too common up to this for me to receive exceedingly faulty specimens of work.

2222. Again you say—"It is irritating to remember that the industrial instruction of future generations of school children may be at the mercy of these incompetents." Who are these incompetents?—Monitresses who have neglected to learn properly how to do the work, and cut out and so forth, and there was nothing to prevent up to this their being passed into the Board's service; of course many of those I suppose even at the present moment are mistresses in schools.

2223. Then you say—"Of all the branches of needlework in which candidates are examined, sewing shows the least improvement during the last five years." Is not sewing the most generally useful branch of the work of this department?—It is the very foundation.

2224. And it is the department that shows the least improvement?—Among the monitresses and teachers.

2225. Darning is a very important branch of the work also?—I think it is, because it conduces to comfort and neatness.

2226. You speak of "carelessness of execution" as being very common, and "a total want of judgment" exhibited in the use of materials. Are the teachers responsible for that?—The teachers are partly responsible, but they have often complained to me that the monitresses—there being no tangible reward in the shape of marks for them at their examinations—have taken very little interest in the subject, and practically refused to give it attention.

2227. You say, "Sometimes the darn forms a clumsy excrescence, sometimes it fills the hole with a cobweb-like fabric without substance or endurance"?—I stated the truth.

2228. Of course, and I think it important that the truth should come out. You speak of the numerous cases "in which utter ignorance prevails." Are these numerous?—Yes; amongst the monitresses it has been formerly the case.

2229. May we not assume that the monitresses represent a higher standard than the ordinary scholars?—Frequently lower. They are often below the sixth class, or have been until lately. Since the rumour went about that they are to get marks for their work they are beginning to apply themselves.

2230. At present you say that monitresses are worse than the ordinary pupils?—The sixth class girls have to be examined by the Inspector and fees are paid on that, but monitresses are not subject to such an examination.

2231. And these are the persons who are in preparation for the office of teacher?—Yes. I think it is six years now since I have been very anxious indeed to have these marks given, knowing the result would be good, and at last it has been managed.

2232. You have stated to us today that these industrial departments are confined to a very large extent to the Convent schools?—Principally, your Grace.

2233. It would seem to represent a very extraordinary state of things in the Convent schools of Ireland if this is the sort of result that comes out from the industrial departments?—Well, the monitresses are common to all schools, and the standard of the monitresses in the industrial departments which I visit yearly is generally decidedly higher than elsewhere.

2234. I find in your report that "thirty-four of these departments are in the charge of nuns"?—Yes.

2235. Is not this correct—"To these belong nearly all the conspicuously successful ones—those remarkable either for high quality or large quantity of the work produced, or for the amount of solid benefit conferred upon the pupils"?—Yes.

2236. So that while the general state of things is so lamentably bad, we have in those places where the department is in the charge of nuns, conspicuous success, high quality, a large quantity of work, and an amount of solid benefit conferred on the pupils?—That does not mean the monitresses alone, but all the pupils.

2237. So in the Convent schools this is true not only of the pupils, but of the monitresses?—I don't find monitresses always perfect even in the Convent schools, but in the industrial departments they are obliged to receive instruction with more care than elsewhere.

2238. Under the care of the nuns?—Yes; but of course there are many convents with no industrial department attached.

2239. Are the nuns who teach in these Convent schools certificated teachers of the Board?—Not always; they are more often under a capitation grant.

2240. But the teachers who teach in the other schools are certificated teachers. They pass an examination and get some certificate in the matter of needlework?—Yes.

2241. Now, comparing the two systems of providing teachers, which has worked the better? On which side of the line do we get the better work—in the schools that are under the care of the ordinary teachers, or in the schools under the care of the nuns?—I sometimes get very good work in schools under the care of ordinary teachers, and sometimes very good in Convent schools.

2242. But take it on the whole?—On the whole I think, perhaps, the Convent schools do the best work, but they have more advantages; the schools are generally larger, and they are better equipped.

2243. But, notwithstanding all this, unfortunately, more poorly paid?—I don't know that.

2244. Now, as to the weaving department, don't you consider that to teach weaving is decidedly teaching a trade?—I suppose it is in a sense a trade.

2245. Is it not as much a trade as shoemaking?—I suppose it is; but, my lord, you must remember also that to be a competent sempstress is to have a trade; to be a laundress is to have a trade. I don't think any person would like to make objection to these things being taught in a school.

2246. I want to have your opinion whether teaching weaving is a trade, and you say that it is?—Yes.

2247. Judge Shaw.—Could you tell us if, in centres where there is a large demand for girls as millhands and mill-workers, you find there is an objection on the part of girls at school to take up this (industrial programme)?—I think there is rather.

2248. Such as Belfast or Lurgan?—Oh, yes; there is a prejudice against it there.

2249. Mr. Richardson.—As a matter of fact is it not taught in any school in Belfast?—It is taught in the [illegible] Miss Prendergast.

[illegible] Convent school and in a very fair manner, too.

2250. Judge Shaw.—Is it not the rule that where a girl looks forward to going into a mill and having her hands occupied all her life she prefers to spend her school days in the ordinary literary work?—As a number of the mill-hands never reach the sixth class at all; it is no [illegible] whatever to them, they leave school after first of fifth generally.

2251. So then they don't come up to the point at which this programme is taken up?—No; but girls who are going into [illegible] shopping and these kind of places in Belfast do prefer having literary training until they are leaving school altogether.

2252. There are a large number of girls that go into [illegible] and other factories where sewing machines are used; do you find, as a general rule, those girls prefer at school to devote themselves to literary work?—They do. Then there are many who wish to become assistants in shops, and so forth, and they also object to anything but literary work; they are very weak with [illegible] beyond all things.

2253. And writing?—And a little book-keeping, and so on.

2254. Most Rev. Dr. Walsh.—You are speaking now, not of needlework teaching in general, but of the special programme known as the "alternative" scheme?—The alternative scheme.

2255. In the ordinary programme for the sixth class, the programme that is called the literary programme, there is a certain amount of needlework, is there not?—Oh, yes; one hour daily.

2256. But the system that has been adopted in so strongly and generally is a different system from that?—Quite.

2257. It is a system under which a considerable portion of the time of the day is given up to such work as would go on in a work-room?—The work time is doubled, and some portions of the literary programme are omitted altogether.

2258. Professor FitzGerald.—And children who want to do arithmetic, such as shop hands, or those things like, like being taught arithmetic in the schools?—Yes.

2259. Each child likes being taught the things inside in the schools?—Enough to say arithmetic is liked in any case. There is a [illegible] passion for arithmetic apparently in this country; I don't know why; it is not that we have so much money to count!

2260. At any rate those who do want to take up an arithmetical occupation afterwards like to be taught this during their school time?—Yes, they like being taught that to the very last moment.

2261. Then not the educational value of a subject depend largely on how it is taught and not what is taught?—I don't know; I would not say that exactly.

2262. Could not arithmetic be taught so as to have very little educational value?—Certainly. It would not be of much use to a girl to be able to do sums on a slate if she could not calculate mentally the price per yard of four yards of ribbon or lace, when she went shopping.

2263. Most Rev. Dr. Walsh.—At Marlborough-street you have a number of distinct schools on the girls' side of the establishment?—Yes.

2264. Could you explain this statement for me, which I find in an official report, that the children in "No. 1 School" have ample opportunities for industrial work and the results are satisfactory?—I am not so sure about that lately. The last time that I examined them the schools had become very large, and one teacher only was in charge of the industrial instruction of each class, and I don't think that any single teacher is capable of satisfactorily conducting the industrial instruction of seventy children, which is sometimes the number in the class—the work suffered.

2265. What I wished particularly to ask you is, not so much about No. 1 School itself, as about the contrast that is drawn in this report between No. 1 School and the other schools. Do you consider that the girls in the other schools are of a class to whom industrial training would be useful?—Yes, certainly; much more so.

2266. Are they of a poorer or a richer class than those in No. 1 School?—They are generally poorer.

2267. And would not industrial training as a rule be likely to be more useful to girls of the poorer class?—All those small schools have not the alternative scheme.

2268. I am speaking now of these poorer children. It would not strike you that there was anything in the class of children in those smaller schools to unfit them for industrial training, so that industrial training while it would be suitable for the children in No. 1 School, would not be suitable for the children in the poorer schools?—I don't see why it should not be.

2269. Nothing occurs to you that would explain such a statement?—No, I cannot explain it.

2270. Professor FitzGerald.—Do poor children stay in school to as advanced an age as richer children?—It depends upon the districts. If there be anything which they can get to do to earn money they leave at an earlier age.

2271. Therefore it might be that the children in 3rd, 4th and 5th Girls' Schools in Marlborough-street did not stay until they came to the sixth class?—Very likely; but the sixth classes in those small schools are all very small.

2272. Will the girls in No. 1 School be able to attend to stay until the sixth class in greater numbers?—Yes.

2273. Mr. [illegible].—Are you aware that the managers of the Central Model Schools wish to make the alternative scheme optional in those schools?—I was not aware of that.

2274. Most Rev. Dr. Walsh.—Has your class the alternative scheme in carried out in all the Marlborough-street schools?—Yes, at present.

2275. When was it introduced?—About six and a half years ago, I think.

2276. What do you think of this statement:—"Industrial school for sixth class is also carried out in No. 1 female school, but in the smaller schools there is only the usual one hour for plain needlework, there being no sixth class pupils in attendance." I ought to explain to you that I am still quoting from an official report. You said that in all those schools, the special "alternative" programme was followed. Now this official report tells us that in those smaller schools, there are no sixth class pupils in attendance?—There was no sixth class pupil at all in one of the schools I remember.

2277. How then could there be an alternative scheme there?—If there had been any pupils there would have been, but in the previous years there was a small sixth class with one or two girls.

2278. Professor FitzGerald.—But the time table was so arranged that if there be any sixth class they would have had it?—Yes.

2279. Most Rev. Dr. Walsh.—Then, is the statement in this official report correct, that the industrial scheme is carried out in Schools 1 and 3, but not in the smaller schools?—I cannot consider that correct, because I certainly had a couple of pupils from one of those smaller schools last May examination in the alternative scheme.

The Commissioners adjourned.

SIXTH PUBLIC SITTING.—THURSDAY, FEBRUARY 25TH, 1897, AT 11 O'CLOCK, A.M. Feb. 25, 1897.

At the Antient Concert Rooms, Dublin.

Present:—The Right Hon. the EARL of BELMORE, G.C.M.G., in the Chair; His Grace the Most Rev. WILLIAM J. WALSH, D.D.; The Right Hon. C. T. REDINGTON, M.A.; His Honour Judge SHAW, Q.C.; The Right Rev. Monsignor MOLLOY, D.D., D.Sc.; Rev. HENRY EVANS, D.D.; Rev. HAMILTON WILSON, D.D.; W. R. J. MOLLOY, Esq.; and Captain T. B. SHAW; with J. D. DALY, Esq., M.A., Secretary.

Miss A. M. KENNY, Organizing Teacher under the Board of National Education, examined. Miss A. M. Kenny.

2280. CHAIRMAN.—What position do you hold in connection with the National Board of Education?—I am Organizer of National Schools.

2281. But what are the duties that you discharge in that capacity?—My principal duty is to go to the schools and try what weak points are in those schools in the teaching of the different subjects, and then when I have discovered the weak points, to do everything I can to strengthen those points by actual demonstration.

2282. That includes all branches of education?—All branches.

2283. Including needlework?—Yes.

2284. Will you give us your views as regards kindergarten as taught in the Convent schools?—As it is taught at present it is principally in the large Convent schools that it has worked out well. It goes in for training all the senses of the children when it is taught as it is taught in the large Convents. It trains the sight, and the hearing, and the speaking.

2285. Tell me exactly what is done under the head of kindergarten: describe it a little?—The kindergarten is divided into four great headings, and the first heading deals with [illegible], the second with surfaces, the third with lines, the edges of the surfaces, and the fourth with points. Under the heading of the first part, solids, the children are taught form.

2286.—Would you illustrate it?—The first form that is brought under their notice is the sphere, the ball, and they are not exactly told anything; they are not given knowledge directly, but they are led to infer the different points.

2287. Most Rev. Dr. WALSH.—Finding it out for themselves?—Yes; for instance I would not tell a child the ball is round, but I would roll it, and give it to the child to feel it. I would educate it more than teach it. To teach it would be to tell it in a dry way, and the child would repeat that like a parrot; but kindergarten trains the child to think and believe for itself. You give the food for thought.

2288. CHAIRMAN.—After you had had the child under instruction for a little while, would you direct it to show you some round object?—You ask them to look around; you illustrate everything; you have round objects, and you teach nothing you cannot illustrate. You leave nothing to the imagination in the kindergarten. You draw the children out, and get them to think. You aid their thinking by means of these illustrations.

2289. Monsignor MOLLOY.—After the sphere what comes next?—The cylinder. Then I show the points of resemblance and the points of difference between the ball and the cylinder; I do not tell them about them, but let them see them, and then if they find a difficulty in expressing the thoughts that have arisen in them by what they have seen I help them to express them in suitable language. In fact, this first part is more a language lesson than anything else, training children to think and helping them to express their thoughts.

2290. CHAIRMAN.—Will you go on please to the next thing?—After the solids the next thing is the surfaces. After the cylinder will come the cube. Each child is given a cube. The little child feels this cube and feels the surfaces, and is led to see the differences between it and the cylinder, and also the points of resemblance which we can illustrate by means of a perforated cube, and before we leave this gift we get the children to build several little things.

2291. Most Rev. Dr. WALSH.—You have cubes that can be taken to pieces into smaller cubes, and so to pieces that are called bricks?—Yes, and the children like this building very much, and even a small child of 2½ years of age, if you give it a box of these cubes and leave it to itself you will be surprised at the forms it will make. But the way we proceed to teach this building is that the teacher has a box of large cubes and makes forms, and the children imitate her. The powers of imitation are strengthened from the beginning. They are always in a child but not always drawn out. Training the imitative powers in the children is a strong point in kindergarten at the first stage.

2292. CHAIRMAN.—What comes next?—The surfaces. These will come after the solids, and the surface we deal with is the square, and we train the child to perform several exercises with the squares; sometimes the laying of tiles, and by giving the children boxes of these little squares, and leaving them to themselves, they very often form pretty patterns; but we do not ask them in the beginning to do that. We put the patterns before them and then the powers of imitation come again into request, and they have to use their eyes. In the kindergarten we do not deal in educating children with dry facts at all. A great deal of that, as applied in the ordinary schools without kindergarten, has the effect of stupefying the child and preventing the brain increasing in strength. After the surfaces we come to the lines, and it I find is a most useful part of the kindergarten—the edge of the surfaces. That takes in principally drawing, and in order to make this drawing very simple in the beginning, as our children are supposed from three to four years of age to have this elementary drawing, we must take care not to press them too much, or we would only defeat the end for which we are teaching them. We give them little sticks, and get them to draw in relief the pattern we put before them. They have just to use their eyes, and we give them very simple exercises at first, and children are then prepared for drawing with a pencil.

2293. Most Rev. Dr. WALSH.—They lay these sticks so as to form an outline?—They lay these sticks on the desk, and the desks are prepared with little grooves in the form of squares to help the child; and the blackboard is also in squares, so the child has very little mental effort to make. The principal advantage of that is the training of the eye and the hand.

2294. CHAIRMAN.—What they do is to take the bricks and lay them parallel with the squares and make patterns with them?—Yes, my lord, but it is little sticks they take and lay them on the lines that are marked on the desk.

Jan. 23, 1897.

Miss A. M. Kenny.

2295. Do you tell them what to make?—We have a figure to correspond on the blackboard, and they have to use the eye and the hand.

2296. You draw on the blackboard, if I understand you rightly, a rectangular figure of some kind, and tell the child to imitate it, and he, with the sticks, and the help of the grooves in the desk copies that pattern?—Yes, fairly well. That helps also to develop in the child precision and method. The ordinary child will not be inclined to put the sticks in the exact place where he should put them, but when the exercise is properly taught the child is compelled to watch what it doing and concentrate its attention on the point. That helps the child.

2297. Most Rev. Dr. Walsh.—It impresses on them the importance of minute accuracy?—Yes.

2298. Chairman.—What is the youngest age at which a child has intelligence enough to carry on this sort of work?—The kindergarten can be started when he is a few months old, but this drawing with little sticks, when a child is between three and four is one start it.

2299. Monsignor Molloy.—Then the points remain. What do you do with the points?—Stitching and pricking. We teach form. We have little patterns and these patterns represent plants and animals and other objects of interest, and these patterns the children prick out with a sort of pricking needle, thereby learning form. The child will have no idea at all of the shape—say of a donkey. It gets a little pattern with a figure of a donkey drawn on it and the child will prick that out itself. The pattern is drawn in ink, and the child will prick out that pattern, thereby getting the idea of the form, and it also has to attend to precision and method. It must prick into the little dots and nowhere else. The child not trained in kindergarten will be pricking at random; the little kindergarten child will go to the exact spot.

2300. Chairman.—Is the outline dotted out?—Yes; and the child stitches the pattern pricked, and will find very little difficulty in doing it.

2301. Do you find the results satisfactory or otherwise?—As a general rule they are not satisfactory.

2302. Will you enlarge on that, please?—There is one point that often struck me about that, and it is that when the kindergarten is introduced into the school, it seems to go no farther than it did the first year. It remains in a groove. As soon as the teacher comes to a certain point, and prepares the children so as to pass the inspector at the results examination, that point is very seldom gone beyond. That is one reason; the results limit the efforts of the teacher, I find. Another reason is that in some cases, not in all, the inspector who examines for results has very little knowledge of the kindergarten, and he, in his examination, I think, injures the subject.

2303. In what way does he injure it—by not examining far enough?—The teacher may be after getting up the kindergarten just as well as she can, and still the pupils will not pass when the examination comes on. I think it injures the subject a great deal, to have a person examining in it who does not sympathise with it or understand it well. They may have a little idea of it, but not much. I do not think they have sufficient, as a rule. There are some very great exceptions to this, but there are some inspectors that have no sympathy with it nor, I think, sufficient knowledge to enable them to examine in it.

2304. How can that be remedied?—By having only those who understand it thoroughly to examine in it, if that could be done.

2305. Monsignor Molloy.—I suppose it generally happens the examiner himself has not been a teacher of the kindergarten system?—The examiner has never been a teacher of it.

2306. And it would be a great advantage if the examiner had for a time been a teacher?—I do not

part from the children?—He would, but still a person that studies it up thoroughly can examine on it without having ever taught it.

2308. Have you taught it yourself?—Yes, very often.

2309. Don't you think you would examine better than these inspectors?—Yes, but I may be prejudiced in my own favour.

2310. Mr. Molloy.—Where did you learn it?—In the Central Model Schools.

2311. Chairman.—Why is kindergarten not more generally adopted?—Because it takes a good deal of money to start it. The result fee is only two shillings, and that won't pay for the amount of that must be expended during the year so as to have it taught properly.

2312. That is with all the appliances?—All the appliances.

2313. And who finds the appliances?—The teacher generally finds them, and they cost more than the amount gained at the end of the year, and that prevents it being taught as a general thing.

2314. Can you make any suggestion as to further extension of the kindergarten?—I would suggest, my lord, that it should be extended to all schools if possible, and as a means of doing that I would have all teachers trained and taught this kindergarten. Up to this they have not all been. On some occasions I asked teachers "Why did you not go in for this kindergarten when in training?" and I was told, "Well, we were not asked to go in," "We could not sing," or something like that. All the teachers should be made go in for kindergarten when training.

2315. There are a great many teachers who are untrained?—Yes, but these will die out after a while. By taking the supply of teachers at the fountain-head—those who are going in to be trained and those who are untrained—it might be possible in the large centres to have instructions given in kindergarten; but there is one thing that would cause kindergarten to spread: if the fee were doubled—made four shillings instead of two.

2316. What have you to say with regard to kindergarten as a foundation for technical education?—The kindergarten trains the eye and trains the powers of observation, and for these reasons it is very valuable as a foundation for technical education. The children are very well able to work with the hands, and they have a fair idea of drawing and a fair idea of design when they leave the kindergarten classes, and all these things tell on technical education, especially the drawing.

2317. Have you any idea of what the amount of results fees for the kindergarten comes to for the whole year?—I have no idea of that.

2318. Most Rev. Dr. Walsh.—You have given us a very interesting description of how kindergarten should be taught, developing the intelligence of the children. Now, in your experience as an organiser, do you find that it is generally taught in that intelligent and useful way?—I am sorry to say, my lord, that it is not generally taught in that way.

2319. It seems to me to be a thing that might be taught in a way that would merely amuse the children—perhaps keep them from falling asleep, or induce them to go to school, all of which would be very useful—but so as utterly to fail in the real object. Do you think the real object of kindergarten training, as intended by its author, is carried out in the kindergarten teaching as we have it in the schools?—In about half the schools it is carried out with that result, and in the other half it is carried out in a mechanical way.

2320. And that comes, I suppose, in a great measure from want of training in the teachers?—Yes, and from want of having an examiner who will be able to really test how it is taught.

2321. And from a want of appreciation on the part of the teacher of the difference between these two

[illegible]

Feb. 24, 1887. Miss A. M. Kemp.

fixing ?—The fee as it is at present would be sufficient then.

2368. CHAIRMAN.—The present fee would be sufficient if the appliances were bought ?—Yes.

2369. Mr. REDINGTON.—Of course you are aware that the Board does not supply any such things (grants except in model schools ?—I am aware of that.

2370. You are aware that the fee for infants is four shillings in the Infant Department besides the kindergarten fee ?—Yes.

2371. Therefore six shillings would be the fee for each infant in the Infant Department; but you do not think that sufficient; you would like to make it eight shillings ?—Yes, I would; there is a lot of work for it.

2372. Monsignor MOLLOY.—The two shilling fee in the present system is so small it acts as a discouragement in the adoption of the kindergarten system ?—It does.

2373. You think that up to the present the results of the kindergarten system have not been satisfactory ?—Not as a general rule, but in special places they have been satisfactory.

2374. The failure is chiefly due to the manner in which the examination is carried out, the smallness of the fee, and the necessity of providing equipment ?—Yes, those are the three obstacles.

2375. And if those three obstacles were removed you think the kindergarten system might be very widely extended ?—I do.

2376. And would be more satisfactorily carried out ?—Yes.

2377. Could you give me a general idea of the number of children throughout Ireland that at present are getting taught in the kindergarten system ?—I could not.

2378. Mr. MOLLOY.—Touching on that last point, according to the Commissioners' Report for 1885, I find that the number of schools in which examinations took place in kindergarten was 362, and that the number of children examined was 37,360. The results fees came to £1,418 6s. for that year on passes earned by 36,135 pupils out of 37,360 examined. That hardly bears out, I think, what you said a while ago, that the examiners were unsympathetic, if 36,000 pupils passed out of 37,000. I thought you rather conveyed the idea that the inspectors were hostile in some manner ?—Well, some of the older inspectors are.

2379. When you are engaged in organizing schools do you not introduce the kindergarten system where it was not in existence before ?—Very often when the manager wishes.

2380. Have you not an opportunity later on of visiting schools organized by you, and of seeing how the thing is working say after six months or a year ?—Not in all cases; sometimes just by chance.

2381. What has been your experience of it in those cases where you visited it a second time ?—Where I started it I found it always in a flourishing condition when I go back.

2382. You mentioned about the fitting up of the kindergarten room that it would cost £30 or £40 ?—Yes, for a large school.

Well, we have had a diversity of statements. One witness said £300, and another £5.

2383. Monsignor MOLLOY.—What would you mean by a large school ?—A school with an average of about 300.

2384. Most Rev. Dr. WALSH.—You mean among 300 children in the kindergarten department.

2385. Mr. MOLLOY.—You are in favour of some modification of the German system of kindergarten—the Froebel system—so as to apply it in Ireland. You do not carry it out yourself when you are introducing it into the National schools; you do not carry out in extenso the system as taught in Germany ?—I apply it so as to suit our little Irish children. I go in more for the hand work. In Germany part of the kindergarten is to take the children out into the actual gardens. We don't do that here. We give them all the work in the schools.

2386. Would you be able to hand in a paper at your convenience setting out the extent and specific modification of the kindergarten that you think would be applicable to Irish schools ?—Yes.

2387. Are you in favour of extending it beyond the third class of children; it never reaches at present beyond the third class, would you extend it beyond the third class ?—I would.

2388. Of course I take it you would have it in boys' classes as well as girls' classes ?—I would have it in a modified form in the boys' school. If you bring the sewing part of kindergarten into the ordinary boys' school, the boys won't go; they would be insulted.

2389. Right Rev. Monsignor MOLLOY.—The boys of two years old ?—Oh, we don't mind those young fellows, but even at four they would not touch a needle for you.

2390. Mr. MOLLOY.—Then, perhaps in the paper you submit, you will introduce the modification that would suit the boys' schools ?—Yes.

2391. You mentioned a while ago that some teachers in the course of training receive no instruction whatever in the kindergarten system ?—Yes.

2392. Is it during their course in the training colleges ?—During their course in the colleges; I do not know what has occurred for the last year or two, but I frequently met teachers who had been trained, and who told me they had not been taken through kindergarten at all.

2393. But is it not an essential feature in connection with the training colleges that all those undergoing a course of training would attend practising schools, especially the infant schools, without exception ?—They might teach other subjects.

2394. Did you witness the instruction in kindergarten in the infant schools of the training colleges ?—It may be only those who are studying kindergarten who would be brought into that work.

2395. Then you really think in a female training college kindergarten is comparatively neglected ?—It was not extended to all the teachers. I know that some get it, but others would not.

2396. Then a student or a Queen's Scholar might be two years in a training college and go out quite ignorant of kindergarten ?—Yes.

2397. Monsignor MOLLOY.—Was I right in supposing that your principal objection to the examination as now carried out is that the method of examination is not such as to bring out the training of the children in the system ?—Yes.

2398. Rather than that it was too severe ?—No, the first point.

2399. That it does not bring out the training they receive. And you think it would be very desirable to have an improvement in that respect ?—Yes.

2400. Most Rev. Dr. WALSH.—Is it not quite conceivable that they do the mechanical things they are supposed to do; the child might do only that and still pass the results examination ?—Very often.

2401. Captain SHAW.—At what age do the children in Ireland leave kindergarten ?—At eight.

2402. And at what age do they enter it ?—About three in the cities and five or six in the country.

2403. Then they have about three years' kindergarten work ?—Yes, and sometimes four.

2404. But the short sketch you gave us in your evidence was only one year's course ?—Yes, the first year's course for infants.

2405. In this teaching of kindergarten do you bring in any writing ?—No, we have no writing; that belongs to the ordinary literary course.

2406. Do you teach them anything in the way of arithmetic or addition ?—We lay the foundations of arithmetic.

2407. What else do the children in the infant schools do a[illegible] out of kindergarten work ?—Reading, writing, singing, and calisthenics.

2408. Could not all those exercises be combined with kindergarten work ?—More or less.

2409. Woven into each other ?—I always try to

the child would know more, and be better able to receive instruction always who had received kindergarten. The brain would be prepared to work better. [illegible] and Miss A. M. [illegible]

2428. May we take it from you that you consider kindergarten instruction as necessary for the primary education of children?—Yes, it is very necessary.

2429. Do you know what the children do at present in the National schools where there is no kindergarten taught?—Yes, the infants sit all day spelling and reading until they become weary and careless, and some of them sleep over it.

2430. Then most of their time is wasted?—The greater part is wasted.

2431. Rev. Dr. Evans.—How many organisers are there?—Three are here.

2432. That is another and yourself?—Yes.

2433. Is the whole of Ireland divided between those two organisers?—No, doctor, it is not.

2434. That is to say you are not limited to any part of Ireland yourself, you may go to Ulster, Munster, Leinster, or Connaught?—Yes.

2435. Do the observations that you have made to the Commissioners about the working of kindergarten apply equally all over Ireland?—I think so.

2436. You said that in the large Convent schools it was well taught?—Yes.

2437. Now, in other schools than Convent schools are they equally efficient, all over Ireland?—There are very few of the schools all over Ireland, very few of the ordinary National schools with kindergarten, and wherever they have it it is not as good as a rule as it is in these large Convent schools, but there is a reason for that. There is a special nun who has this subject in the Convent, and makes it a study, and has nothing else to think of in connection with the school, and who works at it after hours.

2438. Do you think every trained teacher is capable of teaching kindergarten?—I do, she may not have a natural taste for it, but can acquire it if she has not.

2439. I note that you say "she," you exclude the trained male teachers?—I don't think the trained male teachers can teach kindergarten well to the youngest children.

2440. Would you have them attempt it at all?—Not with the juniors, not until a child would be about nine years of age.

2441. Therefore kindergarten should not be taught in schools that were exclusively under male teachers?—No, I would not like to see it either, I know it would be spoiled, you must have sympathy with kindergarten, or it won't succeed, and these ordinary male teachers have not sympathy of that kind, their hands are in the schools generally.

2442. Would it be possible to teach kindergarten efficiently where there was a workmistress?—Yes, doctor, if she knew it.

2443. Would it be necessary that she should have been trained?—She should have got some instructions in it. She should know the subject well, for if she attempted to teach it without knowing it well she would spoil it. A great number of people do attempt to teach it, and that has put the kindergarten into disrepute in some parts of Ireland.

2444. You mentioned that it was costly at first, and that was a reason why it had not been as successful as otherwise?—Yes.

[illegible]

Feb. 25, 1887.

Miss A. M. Emery.

2450. Would it be taken up cordially if the requisites were supplied to them, say, on cheap terms?—I think it would be taken up cordially in schools where there would be an average for an assistant, but it would not be taken up in the smaller schools for the teacher could not give time to it.

2451. Would it be right to ask you, Miss Emery, do the teachers welcome you to the schools?—They always do.

2452. My reason in putting this question is to ascertain whether they have a wish to introduce into their schools the improved and proper methods which you can teach?—They always do welcome me; but there is this point I would like to mention, when I tell them an improvement according to my lights on their methods, they often say to me, "We taught it in that manner last year, and we got all No. 1 passes, why should we go to this trouble now, we will get no more."

2453. But you believe if an increase of fee were paid, and some help given at the start to provide requisites, that kindergarten would obtain very widely?—Yes, I am sure it would.

2454. And the effect would be very beneficial to the higher classes?—It would.

2455. JUDGE SHAW.—I want to know what exactly is taught by kindergarten to children of three or four, or from that to six, that they would not learn themselves if they were out at play?—This kindergarten is play partly.

2456. It is play inside school instead of play outside?—Yes.

2457. But what would a child in school learn about a sphere that he or she would not learn from having a ball outside playing with it?—On that special point the play inside and outside are identical, very little difference.

2458. But an ordinary child that gets ordinary opportunities of playing, say a child in a rural district, growing up in a farmyard or in a farmer's house and going about the haggard, and seeing what is going on, being sent occasionally for the cows, and so on, would you tell me what he would learn in school under this kindergarten system that he would not learn in his own house?—He would learn a very important thing, language. The ordinary farmer's child is a silent child, and when he has an idea he cannot express it without great trouble.

2459. Do you mean he would be taught in school to call a sphere what he would call at home a ball?—The instructions about the ball will take a wider scope than speaking about the shape of the ball.

2460. Supposing he is handling a ball and playing with it, won't he learn all the qualities of the sphere quite as well as he would in school under your supervision?—He learns it at home in a degree, but he cannot express his ideas; it is a language lesson, where the idea is in the child's head, getting it out in suitable words.

2461. A child of six years of age (you say that it is about that age they commence in the rural schools, and you teach them arithmetic by counting balls), is it not your experience that most children of that age will have learned to count objects before they come to school at all; won't they have counted the cows and the sheep and the goats?—No; these children in the country seem to have been living in a sort of passive state until they come to school, especially in the isolated parts.

2462. Suppose a little boy is sent out to bring in the cows and knows he has a certain number to bring in, he has to bring in six, and only has five, does he not know he has the sixth to look for?—Yes, that is the case.

2463. Is not that all you are supposed to teach in this matter by counting balls?—Counting balls is, I think, one part of it.

2464. CHAIRMAN.—Would not a boy often know, not that a sixth cow was missing, but that he had a cow of a particular colour to bring in?—That is often the case.

2465. Monsignor MOLLOY.—They are taught these things systematically, whereas when left to their own resources they don't learn systematically?—I would attach great importance to that.

2466. Judge SHAW.—In what better way is a child taught accuracy of eye and hand in the kindergarten than if he has a knife to make a boat or to spin a tage top; is he not learning quite as much accuracy of hand and eye as he would in the school?—I don't think he is. Give a boy a knife and a piece of wood to make a boat, and if this boy has not been trained in the kindergarten he will very often cut his fingers; but the boy trained in kindergarten is cautious and knows where to stop, and can gauge distances with his eye.

2467. Is not the cutting of his fingers an important part of his education—to be more cautious next time?—His mother would not think so. I think prevention is better than cure.

2468. A child of the better class is furnished with a great many toys that the poorer children have not, but I want to know what exactly is taught to children of three or four in school that they would not learn quite as well out of school?—The children you refer to—the children of parents that are well off—learn just as much at home. But the great bulk of poor children learn nothing at home; they will sit in a passive way, dead and alive, but the school helps them very much.

2469. Have they not a lot of things to do—are they not sent out to look after cattle and do messages, and a number of things that require intelligence and accuracy?—The kindergarten that they will get in school will help them, because it will be more methodical. The different points will be taken up methodically; the information they might acquire by running about and not going to school would be more of a mixed nature.

2470. Do you really think that a child from three to six is better in school four hours a day than it would be at home? Suppose its surroundings at home are respectable, not vicious, do you really think a child would not be better at home from three to six than going to school four hours a day, learning for half an hour this kindergarten and for three and a half hours learning what they call reading?—I think it is much better in school; it will give it habits of going to school, which will be useful to it, and then it will learn discipline—well, not very strict discipline, but even the little it will learn will be useful to it. Children of that age are generally spoiled at home.

2471. Don't you think these little children you are talking to about that fall asleep over their reading would be better playing outside?—These ones would be who have no kindergarten to help them.

2472. But kindergarten is only half an hour out of the four hours a day?—But its influence extends over the other lessons; for instance, reading will be made interesting. The kindergarten teacher will take advantage of all the information she can give them by reading lessons, and in the counting, addition and subtraction will be made interesting for them.

2473. You would advocate then that all children should be trained in this kindergarten from 3 to 6, or from 3 to 8?—Yes, I would.

2474. And that they would learn from that more than they would learn from the ordinary pursuits of children in their play or in their work outside?—Yes, they would.

2475. Most Rev. Dr. WALSH.—Especially as regards methodical habits?—Methodical habits.

2476. CHAIRMAN.—I think you said that in a good many schools it would take about £30 to provide proper appliances?—Yes.

2477. Within certain limits that would be providing appliances, once for all, for a certain number of years?—Yes.

2478. Supposing you take 10 per cent. as the interest on £30 that would come to £3 a year?—Yes.

2479. If you had a school of sixty children, an additional result fee of one shilling would provide that interest?—Yes, it would.

2480. And therefore it would not require a very enormous sum to provide the appliances?—Not in that case.

2481. I see by the report of the National Board that the results fees for Kindergarten come to about £1,070 a year, roughly?—Yes.

2482. Therefore an addition of 30 per cent. to that sum would provide interest upon outlay, if the National Board were authorised to lay out that sum?—Yes.

2483. It would represent £1,500 a year?—Yes.

2484. Captain SHAW.—There is just one question I would like to ask with reference to the boy playing ball outside and the infant playing with the sphere in the kindergarten, you don't insist on their knowing the technical term "sphere"?—We give them the technical term but don't much care whether they remember it.

2485. But the point is that you draw his attention to the fact that the ball would rest in any position in which it is put and that the dimensions are the same every way, and these are things he would not learn for himself?—Yes.

2486. And this quickens his powers of observation?—Yes.

2487. Then as regards the case of the boy cutting a boat, a boy who has not been taught, if he makes a model boat he works to his own dimensions and cuts at his own sweet will, whereas in the other case he has to work accurately to a certain dimension?—Yes.

2488. Judge SHAW.—Do you mean to say that a boy playing with a ball will not find out for himself that it rolls more easily than a cube?—He won't think about it, he won't notice it.

2489. And that if he wants to send a ball along the ground he can send it further than he can send a cube?—Yes, the ball will go along but he won't notice it unless you draw his attention to it, he will be thinking of something else.

2490. CHAIRMAN.—Supposing the means of providing appliances were found by the public authority of the country, do you think there would be an increase in the number of schools in which kindergarten is taught, bearing in mind that in a great many cases it is not possible to have more than one teacher?—

2497. And then they forget what they had learned themselves?—I don't know that, but they give up teaching drawing.

2498. Is there a difficulty in obtaining the supply of drawing materials?—A great difficulty in the country schools, if children get a pencil it will be a little bit about an inch, and they cannot hold it properly, and they find it hard to buy the copies, which is a great obstacle to the teaching of drawing.

2499. Who provides the copies in rural schools?—The children have to buy them themselves.

2500. What do you say with regard to the means of instructing teachers in drawing?—I think all teachers ought to be taught drawing, they should know drawing just as well as they know writing or else they should not be eligible for their post. And then to reach those teachers who don't know how to draw now, I think if centres were opened in Ireland and have the teachers to gather there on Saturdays, have their expenses paid in from the neighbouring schools into the town, and there show them how to teach drawing, that would be suitable for the older teachers, the young ones would of course be all taught in the training schools. I would have drawing in every school.

2501. Would you think the teacher should receive any extra remuneration for going in to learn drawing?—I think not, because he will get extra remuneration when the results fees would be paid to him, but I would pay the teacher's expenses into these centres.

2502. That would be a difficulty if he lived far from a town?—He might be near to another centre perhaps; I would not take those who lived too far.

2503. What distance from a centre would you take the maximum, the distance a person could walk?—If a teacher could go by rail, a greater distance. If he had to go by car, twenty miles by car; he might go fifty or sixty by rail perhaps.

2504. You would contemplate such a great distance as that?—That would depend on the number of centres; I would have as many as possible, but it is very essential that drawing should be taught.

2505. In some of the evidence we had here it has been suggested that schools should be grouped round centres at much closer distances than that, five or six miles at the outside?—I don't think it would be necessary to have them so near as that, the same effect can be produced if the distances were three [illegible]

Feb. 12, 1897.

Miss A. M. [illegible]

[illegible]

Miss A. M. Kenny.

2519. Mr. Molloy.—How many organising teachers are there?—Two.

2520. Those visit the schools, and introduce, do they not, kindergarten and drawing where those subjects were not taught before?—Yes.

2521. If the number of organising teachers were increased would that meet the difficulty?—The number would want to be very largely increased, and it would take a long time to reach all the schools.

2522. What was the greatest number of female organising teachers ever appointed under the Board?—I don't know that.

2523. I may tell you there were three, and they visited all Ireland, selecting particular centres, and then the teachers within a certain radius from, as a rule, three to five miles, attended their instructions on Saturdays. Now, an extension of that, do you not think, would meet the difficulty?—I think it would.

2524. Especially in the case of the female teachers more advanced in age or those who from domestic circumstances might not be able to come up to the training college?—I think that would meet the case.

2525. Captain Shaw.—What is the least time at present in which drawing may be taught in the school?—There is no minimum defined by rule, but one half-hour a week is generally the least time.

2526. What would you consider the proper time?—Two and a half hours; half an hour a day at least.

2527. Do you think half an hour a day is the best distribution of time for drawing?—I think it is.

2528. Would you prefer to give a longer time on any one day?—I don't like the giving of longer time on any one day, the children get tired, and the latter half hour would be waste.

2529. To complete a drawing in the older standards could you do it in half an hour?—It is not absolutely necessary that they should finish the same pieces in one day.

2530. You think a shorter time is better?—Yes.

2531. I did not quite understand about the difficulty of obtaining drawing materials?—Children find it quite impossible to pay for pencils, copy books and india-rubber.

2532. Is it not looked on as the duty of the manager to provide these things?—The managers cannot very often provide them; he has not the money himself, and he is not able to provide them.

2533. Then in Ireland the providing of these has always fallen on the children themselves?—Yes.

2534. Rev. Dr. Evans.—How many schools do you visit in the year, Miss Kenny?—The average, I think, doctor, is about thirty.

2535. And the other lady about the same?—About the same.

2536. Therefore there are sixty schools visited in a year?—Yes.

2537. Any more?—No, I don't think there is.

2538. The organisers come to the schools on the invitation of the managers?—Yes, always.

2539. And do you think that managers are alive as much as they might be to the importance of this?—I don't think they are.

Rev. Dr. Evans.—I remember a school that [illegible] had been very grateful manifestations of the visit and of the benefit to the school which would lead me to wish that your visits were more frequent.

2541. Judge O'Brien.—Upon the drawing materials, don't the Commissioners supply the drawing copy books and pencils at a cheap rate?—Well, the rate is not very cheap when the material is good.

2542. What is the drawing book, one of Vere Foster's?—They can get one penny or two penny books, so they can get very bad material for a halfpenny.

2543. You can get a good book for one penny or two pence?—Yes.

2544. For what can you get a pencil?—Generally a halfpenny or a penny for a good one.

2545. And you are aware that parents now pay no school fees?—Yes, I know that.

2546. And do you think it is a very great hardship that a parent should be asked to pay a penny for a copybook and a halfpenny for a pencil to have his child taught drawing?—It is not a hardship, but since school fees were abolished the teachers tell me they cannot get a penny from the children for anything. They have almost to pay the children for coming to school. I was organising [illegible] outside Letterkenny last week, the teacher's salary is £20 a year, and she has to supply the children with copy books and everything.

2547. So the result of free education is that it has to be fixed on the children?—Yes, people think they should get everything free.

2548. Mr. Bailey.—Do you make arrangements for the instruction of teachers of the outlying schools on Saturdays?—No, we do not, but it would be a good thing if we were allowed to do so or instructed to do so.

2549. It is not an essential part of the organisation?—No, Mr. Bailey.

2550. Most Rev. Dr. Walsh.—Do you make a distinction between the providing of writing materials and the providing of drawing materials?—Yes.

2551. Who provides the copy books, pens, and ink?—Well the parents provide them, they have an idea [illegible] that writing will come in useful, but even parents think drawing is an accomplishment; they will pay for the copy book for writing but not for the other.

2552. Probably they don't know what is meant by drawing. The only drawing that I ever saw anything of when I was attending was the drawing of [illegible] school [illegible] and that sort of thing, but the drawing that you have in contemplation is drawing of a kind

2631. Do you know the nature of the needlework that is done in them?—Yes.

2632. Is it the same through the schools generally over Ireland?—I think it is about the same, it ought to be about the same, for these teachers who come up have been drafted from the schools around, and they bring up samples of what is done in the different parts.

2633. Is it your opinion that the Queen's scholars after they go out of training are capable of making dresses?—Yes, they are.

2634. And can teach them in schools?—Yes.

2635. CHAIRMAN.—You suggested some other heads. I should like to ask you with regard to cookery; do you think that a cookery lesson should be given in every female school, if at all possible?—I do.

2636. What is the practical difficulty?—The same difficulty that arises in all the other cases, materials; they have nothing to cook.

2637. And have they any means of making the proper fire?—They can make a fire just like what is at home in the house of the child, and that is better than having an elaborate range. If a child learns to cook on a range she is helpless when she goes home. But a potato or a cabbage, or any common thing, is not as a rule cooked well in Ireland.

2638. How do the wives of labouring men learn the small amount of cooking that is necessary?—It is just chance. The ordinary labouring man is fed on tea for his dinner, and bad tea, too.

2639. He has something to eat, I suppose, but that is warm?—Yes; I sometimes see the food he gets, some kind of cake, it is exceedingly heavy. The child in school ought to be taught how to make digestible food, how to make vegetable soup and things that would nourish.

Feb. 28, 1898. Miss A. E. Lacey.

2640. Most Rev. Dr. WALSH.—Is there not a programme for cookery in our system?—Yes, I think there is.

2641. You are acquainted with it?—I am not.

2642. Have you any idea on the subject of teaching cookery to boys?—No, your Grace, I have not thought of that, because I don't think they would cook.

2643. A manager of a large school, the parish priest of a seaport town, was with me yesterday, and he said he thought it a lamentable thing that there was no provision made for teaching cookery to the boys, these boys have to go out on ships and cook for the men, and we know what their cooking must be like: then the want of decently cooked food often sends the fishermen ashore to drink; the boys are the ships' cooks, but there is no provision made in the schools to teach them how to cook?—No.

2644. Don't you think that would be a useful thing to organise next time you go round the seaport towns?—I think it would, but the average boy would not come into the cookery lesson.

2645. But would not the fishing boys come in?—Yes, they might.

Feb. 10, 1887.

Br. P. W. Joyce.

2651. Most Rev. Dr. Walsh.—All five are practising schools?—All five are called practising schools. We determined to confine our class in the first instance to the pupils of the smaller schools, and to those pupils only belonging to the fifth and sixth classes, and we called them together on a certain day. I it was that made the statement to them, and they were told all about it. They were told that they would be shown how to plane and saw and make little boxes and brackets and all that sort of thing, and that they would be supplied with tools, knives, chisels, and saws; that they would be charged nothing for it, and that any boy that wished might join the class. But I took great care not to bring any pressure upon them or to make them understand that we wished them to join. They were simply told that they were to come on a certain day, three or four days off, with an account from their parents as to how they received it, and that any boy that wished to join might join and any boy that did not wish was not forced to join. At the end of three or four days the boys were again called together and it was put to them, and it was very remarkable the response the proposal got. There was something like I should say seventy or eighty actually present on that occasion, and they all to a man joined, with one single exception, and that young fellow held out very sturdily, and said he did not want anything of the kind. He was questioned very gently. I questioned him, and he told me that his father, who, I ascertained, was a police pensioner, did not want anything taught to his son except the ordinary reading, writing, and arithmetic. One of the masters of the smaller schools taught the class; it was taught in the morning between nine and ten, and the boys joined as they came in. This class was carried on four mornings of the week, in two divisions, so that it came to this that each little boy got two lessons per week. The lessons were not more than half an hour long on an average. We had tools supplied by the Commissioners of National Education. As to the materials: the master who taught bought them and sold them to the children. They generally had for a penny or a halfpenny or three halfpence enough for the articles they made, and the master sold these materials without any profit to himself. Then with regard to the mode of instruction: the first thing the children were taught was to measure with a two foot rule, and I may remark that it was rather astonishing, even to me, who had some little experience in these matters, the utter deficiency of the children in the simple matter of measuring; nine out of ten could not measure the length of the table, and they had no idea, however, many of them, of estimating lengths. They were taught to measure. We wished to let the thing be as popular as possible, and each child was, as a matter of fact, allowed to make any article he pleased, and we found that little boxes were a great favourite, little bookcases, and brackets; picture frames also were made, generally speaking, to fit a particular picture. In that way the teaching went on for a very long time, and the boys without question began to attain very considerable facility in the use of tools, many at the beginning not knowing how to use them. I have seen a dozen boys attempting to bore a hole with a gimlet and turning it the wrong way, and I have seen boys who could not bore a hole with an awl or drive a nail, but being put under the instruction of this master, they soon learned to use these tools and attain very considerable proficiency, such as must be of great benefit to them afterwards. We made it a point to inquire from the boys often whether they carried these instructions into their own homes; and we found it had very considerable effect; they practised putting on hinges, making boys, or repairing dog houses. It was impossible not to see that the boys took to this thing wonderfully.

2652. Chairman.—It was popular in that?—Most popular, the most popular of all the subjects taught in the school.

2653. You said you had some observations to make upon the programme?—The observations I have to make are chiefly about the programme for boys, though my observations as applied to the boys, apply more or less to the programme for the men. In the first place I should say there are too many subjects, an unnecessary number.

2654. You are alluding to your own programme?—My own programme. The result of my experience was this that, in the first place, we might have confined it wholly to woodwork and the corresponding little details of woodwork, such as locks and nails, and in the second place, even for the woodwork, we soon began to find out that the programme was too hard, that we had expected more from the boys than they could reasonably perform within the time set apart. We found they really could not be expected to perform these things especially in our class that was so irregularly attended.

2655. Rev. Dr. Wilson.—Are these classes of handicraft still continued?—I have reason to think they are, but I don't profess to know anything about them for the last four years. I have been out of the service for four years.

2656. As long as you were principal they continued to be popular?—Most popular.

2657. And you would advise their continuance at the training colleges?—Certainly, and not only their continuance but their extension.

2658. Captain Shaw.—With regard to the programme do you consider it advisable to lay down a definite programme of manual instruction in wood?—I should make the programme less detailed and more general.

2659. Would you draw their attention to what you wish to attain in the instruction and leave to them the best method of attaining it?—Lay down a programme rather suggestive than in such detail.

2660. Drawing is not made a feature in your programme I think?—In connection with the programme for students in training, drawing comes in but not for the boys. Remember I am finding fault with this programme. It wants reform, and I am not going to pin my faith to every point in it.

2661. Don't you think the drawing should be a definite part of the manual instruction in woodwork?—Certainly.

2662. How would you propose to extend the instruction throughout the country, have you formed any opinion on that?—There are various ways I think in which it might be done, but it must be remembered that one is not always prepared to enter on these very important details offhand. In the first place, I should imagine that it ought to be introduced into all the Commissioners' Model Schools. I believe there is plenty of opportunity for doing that, including the whole of the Central Model Schools, and all the District Model Schools. To my certain knowledge there are several of the Model School teachers who are very well qualified to give instruction in it. But wherever an ordinary teacher was not available, then I think the instruction ought to be given by an intelligent carpenter. It is not a good plan, but it is a better plan than none.

2663. Have you studied the methods of instruction in other countries except Ireland?—No, and even in Ireland I have no experience except in this central establishment.

2664. Most Rev. Dr. Walsh.—And that not for the last four years?—Not for the last four years.

2665. Mr. Molloy.—I think you mentioned that all the young men who were students in training in Marlborough-street received instruction in handicraft?—Everyone, without exception.

2666. How is it that so few of them at the end of their course came forward for examination with a view to a certificate and subsequently introducing that subject into their schools?—I really could not account for that, but I think a very considerable number, at one time at least, came forward and got certificates.

Feb. 22, 1897. Dr. P. W. Joyce.

2667. I have the returns here before me for the last eleven years, I find an average of about 30 came forward, although, as a rule, there were 100 under instruction, 30 were examined, and of the 30, 18 received a certificate. In the year 1895, according to the Commissioners' Report there were only fifteen schools in all Ireland in which the subject was taught? —Yes, I see that.

2668. Would you infer from that that it is not popular with the teachers?—I should imagine it is not popular with the teachers.

2669. Would you attribute portion of that unpopularity to what you have already indicated that the programme was not quite a suitable one?—I hardly think so; I don't think that this handicraft work or Sloyd work is popular among the teachers; I only judge from reading the papers, reading their journals and resolutions, but I have no practical experience.

2670. Since you discovered that this programme would not work, have you ever thought of any modified form of programme for teachers and pupils?—I did not say it would not work, but it is a little difficult, a little too extended, and I think it would be not a very difficult thing to draw up a programme for both students and pupils, but it should be as I have already observed less detailed, allowing a little more freedom of action.

2671. Speaking generally, what would be approximately the cost of starting a handicraft class?—This is a very expensive subject, perhaps more expensive than any other subject whatever. I calculate, in order to set handicraft going in a school, not counting the cost of putting up a building, if there is to be a building put up, that the mere cost of tools and materials in the first instance would be about £1 a pupil, or very near it.

2672. In addition to that cost for plant, so to say, would it not be necessary to have also a separate shed or apartment?—Wherever there is anything like a large class, anything beyond ten, I think it would be most desirable to have a separate apartment, but in case of a small class of four or five, I fancy that it might be carried on in the ordinary school-room, but of course only after school hours or before. I may observe with regard to the unpopularity of this amongst the teachers, that is only speaking generally, there are a great many of the teachers who are in favour of it.

2673. Monsignor Molloy.—Do you think it is desirable to introduce into the primary schools generally throughout Ireland some system of handicraft?—I think it most desirable.

2674. What do you suppose would be the special advantage of teaching handicraft in the schools generally?—In the first place it makes them able to work, that is the plainest and most obvious advantage, at least most obvious to the general public. It makes a young farmer able to mend a gate or cart, or to oil a machine; makes him handy. The direct utility of what he does I put first, not as indicating that it is the most important, or as indicating the reverse, but as being of the most obvious advantage to ordinary people, making a young fellow able to use his hands, which they are not able to do at present as a general rule.

2675. Has it other advantages besides that?—Yes, exact cutting, the saw must be set in the right way, the chisel must be set in the right way, the slightest turn will spoil an article, and in that way it trains the attention and leads to habits of attention and accurate observation. Then it cultivates a sense of form; the slightest distortion in the shape of any of those articles made will be at once detected.

2676. I think you said you considered it should be all cases be combined with drawing?—With very simple drawing in all cases.

2677. Suppose handicraft were to be extended to the schools generally in Ireland, what form of handicraft do you consider most desirable?—Woodwork.

2678. The use of carpenter's tools and the working in wood; why do you think that the best and most convenient form to introduce everywhere?—It is the most universally applicable to ordinary life. And also there are better facilities, perhaps, for introducing it. There is one most important difficulty, that is the (initial) expense; if that expense were got over, I believe it would be very easily introduced.

2679. Now, comparing the programme we have got here with the Sloyd system, which do you consider the most desirable to adopt in Irish schools?—The London School Board have a programme, and I fancy if that were adopted with some modification it would apply to Ireland.

2680. That programme is a modification of Sloyd? —Yes.

2681. You think that would be suitable to Ireland? —Something like a mixture of that and ours: the subjects are in this of ours, and if it were modified in such a way as to bear a resemblance to the London School Board programme, I think a very much improved programme could be made out for our Irish schools.

2682. Of course if handicraft were to be introduced into the National schools it would be necessary in the first instance to make it compulsory in the training colleges?—Well, it is, or was, practically compulsory in the Marlborough-street Training College.

2683. But not in the others?—If I don't mistake they teach it in the Church of Ireland Training College. I don't know that they have it in St. Patrick's College, but I am not speaking from book. I should certainly make it compulsory in every male training college.

2684. Most Rev. Dr. Walsh.—Do you think that this existing programme contains those points that we may regard as the essential and distinctive features of the Sloyd system as now understood?—It contains everything essential, there is scarcely a point in the present Sloyd system that is not anticipated in this. In laying down this programme, that educational view that is now forming so important a part of Sloyd was hardly kept in view, in fact we hardly knew anything about it.

2685. The object of this programme of yours was rather to teach them trade operations?—Yes.

2686. Not so much to teach the principles on which the trade was conducted; that point was lost sight of, or perhaps not adverted to?—It was not adverted to.

2687. Is it not strange that so very obvious a principle was not adverted to in the drawing up of the programme?—What principle, your grace?

2688. The principle of dealing rather with the educational aspect of this branch, giving the children

Feb. 25, 1898.
Dr. P. W. Joyce.

this programme, let there be no misunderstanding about it; they are not your own words, and they were not written in 1896; they have been sent down to us from the [illegible] of the National Board. The Fourth Annual Report of the Commissioners for 1837 announced to the public that the Commissioners had it in view to establish in Marlborough-street a department for scientific instruction, to teach the particular [illegible] branches of science which have a practical application to husbandry and handicraft, and there is much of it [illegible] in the same [illegible]. I have just [illegible] quoted for you, "Our object is not to teach trades, "but to facilitate the learning of them by explaining "the principles upon which they depend, and habituat- "ing young persons to experience in the use of their "hands." Having then all this laid down laid down by the Commissioners in 1837, is it not an extraordinary thing that the new programme of handicraft was introduced in 1896 upon very different lines?—Well, we had to be very cautious about introducing the theory and keep the practical and useful to the front.

2701. I thought you said that this other view, the educational view that had been so definitely formulated in 1837, was not even adverted to?—The main thing was to teach the children to perform all these operations; but of course anyone can see that it would be impossible for children to be taught to measure, for instance, or to frame things according to certain angles and forms without educational advantages; it is perfectly obvious that, unforeseen, that there must be an educational effect produced. That we knew, but we did not keep it to the front, though knowing it underlay the work.

2702. So then, in this revised programme of yours the educational aspect is not kept to the front?—No; it is not stated.

2703. Don't you think it is desirable that in a system of handicraft in Primary Schools the educational aspect should be kept to the front?—Most important.

examined before a Royal Commission in England told the Commissioners that this was what the boys had been engaged in, constructing a relief Map of Ireland, which I believe is now in the Museum at Kildare-street. Is that a desirable sort of thing to go on under the name of handicraft in the Primary Schools?—I should prefer the boys should be confined to woodwork.

2705. A relief Map is plainly a thing that could not be made by an individual pupil?—No. But I am afraid it was the teacher that constructed the greater part of it himself.

2706. When was that relief Map made?—In 1883 or 1884.

2707. Was it not made during the very period of the operation of this handicraft system that you have described to us as introduced there about 1883?—I think so.

2708. That is the way in which the principles of handicraft were then applied in the Model School in Marlborough-street?—During the construction of this map the ordinary handicraft teaching went on regularly, this relief map was, as a matter of fact, constructed under the same master who taught the handicraft schools, assisted by a number of boys. I saw them working every day with sprues in [illegible] of the room of [illegible].

2709. I take it you would not recommend that anything of the kind should go on now under any new system?—I don't think so.

2710. CHAIRMAN.—Now we will come to drawing. Will you give us your opinion on the subject of drawing?—Drawing is a [illegible] I don't profess to know much about, but the one point I wish to emphasise is the importance of making object-drawing absolutely compulsory wherever drawing is taught at all, drawing from the real object, drawing a book, or hat, or jug, or ink bottle.

2711. In the Swedish system [illegible], in Sweden and Norway, and in all the Continental countries, as far as I can learn from books, that principle is kept

SEVENTH PUBLIC SITTING.—FRIDAY, FEBRUARY 26TH, 1897, AT 3 O'C., P.M.

At the Antient Concert Rooms, Dublin.

PRESENT:—The Right Hon. the EARL of BELMORE, G.C.M.G., in the Chair; His Grace the Most Rev. WILLIAM J. WALSH, D.D.; The Right Hon. C. T. REDINGTON, M.A.; His Honour Judge SHAW, Q.C.; The Right Rev. Monsignor MOLLOY, D.D., D.SC.; Rev. HENRY EVANS, D.D.; Rev. HAMILTON WILSON, D.D.; Professor G. F. FITZGERALD, F.T.C.D.; W. R. J. MOLLOY, Esq.; and Captain T. B. SHAW;

with J. D. DALY, Esq., M.A., Secretary.

P. W. JOYCE, LL.D., further examined.

The Witness.—My lord, I would ask your lordship's permission to make one observation personally to myself; I have given a pretty strong denunciation of the results system and its defects, and I wish it to be understood that these observations of mine are not made in any captious or faultfinding spirit. We were all in fault. We thought it would turn out a blessing, and it is very much the reverse, and I am of opinion that no reformation can be made in the National system, either literary or general, until the results system is completely abolished and another system put in its place.

3741–3. Now coming on to kindergarten?—As to the description of kindergarten, I have nothing further to say than what is already in my memorandum.

3744. Chairman.—"Objects and Methods," I think, is the first special heading. Can you give us any observations upon "Objects and Methods"?—It is very much the same as objects and methods of the higher classes. The object of kindergarten is to train the children to accuracy of eye, accuracy of hand, methodical habits, and the correct use of the English language.

3745. Before you pass from that, I don't quite follow you as to how it affects the use of the English language. Tell me how? What is in your mind?—It was one of the main methods of the founder of kindergarten, that whenever a lesson is given there is a regular conversational lesson carried on. The teachers question the children. The children answer, and with the teacher—it is her duty—there is the greatest possible care taken of the pronunciation of the children. There are enunciations of consonants and vowels and the correct use of expressions, the children all the time using their own simple dialect. This teaching of kindergarten goes on from week to week and year to year; and the linguistic training is continued, and has an important effect on the education of the children in the use of the English tongue.

3746. It is of advantage to check the child if it uses bad grammar?—Certainly, if it is glaringly bad grammar.

3747. The reason I ask the question is that we had in evidence from somebody the other day, that although the teachers are supposed to know what is good grammar, yet in their conversations, when they are out in the performance of their duty, their own grammar is faulty?—It is quite unnecessary in teaching the correct use of language to children, to refer to technical grammar. As a matter of fact teachers do not refer to technical grammar in teaching children be paid to the strict accuracy specially with regard to eye- or star a small inaccuracy is teacher's and the children's eyes. e children's work consists the hand and eye training. If the and do it inaccurately, there is bit of a very bad kind, so that could make it that the thing ... stringently.

... what the Froebel kinder- kindergarten included a very merely hand work. It included religious training of children, not be introduced into Ireland, ligious instruction. It included ... and their religious training the word.

... ing to that system of kinder- ... you think could be usefully which is not done already? ... of kindergarten that could has been introduced into ... ight to remark that I really the schools except so far as to experience has been entirely ... as it has been taught in the and there I was a close ob- ... effects. I was an examiner

...fied with the results?—Satis- ... doubt, in the Central Model well taught. Kindergarten is ... of manual instruction. You ... then advance to a little more the children of the second and you go up to the manual work ... handicraft, or Sloyd as we ...

—At what age would you ...?—As soon as the children ... years of age.

... that is a proper age at which ... to school?—Among many ... ill regulated as they are, the at school than they are at ... of age.

... could you continue kindergar- ... second class, and then with ... I should cease to call it kin- ... simple form of Sloyd.

... distinctive difference between ...?—I don't know that there ... Sloyd you begin to take the is not put into the hands of

... knives in kindergarten?—No;

... the essential parts of Sloyd is —It is one of the essentials, ... other so gradually that you line of demarcation. There Sloyd, card board and simple ... would catch the second and ... in the higher form, for the classes, but there is no regular nothing like the climates of the ...lly into one from the other.

... ordinary age at which children ... go into the kindergarten ... I have no experience except ... schools, and there we found one ... of age.

... when they get to the stage at ... be known as Sloyd instead ... as they get into the third about eleven. I am not going ... of those figures.

... continue kindergarten from ... until they go into the third class, whatever age that was?—Yes, that is the present rule of the National Board, and I think I should on the whole be disposed to drop the name kindergarten as soon as they get to the Second Book, and give it the name of Sloyd. Mr. ... and Dr. P. W. Joyce.

3762. As I understand you, at a very early age, from three until about six, you regard kindergarten as simply a substitute for home training, the training a child would get in the better class of families?—The training a child would get or ought to get in its home, but never gets in that systematic way, for parents, no matter what is their position, cannot devote themselves systematically to these things.

3763. I understand you to say you would not send your own child to school at that age?—That is a question of private opinion.

3764. It is your opinion that we want to get. You would prefer a child from three to six to be kept at home and under home influences?—I think on the whole I should prefer to keep my child in my own individual home up to four or five years of age. After that I should begin to send it to school. I ought to observe about that, my opinion on this point would be greatly modified by the fact that there was an infant school near me. I am not sure that I should not send my child at three years of age to an infant school if it happened to be near.

3765. But you think that where children have not decent homes, or their surroundings are not very good, you would rather have them at school?—Yes, in the great majority of cases—99 out of a 100—I would rather have them at school, if a school could be got. But it is not very easy to get a school for a child at three years of age. It must be near home.

3766. I understand you proposed a modified Froebel system in regard to this country?—I think this modification I suggest——

3767. That only in reference to religious instruction. Is that the only modification you are suggesting?—In all countries Froebel's original system has been greatly modified.

3768. I only want to know what modification you would suggest, from your experience, in its application to this country?—I don't see any modification necessary further than that to which Froebel's system has been subjected in all countries. He taught kindergarten until six years, and nothing else, then he would have kindergarten altogether and begin teaching reading, writing, and arithmetic. We have modified that.

3769. That is to say you would keep kindergarten and the ordinary instruction of reading, writing, and arithmetic going on concurrently?—Almost from the beginning.

3770. Rev. Dr. Evans.—How long were you professor?—I was appointed in '74, and continued to be professor until the last day of my service in '93, nineteen years.

3771. How many years of that period were you Principal of the Training College?—About three.

3772. Now, is kindergarten taught in all the classes in the Central Model School?—No; it is only taught in the infant schools; there are two infant schools, a large infant school and a branch, the branch being kept mainly as a model of what a small infant school ought to be.

3773. So that out of the ten schools there it is taught in two?—In two.

3774. The other schools afford no illustration or example of the teaching of kindergarten?—None whatever, but it may be observed with regard to the other schools that there are few infants in them.

3775. So that there is very little opportunity of teaching kindergarten in the female schools. Now will you kindly tell me if, during the years you were professor, and in which you had the management of the schools and therefore control over the teaching of kindergarten, you made any recommendation of the changes you have now mentioned to the Commission?—The changes that I now mention about kindergarten, or the position kindergarten would occupy if these changes were carried out, that position kindergarten has occupied, as long as I remember, in the Central Model Schools.

3776. You have written a book which is of much value in relation to school management?—Yes, I have written a book, but as to its being of much value——

3777. Have you in that book set forth the recommendation of the changes that you mention here to-day?—What changes, may I ask?

3778. The changes you have mentioned; that is, you would not call it kindergarten in the second class, but you would call it Sloyd?—We could not do it, because the rules of the Board would not permit it. There is no such thing as Sloyd in the Board's programme. The Board has laid down a results programme for kindergarten, which extends to the first, second and third classes for infants, and we could not alter it because we should alter the rules of the Board.

3779. CHAIRMAN.—I suppose the rules of the Board could be altered. Do you suggest that they could be altered advantageously in that particular?—If they required alteration. I don't attach much importance to a name.

3780. REV. DR. EVANS.—You were examiner in kindergarten?—I was examiner. May I observe that the four professors examined these schools, and we made a rough division of labour, and it fell to my lot to examine in kindergarten, as my tastes lay in that direction.

3781. Did you make any report to the Commissioners?—The ordinary official report.

3782. Did you offer any suggestions as to the improvement of kindergarten, and how it ought to be improved?—There was no need for our offering our personal opinions, for the teaching was quite satisfactory. Perhaps in some of our reports we may have found fault with some of the operations of kindergarten. That is going back for several years. If we found fault we expressed it, and no doubt gave suggestions for the correction of it. I should not like to go into that detail for the past twenty-four years.

3783. REV. DR. WILSON.—Have you any other great objection to the results system beyond that it destroys the power of thinking?—If I were to think about it and write about it, I think I should make other indictments against it, but I think the one item, that it destroys the power of thinking of children, is enough argument to sweep it off the face of the earth.

3784. Then you believe it would be for the interests of education to have done with the results system?—Certainly, and revert to the system before results were introduced—examination by classes.

3785. JUDGE SHAW.—Did you find any such result as want of intelligence before the results system was introduced?—Certainly not. I remember the pupils in the National Schools before the results system was introduced, and I venture to say I would get no such replies as those I gave instances of in the schools of Ireland now. In fact I read some English Inspector's report of similar answers of that kind, and I came to the conclusion that the examiner was exaggerating, or we had brighter children in Ireland; but I have changed my opinion since the results system was introduced, and I have come to the conclusion

...read being high, and I don't think it was a very unnatural answer which he gave. I think if I had been that child, and reared in the surroundings of that child, it might have occurred to me as a natural answer.

Witness.—May I make one reply. I take it that if a word has several meanings, and that a child fails to apply the special meaning to the special passage, that is a total failure of understanding the passage.

3788. MONSIGNOR MOLLOY.—I think you said yourself you could not understand that passage unless you got time for consideration?—You asked me as a joke, and my answer was a joke; I came here to be examined on some useful matters, and I do not want to stand a competitive examination. I decline to answer Dr. Molloy's question.

3789. CAPTAIN SHAW.—Are the Inspectors at liberty to ask such questions at the examinations as you asked?—It is entirely the fault of the results system, and is not the fault of the teachers or the children; but in your system in England precisely the same process was observed. Your Teachers' Union recommended its abolition, and it has been abolished for precisely the same reason as I have given you.

3790. Have you taught any form of Sloyd or kindergarten in any other classes beyond the infant classes under your own management? Have you seen it taught or is it taught in Ireland?—I don't know. I don't think it is. I have no experience outside the Central Model Schools. They teach handicraft in certain classes in the Central Model Schools. This is the only manual training the boys get except the usual subjects, drawing and writing.

3791. You recommended the programme of the London School Board should be adopted in Ireland for manual work?—I don't propose that the programme of the London School Board should be adopted in its entirety, but I mean when compared with our programme a good practical programme, suitable to Ireland, could be made by a union of both.

3792. What do you understand by the London School Board programme? Have they laid down a definite programme for manual instruction?—They have in their last report. I have it. They don't call it Sloyd and they don't call it handicraft, but they lay down a programme not so definite as ours. Ours I consider too definite and detailed.

3793. Could you let us have a copy of that programme?—Yes, certainly. What I call the last is for the year '93. I think it is very likely there is a new report out now.

Mr. MOLLOY.—No; it is in the hands of the printers.

The Witness.—It is a very instructive report. Evidently these programmes have been drawn up by thoughtful, practical men, and would be very useful for us.

3794. Mr. MOLLOY.—Reverting for a moment to the statement about the results system, of course you are aware that you can have in certain branches class examination under the results system. All the infants may be examined simultaneously?—Yes.

3795. And again, apart from the branches or portions of branches that carry results fees, you can have class examination in, say, explanation of the subject matter?—That is under what we call the subordinate heading, but I am afraid it is very insufficient in its action. At least I found that in the exami-

...ave is any exam-
...ce, you are like a
...d retriever never to
...otice of that. A
...r cause too much
...rs from acting or
...the illustration, I
...l in a wholesome

[illegible] pro-
duce certain results. He flings himself just over the threshold of a pass, and once there there is no further trouble.

2512. But if a child did not pass unless it knew the meaning, then the teacher would ask the meaning?—Yes.

2513. Therefore you could retain the results system

Feb. 26, 1897. Dr. P. W. Joyce.

apply to all candidates at examinations from the infants of three up to the divinity student and up to the mathematical student, and, if I may take the liberty of observing, up to the student of your own subject, Physics.

2827. Monsignor Molloy.—Here are the rules for results examinations under the National Board of Education, and in the fourth class there is "(a) To read with ease and correctness Lessons, fourth book. (b) To be acquainted with the meaning of the words and phrases, and also the subject matter of the lessons read." Will you explain how under these rules and regulations the results system prevents a teacher from asking questions as to the meaning of words?—Perhaps you are not aware that under "a" and "b" there is a different mode of marking for each. Under head "a" each child has a mark, 1 or 2 or 3, pass or no pass; but under head "b" each child is not marked, but there is a general statement as to whether the answering is good, bad, or indifferent, in the long column, so that the child is not brought to account for this thing but the whole class in general.

2828. Chairman.—Who made this rule that there should be a different mode of marking? The Commissioners?—Yes. They are marked individually under "a," but they are not marked individually under "b."

2829. Monsignor Molloy.—Taking that rule, and accepting your interpretation of it, does it not show that the defect is in the method of examination, and in the marking, and not necessarily in the system of results fees?—Certainly not. Eighty-four inspectors cannot fall into a vicious mode of examination, and 11,000 teachers cannot fall into a vicious mode of teaching except under an overpowering system. I am not going to explain how it is that the results system has come to produce this total absence of thought, but I know that this absence of thought is there. If a man breaks his leg in a railway collision the broken leg is there; and I don't think it counts in one jot if he is unable to explain how it occurred. In the results system we have a total absence of thought. The total absence of thought is there like the man's broken leg, and it no more mends the results system that we are unable to explain how it occurs than it mends the man's leg that he is unable to explain how it occurred in the collision.

2830. Have you considered the application of the results system in the matter of handicraft?—My objection applies all round in every subject.

2831. Your objection is to the results system as it has hitherto been carried out by the National Board?—Yes.

2832. And it does not apply to a system which would be free from those objections that you make to the present system?—Certainly. I have no objection to a results system that allows children's intelligence free play and allows the teachers' mode of teaching free play, but at present there is neither free play in teaching nor free play of the children's minds.

2833. Most Rev. Dr. Walsh.—Take that rule that Dr. Molloy has read for you—"Fourth Class Reading. (a) To read with ease and correctness the Lessons of the Fourth Book. (b) To be acquainted with the meaning of the words and phrases." Now, I understand you to say that under the results system children are able to read those lessons in some sort of way, but they are not made acquainted with the meaning of the words and phrases?—That precisely is the fact.

2834. Is it not the fact that the fees—the money paid to the teacher is merely for teaching what is under letter "a"?—That is the fact.

2835. Is the teacher paid the results fee for the child simply for the answering under letter "a," without any reference to the answering under letter "b"?—Mainly I should say; as much as that is the answer, the application mainly.

2836. I understand from a former answer of yours said that a child is marked "pass" if it passes in what is under head "a"?—Yes.

2837. When a child is marked "pass" will the fee be paid to the teacher?—Yes.

2838. Without reference to whether the child passes in "b"?—The whole class is taken in lump, and if the general class answers badly, a percentage, in the Office, taken off from the class.

2839. But the answering of the particular child will not be affected by anything that comes under head "b"?—It will not be affected at all.

2840. Would you consider it an improvement to abolish that distinction between "a" and "b," and make the pass dependent not only on the child knowing the lesson but also on his being acquainted with the meaning of the words and phrases?—It would be an improvement, no doubt.

2841. Would the results system with that alteration be destructive of the power of thinking?—I think that individual examination and payment by results will be more or less injurious to the power of thinking as long as it is retained.

2842. You have not answered my question?—I have answered your Grace's question.

2843. Excuse me, you have not. First I ask you do you consider that what I have described would be an improvement?—It would unquestionably.

2844. I ask you then would the system with that modification be, as far as this subject is concerned, destructive of the power of thinking?—I think it would be injurious to the power of thinking to some individuals in any case.

2845. Requiring children "to be acquainted with the meaning of words and phrases" would be injurious to the power of thinking?—As long as there is individual examination I think the power of thinking would not have fair play.

2846. How do you think it is injurious to the power of thinking to require children "to be acquainted with the meaning of words and phrases"?—Oh! no I don't think so.

2847. Then you don't think it would be destructive of the power of thinking?—I should not like to say it would not be destructive.

2848. You are first saying it and then unsaying it. Will you kindly let me know what it is you wish definitely to say on this subject? Would it be an improvement if this distinction between "a" and "b" were abolished?—It would.

2849. And to have the pass made dependent on children having an acquaintance with the meaning of words and phrases?—It would be an improvement.

2850. Would that requirement be destructive of the power of thinking?—I can't say until we have had experience.

2851. Would it be possible for the children to be acquainted with the meaning of words and phrases in the subject matter of what they read if they did not think?—Certainly not. I may observe with regard to that that I remember well at a Conference many years ago certain members of the Conference proposed what your Grace has suggested.

2852. Kindly explain to the Commissioners what is meant by the Conference?—A conference of the chief officers of the Board, of which the professors formed part.

2853. I think it may be well now to mention to you that this very important change that I have described to you, and that I find you are in favour of, has been made in the rules?—That must have occurred since I left the Board.

2854. Quite recently in connection with the new programme, and it is important to know that you consider it an improvement, but I don't think the teachers will be so well pleased with it?—I may observe that one of the main arguments against the adoption of the rule was that it would be a very troublesome business for the inspectors in these examinations.

2855. Chairman.—Is that any reason why it should not be done?—Certainly not.

...d believe you are a professor
...ry and geography in the Baggot-
...ge ?—Yes, my lord.

Dr. Walsh.—Lord Belmore
...few general questions to you.
This may save some time
...r of it. Will you kindly ex-
...t street Training College is ?—
...raining College is a college in-
...ing of female teachers. Candi-
...e teachers who are already in
...from those who intend to take
...ds as a profession, so that we
...two classes, those who have
...ow in teaching, and those who
...come in for a two years' course,
...are in for a one year's course.
...eachers come in for one year's
...didates come in for two years'

...ceived in the college and then
...ed ?—Yes.
...now a professor in the College.
...of students ?—We have 150 ai
...ty-eight are candidates in their
...at quite more of the remaining
...roughly in.
...an explain to the Commission
...ation pursued with the students
...regard to kindergarten ?—The
...partly theoretical and partly
...dergarten classes must twice an
...r instruction in principles and
...ho day they are taken by the
...ess is myself, to the practising
...with the college, and they there
...at they have been taught in
...o during the whole of the one year
...dergarten instruction, which is
...ng in the first year of training, in
...ply trained in the principles of

...n practice ?—No; because they
...nd year. The second year will
...e and principles.
...t in saying that in the case of
...ere they have instruction only
...but students who have yet to
...ve instruction for two years ?—
...he Commissioners will not allow
...in training for more than one

Malley.—Teachers already in

—Is there any other remark you
...he system of instruction ?—Well,
...I wish to say.
...tell us how certificates of pro-
...?—By passing simply a written
...riven out by one of the Board's
...ficers in the subject, sign the
...actical part for trained teachers.
...nts have been with me in the
...ater part of the year practising
...taught, and therefore I can sup-
...of their capacities as teachers.
...ve your certificate from your
...rk of each individual, or do you
...ourse of practical instruction is
...them through a practical course.

2469. Will you give us your opinion of the advantages of kindergarten under these two heads, first, as affecting infant school teaching of the ordinary elementary subjects, and afterwards as affording a basis for subsequent technical training ?—As affecting the teaching of ordinary elementary subjects in infants schools, I think kindergarten is most useful because it trains the teacher to make regular object lessons of what would otherwise be purely abstract subjects, reading, writing, and arithmetic. The ordinary subjects of the elementary schools in the case of the kindergarten become more or less object lessons if the lessons has her lessons properly and carries out the principles of the system.

2470. Would you tell us how she carries these into practice ?—Applied for example to writing, which is an ordinary school subject, the kindergarten child has been taught to observe the form of the lines, to accurately hold something in its hands, and to place them in a definite position. Now all these things are necessary in writing. If a child is learning to form a letter, say the letter "A," there is a definite position in which to hold the pencil, and there is a definite direction in which to make the lines. In other words writing is simply an extension of kindergarten drawing in a kindergarten school.

2471. Then as regards the second head as affording a basis for subsequent technical training ?—The training of the eye to intelligent perception, and the training of the hand to accuracy and precision of movement, all these form in themselves a general preparation for technical training. Then there are particular "gifts" which lead more directly to it than others. We have a child trained to draw ; to observe the form in the first instance, and to draw this form, to fold a paper, to weave, to plait, to model, and all these things are an excellent basis for technical training.

2472. Do you teach anything in connection with weaving ?—Yes ; paper weaving, it is one of the "gifts" of kindergarten.

2473. Do you think the extension of the kindergarten system is advisable ?—Yes, my lord, I think so.

2474. I suppose there are objections to the system. Have you any remarks to make upon them ?—Some say the system is too mechanical, others say it is simply play and that children can play as well outside. Then there are the objections of expense.

2475. Have you any suggestion to make as to how the expense could be got over. Would an increase of the fees meet them ?—I think there might be an initial grant to enable the teacher or manager to start the kindergarten, and after that I think it would be easy to manage a kindergarten, as far as expense goes. It would not take very much to start kindergarten in small schools, nor in large schools.

2476. Do you think kindergarten could be started in the ordinary National Schools through Ireland ?—I think so.

2477. Do you think there would be a sufficient number of children to enable a proper staff to give time to it ?—I think so. In an ordinary country school with an average of sixty pupils, thirty of those children would be in the lower classes, all subjects for kindergarten teaching.

2478. In a school of sixty would there be more than one teacher ?—Not under the present system.

2479. Could the workmistress teach kindergarten, do you think ?—Yes, quite well, if she had been

Feb. 15, 1897.

Miss M. Daly.

course with the teachers, I have not seen any of the work, and I was not long enough in the College to have had experience of it.

2881. Do the teachers as a rule appreciate the value of the teaching while they are going through it?—They do, very much. They become quite enthusiastic.

2882. Would that be almost without exception?—Yes, every class.

2883. The system may be modified to a great extent so as to conform it to other subjects?—Quite so, very much modified. Of course the present programme would afford such a modification of the system.

2884. As long as the principles of the teaching are observed the actual changes need does not make much difference?—No, so long as the principle is understood and carried out.

2885. Mr. Mahaffy.—Do all the students in training at Baggot-street receive instruction in kindergarten?—No, not all. It is what we call an optional subject. There are a certain number of subjects that the teachers may take or may not take, as they wish.

2886. Speaking generally, you have about 150 students under instruction every year?—Yes.

2887. What proportion of that number received instruction in kindergarten?—Well, take the present year as an example. I have a kindergarten class going in for certificates, which consists of twenty-eight at present, and then I have first year's students numbering fifty-eight, that is to say, those who have entered upon the new programme which makes it compulsory.

2888. So that as a matter it is between eighty and ninety?—At present, but it is only this year we have such a number, and it is because of the new programme.

2889. If I mistake not, the College has been in existence about fourteen years?—Yes.

2890. You are the third professor of kindergarten in it?—Yes.

2891. Your predecessors had been trained there, and you have been trained there as well?—Quite so.

2892. If I mistake not the first professor of kindergarten was a lady specially selected from the Notre Dame College, Liverpool?—Yes.

2893. And her qualification in kindergarten was the essential feature of her appointment?—Quite so.

2894. Have you turned your attention to any modification of kindergarten, so as to dovetail it into the ordinary school course—any adaptation that would make it more useful in its application. Do you mean extending it beyond the infant classes?

2895. Extending it beyond the infant classes?—Yes, I think in this way it might be done. For instance there is a great deal of drawing taught in kindergarten that might be turned to beneficial effect when we come to the higher schools by continuing it too, whereas now it is dropped for a whole year. Then one subject is most important, that is the teaching of cutting garments. Children in kindergarten are taught to cut out. It might be taught as a step beyond kindergarten to draw out and cut garments in the higher classes.

2896. You have not put these thoughts on paper so that you could favour the Commissioners with your views?—I have not so far done it.

2897. Would you find it inconvenient to do so?—Not at all.

2898. Professor Fitzgerald.—Is the form of mechanical drawing taught in kindergarten, drawing with rulers?—No, the children have chequered paper which is used as a basis for kindergarten drawing.

2899. Here in the syllabus for instruction in drawing in each of the classes of the first standard, is "drawing, free-hand and with ruler," so as to lead to technical drawing afterwards?—That would come in with the third class drawing; it would not come in with the kindergarten proper.

2900. Is the art side of drawing cultivated at all, that is colouring and so on?—Yes, children for instance are trained to use small crayons, so colour is introduced in that way. If they are sufficiently advanced and show natural capacity for it they are allowed a little water colour, but of course they are very minor children.

2901. Are infant boys admitted here?—Yes, infant boys and girls.

2902. Are the infant boys taught needlework?—Yes, stitching and sewing.

2903. Mr. Thompson.—Are you aware that at present a fee is not paid for kindergarten unless there is an organised infant school or infant department?—Yes.

2904. Do you see any difficulty in teaching it to a small number of infants, say five or six?—Well, it would absorb too much time in proportion to the important classes if there were, but five or six in an average school of sixty.

2905. Take a school of sixty—all six were in the infant class, and if there were a second teacher in the school, could it be carried out?—Yes, decidedly.

2906. Would a monitor be capable of teaching it?—Occasionally, if there was careful supervision, because kindergarten requires careful teaching as it loses its value so much.

2907. It is as difficult to teach kindergarten well as to teach any other subject well?—Infant school teaching is more difficult than teaching senior pupils.

2908. Would you be in favour of allowing fees to be paid for kindergarten teaching in schools where there was a second teacher, or a monitor, if the monitor understood how to teach the subject?—Yes, I would.

2909. Do you think it desirable to extend the teaching of kindergarten by such an alteration of our rules?—I think so.

2910. Chairman.—I want to ask you one question. You said that infant teaching is more difficult than teaching older children. Now, in a large school where there are many teachers, would the more experienced people perform the duty of teaching the infants rather than the older children?—Well, if not, they ought to be, because the teaching of the infant department requires more natural tact for teaching on the part of the teacher.

2911. Then it requires some facility for impressing your own ideas on the mind of the child?—Yes.

2912. Professor Fitzgerald.—May I ask whether kindergarten occupations, even though the children amuse themselves with them, would not be better than leaving the children idle in the way that children are often left?—Very much better.

2913. Mr. Redmond.—How long should the kindergarten lesson last?—It depends upon the class of children. For children from three to five years of age not more than twenty minutes; but there ought to be at least two kindergarten lessons a day in the infant school.

2914. With a break between?—Yes.

2915. Most Rev. Dr. Walsh.—You have a very large infant school in Baggot-street?—We have a very large one.

2916. About how many?—An average of about three hundred. At present they are low on account of the sickness amongst the children in the city.

2917. How many are getting instruction in kindergarten at present?—Every child in the infant school.

2918. How many days in the week is it taught by the ordinary teachers of the school, and how many days by the special scholars under your supervision?—One day in the week for an hour and a half I and my students go to the schools, and every other day of the week, and for the remaining portion of the day I am there, it is in charge of a [illegible] and her assistants.

2919. For how long is the teaching going on at kindergarten?—It is going on continuously. When one class finishes, another takes its place, and it is alternated with the elementary subjects.

2920. How long does it last for each set of children?—Half-an-hour.

Jan. 28, 1897. Miss E. Gray

2921. Then they are in a separate room?—Yes, your Grace.

2922. Mr. Redington.—Is it necessary in order to teach it well that it should be carried on in a separate room?—No; it is advisable if possible; but it is not necessary.

2923. Most Rev. Dr. Walsh.—Singing enters into kindergarten arrangements?—Very largely.

2924. And it would be inconvenient to have these infants singing their songs in the general room?—It would.

2925. So that if you had not a separate room it would be inconvenient?—Unless you take it as part of the general singing lesson.

2926. To what extent is singing taught in the kindergarten department in Baggot-street?—Singing songs accompanies their games for musical drill.

2927. I was sorry to hear yesterday that as a general rule the teaching of singing that goes on in the kindergarten schools in the country is only singing by ear. Is it in your opinion possible to teach even these infants the elements of music?—It is quite possible with children, say, of six, and possibly at five years of age, with what I would call the first steps of the Tonic method.

2928. That is the method for which we are so largely indebted to the late Mr. Curwen, and generally spoken of as the "Tonic Sol-Fa." Of course you are made up in this Tonic method?—Yes.

2929. You think it is much more valuable for use in the infant school than the old five-line Hullah system?—We would not attempt it.

2930. One of the advantages of the Tonic Sol-Fa system is that it renders it possible, and even easy, to teach a certain amount of music to these children and to teach it to them on really scientific lines?—Quite so.

2931. But you would not attempt to teach it to them formally as a science?—Oh, no.

2932. I think it is one of the fundamental elements of the kindergarten system that as it is brought before the child it proceeds on thoroughly scientific lines, but there is no attempt made to make the child grasp scientific principles as such?—No; that would be a mistake on the part of the teacher.

2933. So that it would not be necessary to burden the child with the theory of music; but what the child learns really is the theory of music?—Quite so. For instance, a child could sing by note from what we call the hand signs. That is an introductory step to singing afterwards from what we call the kindergarten modulator.

2934. Do you make any attempt to get the infants to sing from the modulator?—Yes; they also sing from the hand signs.

2935. That is really a form of singing by note?—Yes.

2936. Up to this it was only a comparatively small number of teachers who went in for kindergarten in Baggot-street?—Yes.

2937. What percentage had they to get in order to qualify themselves for a certificate to teach it?—Thirty per cent.

2938. Don't you regard that as a great difficulty in the way of taking up kindergarten?—A very great difficulty indeed.

2939. A teacher has to score 50 per cent. all round in order to pass the qualifying examination at all. teaching kindergarten unless they score 60 per cent. in it?—No.

2944. So a teacher may pass in kindergarten on the same marks as she may pass in arithmetic, and she is qualified to teach arithmetic, but not qualified to teach kindergarten?—That is so.

2945. You consider at all events, that there is an improvement in having marks that are scored for kindergarten or any optional subject count towards classification?—Certainly, your Grace.

2946. Professor Fitzgerald.—Do you think that teachers who have passed at 20 per cent. should be considered qualified to teach kindergarten—would that be a sufficient qualification?—Quite so, if they are able to pass the practical examination. Twenty per cent. only on the theoretical part, as examined in writing, ought to be sufficient.

2947. Do you think it would be advisable to give a certificate to those who have got higher marks?—Oh! certainly.

2948. Most Rev. Dr. Walsh.—For instance, in an important school like Baggot-street, if the nuns were looking for a teacher they would naturally look for a teacher who had as high a qualification as 60 per cent. and not one merely qualified by 20 per cent.?—Yes.

2949. Have you thought what percentage would be desirable to qualify for a high class certificate, as distinguished from a mere certificate qualifying a person to teach?—Perhaps you would deal with that in the paper that you have promised to send in?—Yes. There is one subject I would like to mention——

2950. Chairman.—Suppose a young teacher were appointed to a school where there were many teachers, what class would it be likely that she would be appointed to begin at once?—That would depend entirely on the principal teacher in charge.

2951. What would be likely, a class in the middle course or the junior course?—I am afraid if it were an ordinary national school she would be put to teach the infants in the first place.

2952. And you think that would be a wrong arrangement?—Yes.

2953. Most Rev. Dr. Walsh.—You said just now there was one subject that you wished to speak about?—Yes, the examination in kindergarten.

2954. Is it the examination of the students in training or of the pupils?—The pupils.

2955. What do you wish to say about them?—I think specialists in the system would be better for the development of it, because very often it is the result that is looked to rather than the method.

2956. In the kindergarten system, I take it, the method pursued is the important thing?—It is the important thing.

2957. The results are worth something, but the method of teaching is the important thing?—Yes.

2958. But the present system of examination looks rather to the results than the methods?—Yes, your Grace, and in that way I think it requires reformation.

2959. You were a teacher yourself in an ordinary national school in the city. Did it strike you as a great defect in the results system of examination generally that it necessarily looks rather to results than to methods?—Yes, your Grace, in all the schools.

2960. You think it desirable there should be specially qualified examiners in this particular depart-

[illegible]
Miss E. Daly

2965. Do you think it is any indication of the effect of kindergarten teaching of children, when examined they come up?—No; if they have gone through the National schools. The ordinary National school programme permits some children remaining in kindergarten—well, no, it does not recognise, but it allows them remaining in kindergarten up to the third class, but as a rule you will find that kindergarten is not continued to that extent, and then when children come to the third class they are treated just the same as in the ordinary school, and kindergarten is entirely neglected.

2966. Most Rev. Dr. Walsh.—We see by the returns that very few were examined, either boys or girls, in the third class?—Yes; they come into the infant school at a certain age, and that age is generally exceeded when the child has reached the third class, so that excludes them from the benefits of kindergarten. Then you ask me as to the result of a child's training in kindergarten; the result on the child's general intelligence is most marked. They are more intelligent, they are receptive, and their faculties have been more developed. Their eyes and hands are trained properly, if the teaching has been done properly.

2967. In other words, they are more capable of being educated properly afterwards. I am not quite [illegible] about the extent to which boys are taught in kindergarten. You have only an experience of Baggot-street?—Yes, but we have boys there.

2968. Well, I find that 15,000 boys were examined and 21,000 girls, in our last report. That would show that the teaching of boys in kindergarten goes to a fairly large extent?—Yes.

2969. In the second class there were 1,633 boys and 1,637 girls, so that there were nearly the same number of boys as girls?—Yes.

2970. Rev. Dr. Evans.—May I ask you do you take any part in the teaching of the practising schools connected with the Training College in which you are a professor?—Not with a view to the direct instruction of the children, but with a view to practising students in teaching I do.

2971. You don't do anything there in the capacity of a teacher of the school?—Oh, nothing whatever.

2972. Most Rev. Dr. Walsh.—Your work is confined altogether to the Training College and to the instruction of the students in that college when they come into kindergarten department in the practising school one day a week?—Quite so, your Grace.

2973. The children of the school derive no advantage whatever from your power of instruction as a teacher of kindergarten?—No; none whatever.

Mr. F. [illegible] Vere, Professor of Drawing in St. Patrick's Training College, Drumcondra, examined.

Mr. F. [illegible]
Vere.

2974. Chairman.—You are the professor of Drawing in St. Patrick's Training College, Drumcondra?—Yes, my lord.

2975. Have you any observations to make in reference to the teachers' programme?—My connection with Drumcondra is one of very long duration. I have been there a little over a year, but on going there the first thing that struck me with regard to the teaching of drawing was the absence of a detailed programme as a guide to the teacher. For instance, we have among our subjects practical geometry, perspective and freehand drawing, and with regard to the practical part of the course we had no guide, as far as I could see, as to how far perspective was to extend, whether it was to be confined to mere perspective drawing of a cube or whether the students might be expected to draw in perspective a steam engine. The same, of course, applies to practical geometry. We had merely the heading, and I think the first difficulty I experienced with regard to taking up the subject was really to know what course exactly to follow in the teaching of it.

2976. Can you suggest any steps that might be taken to make the present programme more practical?—Well, I think if you contemplate the introduction of manual instruction on anything like a large scale you will have to considerably alter the present scheme under which drawing is carried on.

2977. In what direction?—At present I think as far as I can judge—I have no experience of the ordinary day schools under the Board—but from what I have heard of the evidence so far with regard to drawing, I understand that drawing consists of simply copying a number of curved line patterns from paper. Of course that would be of some use later on. But if we want drawing of practical use we have to add considerably to that programme, and to diversify it to some extent.

2978. Most Rev. Dr. Walsh.—Your first fault with the programme is this, it is not sufficiently detailed?—Yes, your Grace.

2979. It is hardly detailed at all?—A mere statement "Perspective" is rather insufficient, I think, in dealing with a subject like that.

2980. Of course this programme comes to the college authorities from the Commissioners, so that it would rest with the Commissioners to work out a more detailed programme?—In fact I may mention that in preparation I had to be guided by the former papers.

2981. I was just going to ask you what else you got as to the sort of thing you should teach?—The suggestion as to the programme to be carried out was entirely derivable from the papers set in former years.

2982. They are published in a series of blue books, and it was only by going through these you could find out whether your students would draw coins or steam engines?—Yes, your Grace.

2983. You mentioned a second difficulty in the programme, that it was not sufficiently practical?—Yes.

2984. As to freehand, do you think it practical?—Yes; it would form an essential part of the course.

2985. That consists in copying straight and curved line objects from one piece of paper on to another?—Yes.

2986. Would that sort of drawing be of much use if drawing was to be applied for practical purposes? Suppose, for instance, that a carpenter sees a particular kind of chair and it occurs to him that if he had that chair at home he could make something like it, but he hasn't it at home, he is perhaps twenty miles away from home—now does our system give any real help to a man who wants to construct a chair in that way?—If the drawing is confined to mere copying from the flat of curved line objects I take it that the student, no matter what perfection he arrives at, will be incapable of producing a drawing of the object which he could send to a tradesman and say "I want that made."

2987. What kind of drawing do you suggest should be brought into our system for this purpose?—I would suggest that instead of devoting time to this sort of work the student should be brought face to face with a simple object and make a sketch of it.

2988. Have we any object drawing at present?—Yes, but one to scale of measurement.

2989. What we have is in the artistic direction, and drawing to scale would tend in the practical direction?—Yes, which, of course, with manual work would be the first step.

2990. Could it be illustrated in what we get from architects in reference to church buildings. The architect may give a picture of what the church may be, but he also gives us a very inartistic thing, a mere elevation of the church, or a section or ground plan. Is that what you contemplate when you speak to think they will come up more in one than in the other?—I have every reason to believe they will come up almost entirely in freehand.

3008. Which do you think it would be most desirable for us to encourage them to come up in?—Decidedly in practical geometry. That is, I mean solid geometry of the kind I have referred to.

3009. Do you think that in the Training Colleges and in the schools it would be better for us to encourage a combination of both?—In the mere sketching of an object for the purpose of making a drawing to scale there is any amount of training as to eye and form, because when the student makes the drawing by his eye and then makes the drawing with instruments very often his proportions clash with his measurements.

3010. CHAIRMAN.—I don't quite understand you?—He actually makes measurements and he has made a rough sketch. If the measurements clash with the rough sketch of course it is at once a check on his eye; that is, he will find the original sketch was incorrect, whereas of course he must have constructed his drawing with rule and compass exactly of the dimensions.

3011. Would he not begin by making a drawing to dimensions?—He would begin with a rough sketch of the object marking his dimensions on it.

3012. And he would then test them?—Yes.

3013. And when he found them incorrect he would alter his drawing?—Yes.

3014. MOST REV. DR. WALSH.—He would work so as to get everything into scale, when making the finished drawing?—Yes.

3015. PROFESSOR FITZGERALD.—You think he ought to be able to make a rough sketch and a finished drawing?—Yes; but I would require no high artistic merit in the rough sketch.

3016. But it should be recognisable as being the original object?—Yes.

3017. You said it would be desirable to have the programme more detailed. Would it not be desirable that the teachers in the different colleges should confer together and make suggestions?—I think it would be very desirable.

3018. Do you think it would be possible for the teachers to confer together and provide us with their suggestions?—I think it would.

3019. In one of the syllabuses which has been issued by the Department of Science and Art in England for the Practical Physics course, it is recommended that some of the apparatus required can and ought to be made by the students themselves, in the second and third year's course of manual work, that is the apparatus required for science teaching? Do you think that would be a possible arrangement here?—A good deal of that would depend on the natural skill of the teacher in rigging up the apparatus, but if we take the introduction of elementary science as an extension of the kindergarten system the teacher can go a very fair way towards arriving at very important scientific results.

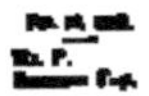

drawing, as carried out at present, the repeated copying of curved line outlines.

3054. Most Rev. Dr. Walsh.—The pupils in the practising schools derive no benefit whatever from your connection with the college?—I have never been in the practising school.

3055. Your position is altogether in the college and the salary you receive is for work in the college?—Yes, your grace. Dec. 20, 1897.

3056. You are not paid by the National Education Board for any work to be done in the school, and in fact you have no opportunity of exercising your teaching to the children in the school?—None, whatever. Mr. E. [illegible], Esq.

Mr. P. Goodman, Examiner in Music to the Board of National Education, examined.

3058. Chairman.—You are an examiner in music under the National Board of Education in Ireland?—Yes. Mr. P. Goodman.

3059. I think you can give us some information on the subject of the Tonic Sol-Fa system in connection with kindergarten?—Well, I have very little knowledge of kindergarten, but I have seen what the Tonic Sol-Fa did in connection with kindergarten in one of the Convent schools, and the results there were simply splendid.

3060. Most Rev. Dr. Walsh.—You consider that it is possible to teach the elementary portions of the Tonic Sol-Fa system even to young children?—Quite possible.

3061. At what age do you think they could begin to learn?—The children I saw at work were about six.

3062. You think the system is much more applicable in the case of young children than the old Hullah system?—Much more. The Hullah system would be quite a mistake.

3063. And teaching even these young children on the Tonic system is not only possible but easy?—Easy and delightful.

3064. The kind of music these children would learn in kindergarten would be of use to them afterwards?—Surely.

3065. There is nothing in it that they would have to unlearn afterwards—it would all remain with them even if they were to become equal to Wagner or any other musician of the highest eminence?—Quite so.

3066. Do you think the Tonic Sol-Fa system an educational system in itself?—Quite so.

3067. Just as the kindergarten system is in its way?—Yes.

3068. What do you consider are the educational advantages of the Tonic Sol-Fa system?—In the first place it teaches them to observe, and in the next place it teaches them to read music.

3069. There is a book written by Mr. Curwen which I have always regarded as a most useful book for persons engaged in teaching in any department; it is called "The Teachers' Manual;" it lays down most useful principles of teaching?—Certainly.

3070. One of these is to teach the "thing" before you teach the "name" of it?—Yes.

3071. That is a common principle of the Tonic Sol-Fa?—Quite so. Another is "the easy before the difficult."

3072. And another, I think, is the "simple before the complex"?—Quite so.

3073. And another and a very important principle is, "one thing at a time"?—Most certainly.

3074. These are all most useful educational principles?—Quite so; in music as in everything else.

3075. Then it is a special thing to put these in operation, as embodied in this Tonic Sol-Fa system, through all our schools?—Yes, and it would be very desirable if it could be taught to our infants. At present children only from the second class up are taught, and I would strongly recommend that children in the first year should be taught.

3076. I believe that in England singing is taught on the Tonic Sol-Fa method to very small children?—Yes; and the children understand it. It is quite possible to teach a child who does not know his letters to sing the Tonic Sol-Fa, beginning with hand signs.

3077. I believe you have experience of the wonderful results produced in Dublin schools by this system?—Quite so.

3078. Mr. Redington.—Do you think it would be useful to teach music by ear to little children?—I think it would be very much better to teach it by note. By this system it is quite possible to teach it by note.

3079. To children of that years of age?—Well, of course something must be taught by ear then, but there ought to be a little teaching by note.

3080. From as early an age as that?—Yes. Of course teaching by ear is better than nothing.

3081. Professor FitzGerald.—The whole of the Tonic Sol-Fa consists in providing the children with the facts, namely, musical intervals?—Yes, teaching by chord.

3082. Ultimately you go through very elaborate and complicated generalities?—We go over the whole scale and transition.

3083. Transition is very complicated?—But in Tonic Sol-Fa, we show it very easily.

3084. Because the children are familiar with the facts first?—Yes; the notation is very simple.

3085. Most Rev. Dr. Walsh.—The knowledge of the notation comes after the knowledge of the facts?—Quite so.

3086. Professor FitzGerald.—Then Tonic Sol-Fa may be described as providing familiar facts, and going from them to scientific generalities?—Quite so.

3087. And the science of music is taught in a proper way from the facts?—Quite so; from the very beginning. It is taught at present in England in first infant classes.

3088. Most Rev. Dr. Walsh.—I believe Professor Helmholtz expressed strong approbation of the Tonic Sol-Fa system?—Quite so; and, better even than Professor Helmholtz, I think, is the testimony of the teachers who use the methods.

3089. Then we have high scientific testimony in favour of it, and also the practical experience of the teachers?—Certainly.

3090. Professor FitzGerald.—Is there any use in teaching children this system black notes made on lines and called Tithes and Thirds?—Not a bit of use.

3091. Isn't that system adopted by the Intermediate Education Board?—Well, that is of no use in teaching children; it would not teach them to sing.

3092. There is no use in our adopting any system of that kind?—None whatever; it was long enough tried.

3093. Most Rev. Dr. Walsh.—You would not have a system of teaching music under which a deaf and dumb child could obtain the first prize, which, I am sorry to have to say, is still the case under the Intermediate Education Board?—No, your grace.

The Commission then adjourned.

INDEX TO EVIDENCE.

[NOTE.—The Figures refer to the Numbers of the Questions.]

15th *March*, 1897.

Sir,

I am directed by the Lord Lieutenant to acknowledge the receipt of your letter of the 10th instant, enclosing six copies of the First Report of the Commission on Manual and Practical Instruction; and I am to acquaint you, for the information of the Commissioners, that His Excellency has given orders for the presentation to Parliament of the Report and the Minutes of Evidence referred to therein.

I am,

Sir,

Your obedient servant,

D. HARREL.

The Secretary,

Manual and Practical Instruction Commission,

120, Lower Baggot-street.

www.ingramcontent.com/pod-product-compliance
Lightning Source LLC
Chambersburg PA
CBHW030546270326
41927CB00008B/1539
* 9 7 8 3 7 4 1 1 9 9 8 0 6 *

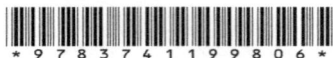